JOHN TOVEY'S
Feast of
Vegetables

JOHN TOVEY'S
Feast of Vegetables

The Perfect Accompaniment
——— to Any Meal ———

CENTURY PUBLISHING
LONDON

First published in Great Britain in 1985
by Century Publishing Co. Ltd,
Portland House,
12–13 Greek Street, London W1V 5LE

British Library Cataloguing in Publication Data
Tovey, John, *1933–*
Feast of vegetables: the perfect accompaniment
to any meal.
1. Cookery (Vegetables)
I. Title
641.6′5   TX801
ISBN 0 7126 0780 3

Designed by Robson Lamb Design Associates
Illustrated by Rob Shone
Jacket photography by David Parfitt

Photoset by Rowland Phototypesetting Ltd,
Bury St Edmunds, Suffolk

Printed in Great Britain in 1985 by
Purnell (Book Production) Ltd,
Paulton, Bristol

CONTENTS

INTRODUCTION	2	GLOBE ARTICHOKE	81
ABOUT THE BOOK	4	HOP SHOOTS	82
ABOUT VEGETABLES	5	HORSERADISH	83
BASIC PREPARATION AND COOKING	6	JERUSALEM ARTICHOKE	84
BASIC RECIPES	11	KALE	86
ASPARAGUS	22	KOHLRABI	87
AUBERGINE	24	LEEK	90
BEANSPROUTS	27	LETTUCE	95
BEETROOT	28	MANGE-TOUT PEAS	98
BROAD BEANS	30	MARROW	100
BROCCOLI	33	MUSHROOMS	102
BRUSSELS SPROUTS	36	NETTLE	106
CABBAGE	39	OKRA	107
CARROTS	45	ONION	108
CAULIFLOWER	51	PARSNIP	112
CELERIAC	54	PEAS	115
CELERY	58	PEPPER	117
CHICORY	61	POTATO	120
CHINESE LEAF	64	PUMPKIN AND SQUASH	126
COURGETTES	65	RUNNER BEANS	128
CUCUMBER	70	SPINACH	129
DANDELION	72	SWEETCORN	133
ENDIVE	73	SWEET POTATO	136
FENNEL	74	TOMATO	137
FRENCH BEANS	77	TURNIP AND SWEDE	141
GARLIC	79	INDEX	145

INTRODUCTION

I WAS ASKED ON SEVERAL occasions while being interviewed during the writing of this book whether it was purely for vegetarians, and whether I had become a vegetarian. To which the answer is emphatically 'no, no, no'.

Vegetables to me are fun food. They're also one of the ultimate health foods, and we should eat many, many more than we do. Vegetables come in a glorious variety of shapes, colours and flavours; they are relatively inexpensive, easy to buy and to grow (for those who have greener thumbs than I); and there is no excuse – particularly after looking through the pages in this book – for not serving an interesting selection at every meal. Vegetables add a splash of colour to the main-course picture, and provide contrasting textures and tastes to the meat or fish served. They can be made into a delicious starter, or soup, and can often take the place of meat as a light lunch, or indeed a vegetarian main course (for I believe the health pundits do say the occasional meat-free meal is good for the body – and the figure).

I have spent many happy hours doddling away without becoming gimmicky, and my test cooks and I have, believe it or not, turned out many right disasters which have found their way very quickly to the waste disposal unit. Even our beloved sixteen-year-old sheepdog, Mutley – commonly known in the household as the animal hoover, as everything but everything will go down her throat – turned up her nose at some of the vegetable concoctions appearing, and tended to keep out of the kitchen on test cooking days.

But don't be put off! All the recipes included in the book have been well received by dinner-party guests at Brantlea, and the general air of contentment and approval has been a joy to watch and listen to. And at Miller Howe, when one table has praised to the hilt a particular vegetable, I've purred like a well-stroked cat only to be brought down to earth with a bang when some other guests a few tables away have heatedly denounced the same new vegetable! (It's all a matter of personal taste after all.)

From my own point of view, though, the sad thing is that I managed to put on seven pounds in weight testing the ruddy recipes – bearing in mind that each recipe had to be cooked three times, for the crisp, firm and soft stages. For this is one of the elements which most particularly characterise this book. Used as I am professionally to pleasing as many people as possible at one time, I have also decided to do that in the book! Whether you like your vegetables crisp, firm or soft, you will find the necessary timings here. Now you can understand why I put on so much weight! When the end result was superb, nobody but nobody had the opportunity to finish off the dish except me. In fact, when recently interviewed by an old friend, I was asked why I had developed such a prominent paunch, to which I replied, 'I've been writing a book on vegetables.' The interviewer's eyebrows and intonation went several degrees higher: 'Vegetables?' To which I then had to retort, 'Ever seen a skinny rabbit?'

We have to eat to keep our batteries charged, so for me the way to eat is invariably totally opposite to what the health pundits say one should consume. Sweetcorn without masses of salted butter, asparagus minus the lashings of rich Hollandaise, vegetables without various rich oils and sauces – all these are definitely not on the agenda. But of course one doesn't live or cook at this level day after day – so, when entertaining, I do hope you will try some of the more unusual and slightly expensive recipes (beetroot fried in walnut oil and orange juice for one), and for the daily feeding of the family I hope some of the hints will broaden your and their appreciation of the glorious greens provided in abundance for us.

The thing about cooking, I find, isn't what I know but what I still have to learn, and, by golly, I learned a great deal working on this book. The hostess trolley is never used now except to keep the plates warm or possibly for a purée of vegetables and sauce. I have learned at home to plan my entertaining routine whereby, as I sit down myself to the course prior to the main one, I have each ring on the stove bringing pans of water to the boil, the frier turned on to the final cooking temperature, and the steamer ready and waiting. Thus, during the process of clearing plates from the table, serving the wine to go with the main course, and actually carving the roast or finishing off the main dish, the vegetables can all be cooked nice and crisp. Occasionally I time it slightly wrongly, and find myself dishing up a veg that is very, very *al dente* – but the concensus of opinion is that guests these days would rather crunch away on a veg than simply let an overcooked tasteless mush float down their throats.

Mind you, cooking is terribly personal and when the odd guest isn't too pleased with a vegetable at home or at Miller Howe, I still find it hurts as I would so like to have *all* my clients or guests satisfied one hundred per cent of the time. (I think this would be living in a fools' paradise.) There *will* be ideas in this book which will make your eyebrows rise. But unless you try them you won't really know how your tastebuds and stomach are going to react. I hope you enjoy them.

3

ABOUT THE BOOK

BASICALLY THROUGHOUT THE book the amounts of vegetables to be purchased and cooked are for a party of six people sitting down to eat, usually having *three* vegetables on their plates along with the main course. (At Miller Howe, as many people know, we have *six* vegetable accompaniments!) This means that the vegetable portions are *smaller* than you might normally serve if only presenting *one* vegetable. However, it takes very little effort or imagination to adjust the amounts and cooking times to your own particular liking as, after all, you are the person who is going to eat the end result.

So most recipes are for *accompanying* vegetables, but I have included several which could be served as a starter or a light lunch or supper. What I *haven't* done is give recipes which use vegetables as an ingredient: I give you a multitude of carrot recipes, say, but I don't tell you how to cook boiled beef and carrots. I have stuck to vegetables pure and simple, and I hope my ideas will inspire you.

Don't be timid about trying something for the first time, but remember never to do it when you are entertaining – this can be embarrassing. Always be honest with yourself about the end result: if you hate it, simply discard the recipe; if you like it, try it the next time friends are round; and, if you are like me, the third or fourth time you make the dish you will, more than likely, even change the recipe slightly!

Do, however, constantly be aware of the *overall* taste of the goodies on the plate. Think about which vegetables will go with which other vegetables – their colour contrasts, their contrasting textures and shapes – and think about what they will most happily accompany. I have one firm rule when it comes to the exotic variations of vegetables I serve at Miller Howe, and that is to constantly bear in mind that *white* meats will stand more adventurous vegetable flavourings than *red* meats. The carrots with pernod on page 49, for instance, go superbly with breast of chicken, veal or pork, but just do *not* marry happily with roast beef. Red meats deserve a little more caution, and carrots with my roast beef would have a herb butter with them, or perhaps just a touch of curry powder or preserved ginger.

4

ABOUT VEGETABLES

VEGETABLES, LIKE FRUIT, ARE the edible products of plants and are an important part of our diet. Most vegetables consist of about eighty per cent water, the remainder being carbohydrate, protein or fat. Some contain sugars – carrots, for instance – and many are valuable sources of minerals and vitamins: dark green leafy vegetables contain Vitamin A as do the orange and yellow vegetables; most vegetables contain Vitamin C. It is the cellulose in plants that the human digestion cannot cope with (that must be why cows have four stomachs), so vegetables are one of the prime sources of dietary fibre.

In many cases nowadays, vegetables are deprived of their true seasons, with modern packaging and transportation. French beans, which used to be a summer vegetable available only during a few months, can now readily be bought more or less throughout the whole year, as they are flown in from Kenya, South Africa and the southern parts of America. Mange-touts as well, once a brief highlight of an English summer, come from Morocco, Spain, Italy, Kenya and Guatemala. All are good – we wouldn't buy them if they weren't – but home-grown or locally grown are best, as they will be fresher.

For, to take full advantage of all that goodness that vegetables contain, they must be as fresh as possible. The *minute* a vegetable is pulled from the ground or plucked from the plant, its vitamin and mineral content, its original composition even, begins to alter.

The whizz kids who actually design modern packaging methods have – in many cases – much to answer for. Plastic seems to be their preference and if vegetables covered with plain plastic look more desirable to the shopper, then plain plastic minus holes is used. Try putting *your* head in a sealed airtight plastic bag and see how long you stay fresh. Vegetables need to breathe to stay as fresh as possible, and it never ceases to amaze me how poorly we are served in this respect. Next time you go into your big, spotlessly clean, bright and cheery supermarket, edge your way slowly towards the vegetable section. The well-heeled, blue-rinse ladies will all eagerly go for the pre-packed, lightly chilled veg stored under brilliant lighting, which need little or no preparation at home. Just *think* of what those vegetables have gone through before you lay your hands on them – and how long it has taken. More canny, down-to-earth folk will gravitate towards the open vegetable counter where, even if there is a bit of soil clinging to add to the weight, you can personally pick what you want, and as *much* as you want. You may have to tear off a clingfilm wrapping and go to a scale to have your produce weighed, but eventually you will have a better vegetable, and anything you cut off in preparation can go into the stock pot.

5

BASIC PREPARATION AND COOKING

IN THE INTRODUCTION TO each vegetable, I have given details of individual selection and preparation – and in the recipes, too, of course – but here a few further words may be helpful as an insight into many of the techniques and methods I employ throughout the book.

CUTTING, SLICING, CHOPPING AND SHREDDING

Knives are an important part of any kitchen, and *good* knives are essential. Personally I prefer stainless steel to plain steel, and have only got Victorinox (made in Switzerland) and the newer Richardson of Sheffield stainless steel laser knives. The latter I approached at first with awe when I heard that 25,000 sets had been ordered by the Japanese. Having worked in Japan and seen how deft the chefs are with their knives – creating paper-chain effects from a potato in about ten seconds – it did enthuse me to try them out. They are excellent.

I find that my knives keep their edge longer if I store them in the wooden slanting knife racks that have come very much into vogue in the last few years. And you must keep them sharp – more damage can be done to food (and you) if they are blunt. Buy a knife sharpener of some proven sort, and always, but always, use a wooden or rubber board for cutting. Never cut on stainless steel or slate as they will very soon dull your knives.

However it is in the use of the knife where patience initially will very soon turn you into a skilled manipulator of this important kitchen item.

Always hold the vegetable to be cut half-way along its length, with the fingertips tucked under, and then the blade is able to slide down against the middle knuckle section of your fingers. Slice up and down, but don't look for speed in your initial efforts – try to get evenly shaped pieces. Your cutting hand will soon begin to increase its speed, and your holding hand will move back instinctively, and very soon you'll be able to prepare vegetables fairly fast.

To slice a carrot, courgette or aubergine into strips, hold the vegetable very firmly down on

6

your cutting board with the tips of your fingers and then simply cut lengthwise into equal slices. Stack three or four thin slices on top of each other and, using the same technique, cut into square sticks. Then, if you need to have finely cubed vegetables, simply cut once again through in the other direction. All terribly simple.

To slice a potato thinly it is often necessary to nick a thin slice off first in order to make it lie flat on the board (remove this from the flattest side). The fingers holding the potato then act as the guide for the thickness of the potato slice as the knife goes through.

For chopping herbs and parsley I find it easier if I use a bigger knife with a plain blade. Simply put the cleaned parsley or fresh garden herbs on to the chopping board and, before chopping quickly in all directions, hold the tip of the knife's blade firmly against the board, to act as a pivot. It takes hardly any time at all, and chopped herbs of whatever kind, always add to the look and taste of a dish.

To shred a leaf vegetable such as spinach, separate it into individual leaves and remove any thick central stalk. Roll up from the uncut end (opposite where the stalk was) into a cigar shape, and hold firmly while you cut the 'cigar' across into ¼inch (5mm) thick slices.

GRATING

Being, in many ways, rather old-fashioned and set in my ways – well, at nearly fifty-two, one should have formed likes and dislikes, and have strong views on certain matters – I found it rather heartening to discover that I had been wrong about one small thing in question – the usefulness of electric grater attachments on commercial mixers/liquidisers. For years, any vegetable that needed grating was duly prepared and wiped and then time-consumingly done by hand on a stainless steel run-of-the-mill grater.

I have always used the Kenwood Chef mixer, and have mentioned it in all my previous writings (not through a commercial hand-out from the makers, Thorn EMI, but because I really believed in the machine), so it took some persuasion from the same company for me to make a half-hour video soft sell for their new Kenwood Chef Excel. I took to everything new about this piece of equipment – the sensibly sized D-shaped bowl, the quiet but powerful motor even at low speeds, the looks – but I was still sceptical about the grater. I remember saying to the director when it came to shredding vegetables: 'I've never used an electric grater and feel that I won't be able to appear enthusiastic about this on the film.' As I was saying this I was rehearsing the piece. I had to eat my words more or less immediately as I was literally speechless (and that's something terribly difficult for me to be) when I realised that two whole courgettes had gone through the machine in as many seconds as it took me to make my statement. The outcome was perfectly grated courgettes! I immediately tried out a couple of carrots and then some celery sticks. When the edited video was shown to me I am sure that this part of the track was the happiest.

Now all grated vegetables at Miller Howe are done with this machine and I find that every single night, one of the six vegetables is grated.

At home vegetables can be grated earlier on in the day and stored in screw-top containers or polythene bags in the fridge, and then simply stir-fried Chinese style while the main course is coming to the end of its cooking time. For a quick vegetable, or selection of vegetables, this is a very good way of cooking. A great time-saver, and looks so unusual as well. See pages 9 and 10 for some hints about the quantities of oil and/or butter, and types of oil to use.

Flavourings for grated, stir-fried vegetables are endless: ginger (preferably the sweet preserved ginger), spices or rind of citrus fruits (next time you intend to squeeze a fresh orange, first grate off the rind, finely or coarsely, as no matter what you are cooking that day, it could be used). Exotic fruits can be incorporated too at the stir-frying stage, and you can throw in desiccated coconut, sultanas, those delicious dried banana slices broken up, a shot of Pernod or Ouzo from your sunny holiday. . . . But do see the individual recipes for a few more ideas.

BOILING AND STEAMING

These are the most basic methods of cooking vegetables, and probably the best from a health point of view – no fat or oil is used in the cooking process itself. Steaming is better than boiling because the extreme heat of the boiling water with which the vegetable comes in contact leaches out many of the vitamins and minerals. The indirect heat of steaming – when the actual water never touches the vegetable – retains all these goodnesses to a greater extent. Steaming, which takes in general a little longer, also means that you can make fewer mistakes: it's a *gentler* process.

Little needs to be said in detail about boiling, and I expand on the process in each recipe. Basically, the vegetable to be boiled should be *covered* with boiling water, and do remember to cut your veg into equal-sized pieces so that the recipe timings can work properly. You can use the cooking water afterwards for stock, in a soup base, or sauce.

For steaming, special equipment will be needed. Commercial steamers are available, metal sieve-like objects with lids which stand on a sturdy pan, and many have more than one tier or compartment so that a selection of vegetables can be steamed at the same time. Chinese bamboo steamers are also useful, as they can stack on top of each other. But you can easily improvise with a sieve or colander on top of a saucepan, and foil instead of a lid if the lid won't fit. The basics are that the foot of the steamer, and thus the vegetable, must not touch the water; the water must bubble to create the cooking medium of steam; and you must always be aware that the water level may need topping up.

STIR-FRYING

Whether stir-frying a vegetable as the sole cooking method, or frying it off for a last-minute flavouring and/or cooking, you must observe certain 'rules'. If you use too much butter or oil, the vegetable will be swamped (and it's very fattening, apart from anything else); if you use too little, it won't taste so good, and might burn. The size of the pan is important too, as is the quantity of vegetables you put in it: too much in a small pan and the veg might *stew* instead of stir-fry.

SIZE OF FRYING PAN	OIL/BUTTER QUANTITY
9 inch (23cm)	1 tablespoon oil 1oz (25g) butter
11 inch (28cm)	2 tablespoons oil 1½oz (40g) butter
12 inch (30cm)	3 tablespoons oil 2oz (50g) butter

As a rough guide, the 11 inch (23cm) pan is the best size for, say, courgettes for six people. See also the following pages for a few ideas on fats and oils and mixtures to add a new dimension to the frying pan.

FATS AND OILS

You all know that the kind and quality of fat or oil used makes an enormous difference to a dish – and nowhere more so than with vegetables. You can use various oils according to your personal taste or, more important still, particular whim at that moment: good expensive or inexpensive olive oils, corn oils, commercial 'non-fattening-good-for-you' oils, through to the upper end of the market – walnut, hazelnut and avocado. And don't forget about the flavours given by duck or goose fat, or even that good old faithful standby, bacon fat.

BACON FAT

Bacon fat, smoked bacon fat in particular, adds a new richness to certain aspects of vegetable cooking. I *bake* my slices of bacon on a baking tray in the oven and then carefully make sure none of the fat is thrown away but diligently strained and stored in a jar in the fridge for future cooking purposes – mainly for vegetables.

DUCK FAT

When cooking a duck, the fat should be collected and looked after like a mother duck looks after her ducklings, for it is excellent for roasting and frying many vegetables. Each farm-raised fresh duck will produce about ¼ pint (150ml) duck fat if you take the roasting pan out of the oven each 15 minutes during cooking time and pour off any excess fat (you'll get a lovely crisp skin as well). Store in a jar in the fridge when cool, and label meticulously.

9

GARLIC OIL

This is something you should always have to hand as it makes all the difference when stir-frying several of the vegetable recipes in the book, or when wanting strong-flavoured croûtons for a soup.

You will need a 1lb (450g) jar with a screw top. Place six to twelve cloves of peeled garlic in the base of the jar, and then simply fill up with any favourite olive oil. I am a garlic freak, as I am convinced it has good medicinal properties for my ageing body, so at home you will find *at least* twelve whole cloves of garlic in the bottom of my jar.

Each time you use some oil, simply top up the level again – you will be surprised at how long the flavour lasts in the oil and, hopefully, delighted when using it in cooking. When you find the flavour going – and it *will* ultimately, if kept too long – don't discard the garlic cloves, but use them in a casserole or soup.

SESAME OIL WITH RASPBERRY VINEGAR

This is a mixture which has proved very useful with vegetables, a cooking and flavouring medium that is easy, delicious and very unusual. Mix together ½ pint (300ml) sesame oil and 2 tablespoons of raspberry vinegar – more than you'll need in any one recipe – and store in a screw-top jar in the fridge to use as required. After frying, always put the vegetables on kitchen paper as sesame oil can run into and flavour other vegetables on the plate.

SOYA SAUCE WITH RASPBERRY VINEGAR

This is much the same as the above, but uses ½ pint (300 ml) soya sauce instead of the sesame oil.

SEASONING VEGETABLES

Recently at Miller Howe I had to join a party of six at the main-course stage of dinner, and was quite proud of what was put down in front of each person. I could feel myself smiling contentedly, knowing inwardly how delicious each item on the plate was going to taste. The smile was soon (oh, how soon) wiped off my face as two of the six guests – *without tasting anything* – immediately ground lashings of black pepper on to their food and generously layered salt over everything!

Apart from being rather an insult to the chef, salt in particular is bad for you added in this way. It's better for your health added during the *cooking*, and even then should be minimal. But, as with almost everything, it's all a matter of personal taste.

I can only advise you to always, but always, *taste* what is put down in front of you before seasoning further. Or, for that matter, if you are in the kitchen, to taste again yourself before you finalise seasonings. In the book I have been extremely general in my approach to both salt and freshly ground black pepper, and maybe for you I haven't used sufficient salt. I'm sorry, but only you yourself know exactly how much you and your family like. You must adjust each and every recipe accordingly.

And while talking about seasonings, I have *three* mills in my kitchen: one for sea salt, one for black peppercorns, and the third for whole coriander seeds. The latter grated into or onto some dishes adds an intriguing taste.

BASIC RECIPES

IN ALL MY BOOKS THERE HAVE been certain recipes which can be called central to my way of cooking. This has involved a certain amount of repetition, for which I apologise, but I can't have you rushing between books to find the correct reference! There *are* a number of new ideas here as well, though, and I hope you'll enjoy all of them, and use them to add to the deliciousness of your versatile vegetables.

BASIC VEGETABLE SOUP RECIPE

In a book on vegetables, the soups must bear pride of place, and coming from the north of England, soups feature prominently on my dining table anyway. For they're not only cheap and cheerful, but with a little imagination and hardly any financial strain, they can be such fun too!

The basic essential item (and I truly do believe this) is your own home-made stock, so please don't, at this stage, immediately turn the page and say, 'That's not for me – too time-consuming.' For if you do you will have lost a lot of the money's worth to be obtained from this book.

So many items that you chuck down your waste disposal unit or even into the bin or on to the compost heap can provide the basis for a good home-made stock. When you know you're going to have roast chicken or cook chicken breasts (always cheaper when bought *on the bone*, and the bones can be used for stock), a couple of days before start to fill up a polythene bag in the fridge with things such as onion skins, garlic skins, outside lettuce leaves, celery tops, parsley stalks, fairly clean peelings from carrots (if you've dared to peel them), outer leaves and stalks of cauliflower, fluffy green carrot tops etc. These, slowly simmered, are all you need.

Simply place the cooked cold chicken carcass or raw chicken bones into a large saucepan along with all your 'harvestings', cover with water, and slowly simmer away for several hours – adding further suitable ingredients to the stock pot as your daily cooking tasks 'bear fruit'. As the water draws out the goodness and flavours from your conglomeration of ingredients and reduces, so you simply top it up with more cold water until you – and only you – are truly satisfied that it will be a waste of time and costly energy to carry this process any further. Strain your stock and use for the soup – each soup throughout the book needs 1½–2 pints (850ml– 1 litre) home-made stock.

Now at turkey time, you will have a field day as you should – using a preserving pan as a stockpot – end up quite easily with a gallon *at least* (over 4 litres) of super, slightly murky, but so flavourful stock. This could be a nuisance to store in your freezer so use your first stock fresh for your first soup and then put the strained balance into a saucepan and slowly simmer this without a lid on until it has reduced to about 1½–2 pints (850ml– 1 litre). When cold pour into ice-cube trays and freeze. When completely frozen turn out into a polythene bag and store in the freezer. Next time you wish to make a home-made soup, instead of going through the rigmarole of stock-making (which isn't, now is it, a difficult task?), you simply take out a couple of cubes, bring them back to life with boiling water and, hey presto, instant home-made good stock, ten times better than those little cubes full of monosodium glutamate!

Having gone to great lengths over the actual stock, here is the basic recipe for *every single vegetable soup* mentioned in this book. Each recipe makes enough soup for 12 small portions – as a course in a five-course meal – or 6 hearty portions as part of a simpler three-course meal.

4oz (100g) butter
8oz (225g) onions, finely chopped
2lb (900g) prepared vegetables (see under individual
    sections, and below)
¼ pint (150ml) cooking sherry (optional but
    preferable)
1½–2 pints (850ml–1 litre) good home-made stock

In a 9 pint (5 litre) saucepan, melt the butter. Add the finely chopped onions and cook until golden. Then add the vegetables. Here I wish to digress a little. It is of the utmost importance (and also basic common sense) to see that when you prepare the vegetables they should all basically be the same size. It is no use being clumsy over this as you want each veg to be cooked to the same degree.

With the vegetables, pour in the sherry – essential when entertaining, optional when feeding the family. At this stage some of the individual *added* flavourings of vegetable soups throughout the book are incorporated. Take a double thickness of dampened greaseproof paper and press this down on top of the vegetables and simply simmer away over a low to medium heat on top of the stove for about 35–40 minutes (occasionally looking at the contents of the pan to make sure they aren't burning or drying out).

After the cooking period, when you are satisfied the veg are soft enough to be liquidised you will, I am sure, be agreeably satisfied as to how much liquid there still will be in the saucepan. To this add your home-made stock and then liquidise the soup. Don't overload the liquidiser (you can do it in a food processor, but the end result isn't quite so good), and whatever you do, make sure you add even parts of solid to liquid, and fill the machine only two-thirds full. Put your hand firmly on the lid of the liquidiser, turn the machine on, and give each bowlful about 2 minutes on high speed.

The next thing is extremely important as you *must* get into the habit of constantly sieving your finished soups or, right at the beginning of your dinner party, some poor unsuspecting guest with ill-fitting false teeth will get a string of celery or piece of tomato skin lodged uncomfortably in his mouth! The easiest way to sieve soup is to place a fairly large, round metal sieve over another saucepan (one that the handle and the round end can rest easily on). If you use your *soup ladle* to force the soup through, you will find this takes half the time than when messing around with a wooden spoon.

Soups are always seasoned when they are reheated prior to serving, and a tip here is that should your soup end up too sweet (and nobody will know what the actual final soup will taste like in some of the recipes until all the various ingredients have come together), add salt. If too *salty*, add sugar to counteract this. At this stage, too, many flavourings are added to individual soup recipes throughout the book.

Leftover soups should, like stock, be frozen in ice-cube trays which, when they become solid, can be stored in a plastic bag. Then, should you have unexpected guests, a starter course can be on the table literally in 10 minutes. All you have to do is simply take the soup cubes from the bag and warm them in a double saucepan – or in a Christmas pudding type bowl over a pan of boiling water. (They might burn if heated in a pan over direct heat.)

SIMPLE ROOT VEGETABLE SOUP

This is an ideal filling supper dish for the family. Use a single root vegetable, or a mixture – carrots, potatoes, turnips or swedes, parsnips etc – and cut them into ¼ inch (5mm) cubes. Instead of boiling in salted water use a good flavoursome chicken (or beef) stock. See individual sections for timings. Everything is ladled out into soup bowls and eaten with thickly buttered bread. What could be simpler!

VEGETABLE PURÉES

The Good Food Guide once said – when I had just discovered the luxury of puréed vegetables – that we were beginning to cook for toothless octogenarians. When I went painstakingly through that particular season's menus on file, they were right.

But one puréed vegetable at a dinner party will be very much enjoyed by your guests and, more important still, as it can be done earlier in the day (or for that matter the day before), it makes entertaining easier.

FOR 6 PEOPLE
1lb (450g) vegetables, prepared as appropriate
1oz (25g) butter
¼ pint (150ml) single cream

Basically, the vegetable should be prepared and cooked to the *soft* stage (see individual boiling or steaming instructions). Drain well and return to the dried pan with the butter and dry out over a low heat.

Liquidise with the single cream and then pass through a fine hair sieve into the buttered top of a double saucepan. Reheat when needed over hot water.

You could also put the cooked, liquidised and sieved vegetable into buttered and seasoned individual ramekins in a small roasting tray. When you have to reheat them, put boiling water in the pan, half-way up the sides of the ramekins, and put the pan into a preheated oven at 350°F/180°C/Gas 4. They will take 15–20 minutes to really heat through, ready to serve either as a small tasty starter or as a veg in its ramekin on the plate.

SAVOURY PASTRY

This is the pastry that is used for quiches and flans, and this quantity is enough to make three 10 inch (25cm) quiches, or sixteen individual 3 inch (8cm) quiches. If you don't want to use it all at once, it freezes well.

1lb (450g) plain flour
Pinch of salt
2 tablespoons icing sugar
10oz (275g) butter, softened
2 eggs, at room temperature

Sieve the flour with the salt and icing sugar on to a clean board or working surface and make a well in the centre. Put the soft butter into this, and then break the eggs on top of the butter. Now, with your hands, pat the egg into the butter. Don't squeeze, *pat*, and it doesn't really matter if you incorporate the odd bit of flour. Pat and tap away for about 8 minutes.

When they are mixed together and looking like fluffy scrambled egg, scoop up the flour with a palette knife and parcel it over the butter/egg mixture from all four sides. Blend it all in with the knife until you see it beginning to form larger crumbs. When it starts to have a texture like shortbread dough, take it in your hands and press the pastry gently together into three separate balls. Don't squeeze, just gently bring it together so that it looks like dough! Place in a polythene bag, tip up, and leave to chill.

When you wish to use it, let it come back to room temperature before rolling out.

SAVOURY CHEESE PASTRY

This is easily made in a Kenwood mixer using the K beater, and it stores well in fridge or freezer.

1lb (450g) plain flour
1lb (450g) butter, softened
1lb (450g) strong Cheddar cheese

Sieve the flour, cut the butter into walnut-sized pieces, and grate the cheese finely.

Put them all into the Kenwood, mix, and the dough will soon come together. (Or you can put the ingredients in a large bowl and mix by hand – but that, naturally, takes longer.) Chill the dough well, and let it come round to room temperature before using.

A pinch of curry powder makes an interesting change!

VEGETABLE SAVOURY PIE

The Food Minister, Lord Woolton, gave his name to a similar dish to this during the Second World War when frugal recipes were concocted to eke out the meagre weekly rations. I occasionally tell my (young) staff how much butter, sugar and tea *each week* we had to exist on – to their disbelief – but exist we did, and seemed none the worse for it at the end of the war. Some say we were a damned sight healthier. In 1940 those weekly rations per adult were: 2oz (50g) tea, 8oz (225g) sugar, 4oz (100g) bacon or ham, 1oz (25g) cheese, a shilling's worth of meat (the present-day 5p!), 8oz (225g) fat (of which only one-quarter was butter), and 3–4oz (75–100g) sweets or chocolate. Eggs were on allocation but in very short supply; and a monthly 'points' system allowed you to buy tins of Spam (low-point rated) or a solitary tin of salmon!

However, back to the vegetable savoury pie. Any vegetables can be used, and they should be cooked to the *crisp* stage (see individual recipes), and immediately refreshed under cold running water to arrest the cooking. Simply combine the cooked

vegetables with white sauce (see page 17), put in a casserole dish up to the top, and then cover with savoury cheese pastry (see previous recipe). Bake in the oven at 375°F/190°C/Gas 5 for about 30 minutes. Better still, use small to medium ramekin dishes for individual pies, and cook for about 20 minutes. Serve as a starter.

VEGETABLE QUICHE

I won't repeat the full instructions for quiches here – and you know the basics anyway. Vegetables are an ideal filling for a quiche, and just looking at the list below, you'll appreciate how you can ring the changes!

The basic recipe requires the savoury pastry (see page 13), and a pre-baked flan case (35 minutes at 325°F/160°C/Gas 3, with edges carefully covered with foil). The other ingredients are:

2 eggs
1 egg yolk
Pinch of salt
Turn of freshly ground black pepper
Pinch of freshly grated nutmeg
½ pint (300ml) double cream

Mix these together and pour into the pre-baked case over or under the vegetables. Bake for 35 minutes at 375°F/190°C/Gas 5.

Each vegetable in the following listing should be prepared basically as sense or the individual sections dictate, and the weight quoted is for *prepared* vegetables.

VEGETABLE	8 INCH (20CM) LOOSE-BOTTOMED FLAN TIN	10 INCH (25CM) LOOSE-BOTTOMED FLAN TIN
ASPARAGUS, fresh	8oz (225g)	12oz (350g)
BROAD BEANS	10oz (275g)	14oz (400g)
BROCCOLI florets	8oz (225g)	12oz (350g)
CAULIFLOWER florets	8oz (225g)	12oz (350g)
COURGETTES, sliced and fanned	5oz (150g)	9oz (250g)
FENNEL, diced	5oz (150g)	8oz (225g)
FRENCH BEANS, chopped, 1 inch (2cm) long	8oz (225g)	12oz (350g)
JERUSALEM ARTICHOKES, peeled and sliced	7oz (200g)	10oz (275g)
LEEKS, sliced	6oz (175g)	12oz (350g)
MUSHROOMS, sliced	6oz (175g)	12oz (350g)
ONIONS, finely chopped	8oz (225g)	12oz (350g)
PEPPERS, diced	6oz (175g)	10oz (275g)
RUNNER BEANS, sliced	8oz (225g)	12oz (350g)
SPINACH, coarsely chopped	1½lb (675g)	2lb (900g)
SWEETCORN kernels	6oz (175g)	10oz (275g)
TOMATO, peeled, seeded and chopped	8oz (225g)	12oz (350g)

FLAVOURED BUTTERS

The butter mountain in the Common Market would soon become a mere hump on the horizon if I had anything to do with it, as I would urge all and sundry to use it. It seems nonsensical to me, a mere taxpayer, that they find money to sell the commodity at a ridiculously low figure to everyone else, and make *us* pay through the nose for it! And all this bombarding with bumph about the terrible things butter does to you can go by the board – in fact such literature popping through my letter box immediately goes into the nearest wastepaper basket. No matter what we do or how we live, I firmly believe that only when the Great Man Himself (feminists will be saying, why not Herself) calls 'Come in, JT, your time is up', will I be whisked away to the wonders of heaven or the wickedness of hell.

I have often been involved in joint interviews in the media with the so-called food pundits who bewail the fact that we eat too much of this and not enough of that, that fats clog up the arteries, commercial flour does something else, egg yolks are terrible for this and oil shocking for that. And so often each pundit looks as if he or she could do with a damn good meal of normal, day-to-day things. It *may* be fattening, clogging and all that, but *nothing* can replace the flavour of butter, in cooking, in sandwiches, in sauces, or as a savoury topping for vegetables in particular.

The following ideas for flavoured butters are all easily made in a food processor, provided the butter is nice and soft (always remember that you mustn't flog your machine to death – this way it will be your trusty friend for so much longer).

Some people spread their soft butter out like a long fat sausage on greaseproof paper and then roll it up like a large Swiss roll before popping into the fridge or freezer. I personally like to put the soft butter into a piping bag and then make small or large stars on a flat tray. These I open-freeze, then, using a spatula, scoop off and into a plastic bag and label. So easy then on the day you are going to have a party to take out whatever flavour you want, count the stars you require, and then transfer them to the fridge to

16

use at the last minute with whatever veg you fancy.

I have given each flavoured butter recipe in a 1lb (450g) quantity and you may well say to yourself, that's a lot – but you will only use it in approximately ½oz (15g) portions, and the butters will certainly enhance the dullest of vegetables!

For each 1lb (450g) of butter

GARLIC
6 cloves garlic, finely crushed with 1 teaspoon fine salt
HORSERADISH
2 tablespoons horseradish cream
LEMON
Juice and rind of 1 lemon
LIME
Juice and rind of 1 lime
ORANGE
Juice and rind of 2 oranges
TOMATO
4 tablespoons tomato purée
TOMATO AND MUSTARD
2 tablespoons tomato purée and 2 tablespoons English mustard powder
RELISH
2 tablespoons Worcestershire sauce
WALNUT
4oz (100g) finely chopped walnuts
HERB
With individual herbs, be as generous as you fancy and as your palate will take

CHEESE AND HERB PÂTÉ

Like the mushroom pâté in the mushroom section, this is a basic of mine, which can be used and adapted in a seemingly infinite number of ways. With vegetables, it can serve as a topping for a salad, it can be used instead of a savoury or plain butter on hot vegetables, it can be baked with cabbage, chicory, courgettes, served with mushrooms, stuffed inside cucumbers, peppers or tomatoes. It is a very versatile mixture.

5oz (150g) butter
1lb (450g) cream cheese
3 cloves garlic, crushed with a little salt
1 tablespoon each finely chopped chervil, parsley and chives

Melt the butter slowly in a saucepan. In a large bowl mix the other ingredients together carefully, or you can mix them in your blender or processor. Do make sure that the herbs are evenly blended.

When the melted butter has cooled, pour it gently and slowly (not all at the same time) into the cheese. Fold it in very carefully as the mixture could curdle. Transfer the mixture, when all the butter has been absorbed, to a loaf tin for it to cool and set. (Or leave it in the bowl if you just want to use it in scoops.) It will keep for up to 10 days in the fridge, but I can't say that it freezes well.

PORT AND STILTON CHEESE

This is a wonderful filling for baked potatoes – allow about 1oz (25g) per potato – as well as a good way of using the end bits of Stilton.

4oz (100g) old ripe Stilton
2oz (50g) butter, softened
2 tablespoons port

Simply bring together all the ingredients in a food processor and scrape into jam jars, or other suitable containers. If it's not going to be used within a day or so, seal with a little cool melted butter after chilling.

BASIC WHITE SAUCE

I'm sure everyone knows how to make a white sauce, but here's how I make mine! It can be adapted in a number of ways, as you'll see from the variations below.

MAKES ¾ PINT (425ML)
1¾oz (45–50g) butter
¾ pint (425ml) milk
Pinch of salt
1½oz (40g) plain flour, sieved

Melt the butter in a deep, narrow saucepan, and heat the milk with the salt gently in another saucepan. When the butter has melted, add the sieved flour all at once, and stirring vigorously, blend together until smooth.

Add the warm milk in spoonfuls (I use a small ladle) to the flour and butter roux, beating well between each addition. Do make sure that the milk is absorbed before adding any more. Whisk and whisk until all the milk is in and the sauce is smooth. And just in case there are any lurking lumps, I usually pass the finished sauce through a sieve.

Store in a double saucepan, covered with a butter paper to prevent a skin from forming. It will be fairly thick at this stage, and will thicken up with cooling, so you can add more milk – or better still, cream – when you come to reheat it for use.

CHEESE SAUCE

Add about 4oz (100g) grated cheese to the basic white sauce.

CHEESE AND MUSTARD SAUCE

Add about 2oz (50g) grated cheese and 2 tablespoons Moutarde de Meaux to the basic white sauce.

MUSHROOM SAUCE

Add about 4oz (100g) mushroom pâté (see page 104) to the basic white sauce.

WHITE WINE SAUCE

Reduce half a bottle of white wine with a few black peppercorns down to about 4 tablespoons, remove the peppercorns, and mix the reduced wine with the basic white sauce.

HOLLANDAISE

Either a liquidiser or a food processor is necessary for this quick, never-fail adaptation of the difficult, time-consuming classic Hollandaise sauce. It should be made at the last minute, however, but it does hold its texture and heat in a double saucepan providing the water underneath merely simmers and doesn't boil.

The following recipe is ample for six people. If you have any left over, leave it in a bowl to set and use it for buttering bread for sandwiches.

4 egg yolks
1 teaspoon castor sugar
Pinch of salt
Juice of 1 lemon
1–2 tablespoons white wine vinegar
8oz (225g) butter

Put egg yolks, castor sugar and salt into the machine and lightly whizz around. Heat the lemon juice and vinegar in a small saucepan and slowly dribble this boiling liquid on to the combined egg yolks, using the machine at its highest speed.

Cut the butter into 1oz (25g) pieces and bring to a bubbling boil. Slowly dribble it on to the mixture, with the machine once again running at top speed. In a matter of minutes the sauce is ready.

Herbs may be added according to personal taste, as can curry powder, purée of spinach (see page 131) or mashed avocado.

BASIC DOUBLE CREAM SAUCE

This – although terribly fattening, I'm afraid – is one of my favourite sauces and it goes wonderfully with many vegetables. It can also be varied in a number of ways.

1 pint (550ml) double cream
1/4 teaspoon sea salt

Pour the cream with the salt into a large saucepan and place over a low heat. Leave to barely bubble until the cream has reduced by half. Do watch it though, as cream has a nasty habit of suddenly creeping up over the top of the pan and wasting itself all over the top of the cooker!

Keep this basic reduction warm in a double saucepan at the side of the stove, and add flavourings to taste or as appropriate.

TARRAGON CREAM

Beat together 2 eggs with 4oz (100g) castor sugar in a Pyrex or Christmas pudding bowl. Slowly add 1/4 pint (150ml) tarragon vinegar, still beating. Place bowl over a pan of simmering water and, stirring from time to time, over a period of 12–15 minutes, the mixture will thicken like lemon curd. Pass through a sieve into the warm reduced cream, beat until smooth and serve at once.

If you want to serve the tarragon cream cold, simply beat the sieved mixture to the thickness desired with 1 pint (550ml) of *un*reduced double cream.

Ring the changes with vinegars *other* than tarragon. Use garlic or mint vinegars or reduced wine.

TOMATO AND MUSTARD CREAM

Mix together 1 tablespoon of English mustard powder with 2 tablespoons of good tomato purée. Beat until smooth and then gradually beat into the reduced cream.

FRENCH DRESSING

This basic dressing is my favourite with vegetables and salads in general, but I often vary it: you can add finely chopped herbs, honey, redcurrant jelly, garlic, onion, or even apple. You can experiment with different flavours of vinegar, or you can replace some of the oil with another oil like walnut or hazelnut. Use 1/4 pint (150ml) bacon fat, hazelnut or walnut oil to 3/4 pint (425ml) olive. All these flavours will come through to tempt the palate or, to make the dressing somewhat thinner, simply add 1/4 pint (150ml) dry white wine. I personally find that the most important thing needed when making a French dressing is a finger to dip in to taste the mixture!

I make it in a 1 1/4 pint (700ml) quantity at a time, purely for convenience, as it stores well in the fridge for up to a week, but you can halve the quantity if you like – just remember the basic balance of four parts oil to one part vinegar.

1 pint (550ml) good olive oil
1/4 pint (150ml) white wine vinegar
2 generous teaspoons soft brown sugar
Pinch of salt
2 level teaspoons English mustard powder
Juice of 1/2 lemon

Simply blend all the ingredients together in the liquidiser for a few seconds until everything is perfectly combined. Decant into a lidded jar and store in fridge. Shake well before use.

SAVOURY CHEESE BREADCRUMBS

This is another basic of mine, *so* much more interesting than plain breadcrumbs. With vegetables, it's invaluable: as a coating when you're shallow- or deep-frying vegetables; as a stuffing; or as a topping for plain buttered cauliflower, broccoli, French beans, or any vegetable purée.

6oz (175g) Cheddar cheese, grated
2oz (50g) fine breadcrumbs (brown or white)
1 tablespoon chopped parsley

Simply mix all the ingredients together. Store in the fridge if not using straight away.

SAVOURY HAM FILLING

This basic recipe is good for many vegetables – tomatoes, marrow, cucumbers, peppers etc – and any left over stores well in the fridge. It could also be made into fritters or rissoles.

1lb (450g) leftover cooked ham or pork, cut in small
  pieces
8oz (225g) Cheddar cheese, coarsely grated
8oz (225g) breadcrumbs (brown or white)
1 medium onion, roughly chopped
4 tablespoons fresh seasonal herbs, chopped
4 tomatoes, skinned, seeded and chopped
1 teaspoon English mustard powder
2 tablespoons sherry
1 egg, beaten
Salt and freshly ground black pepper

Purée everything in the food processor, which takes all the hard work out of making this delicious filling. Make sure that your pieces of meat and onion are not huge, otherwise this will strain the motor on the machine.

OTHER SAVOURY FILLINGS

Anything can be used as a stuffing or filling for vegetables. It is basic imagination and the courage to use up leftovers which characterise them, and once again (as with French dressing) it is all the joyous tasting, little by little, stage by stage, which allows you to finally achieve a stuffing to your liking. Often the simplest made-up dishes like these are the ones which please most.

As a rough guide, the basic ratio should be as follows:

4oz (100g) onions
12oz (350g) meat
4oz (100g) breadcrumbs
1 or 2 eggs

Put these into the food processor or blender and whizz round to a purée and mix. Then mustard/curry powder/ginger/paprika/tomato/herbs/chutney/sauce/cheese/seasonings can be added to taste. And I mean *taste*, for you should then wield a teaspoon and taste the stuffing.

Leftover cold lamb can be enhanced with some apricot jam or redcurrant jelly, and to add flavour, some fresh mint or (a last resort) the bottled vinegary mint sauce.

Chicken or turkey leg meat can be used too. Whizz round in the food processor, adding nuts, curry powder, mustard, red peppers, skinned tomatoes, celery, stale bread, horseradish . . .

Use some orange or lemon rind, the last spoonful of apricot jam left in the pot – or some of your favourite honey. Just go on dabbling until you create something to satisfy your own personal palate.

MELBA TOAST

When I am going through my all-too-infrequent fruit-and-veg-no-booze phases of life, I consider myself truly virtuous when I forego my daily dose of home-made wholemeal bread or oven-hot rolls filled with dripping and jelly from the previous day's roast – and prepare melba toast.

19

20

It is a relatively simple task provided you have a good hot grill. I experimented with doing both stages in a domestic two-piece bread toaster. The first stage was easy but I think I still have remnants of the thin pieces jammed in the ruddy machine from the second stage. As the toast curled, it wound its way round the thin coils of hot wire! Not to be recommended.

Toast your regular slices of bread (brown or white) on both sides under the grill. Cut off the crusts, then, keeping the slice flat and using a very sharp, thin-bladed knife, simply cut through the middle horizontally to split the slice into two flat halves (quite easy as both outside pieces are firm because of the toasting).

Place these slices, soft side up, once more under the grill, and they will very quickly begin to curl up and brown. *Do* watch them though! When stone cold store in an airtight tin.

DEEP-FRIED PARSLEY

Deep-fried parsley is a much more interesting accompaniment than raw. It goes with almost anything, but particularly well with vegetable soups and purées.

Use parsley sprigs as large as possible, as they will shrivel when deep-fried. Heat the fat in the deep-fryer or pan to 365°F/185°C, and carefully check over the sprigs for dirt and grit (if you wash them, drain and dry *very* thoroughly before frying).

Arrange the sprigs on the foot of the deep-fryer basket and, just before you wish to serve, submerge in the oil. There will be a lot of sizzling and frothing, but in a matter of seconds this ceases and the parsley is ready. It tells you itself when it's done!

Transfer immediately to a double thickness of kitchen paper to drain, and serve at once, placing on the dish or plate with tweezers.

CITRUS TWIRLS

A slice of orange, lemon or lime can enhance many vegetable dishes, and if it's tarted up a bit, it looks even better!

Wash your fruit well, and then score the peel evenly round from top to bottom. (Keep the parings for garnishes, salads, sweets; they'll freeze or dry too.) Cut the fruit half-way through from top to bottom, then turn on its side and halve through its equator. As the slices fall, the cut through to the centre of the slice will open, revealing how they can be twisted decoratively.

RECIPES

ASPARAGUS

ASPARAGUS OFFICINALIS

22

A MEMBER OF THE LILY FAMILY, asparagus was eaten by the Ancient Egyptians, by the Greeks (whose legends say it grew from a ram's horn stuck in the ground), and by the Romans – who liked it crisp as we do today, evident from the saying *Velocius quam asparagi coquantur* (as quickly as it takes to cook asparagus)! After the Romans left Britain, it was not until Elizabethan times that asparagus was reintroduced, from France. It was known as sparrow-grass (thin varieties of asparagus, or sprue, do indeed look like grass), and 'grass' is the name by which it is still known in the trade. It is a stalk or shoot – along with cardoon, celery and rhubarb – and given their shape, it is not surprising that, historically, they have been thought of as aphrodisiac.

Asparagus grows plentifully in Europe, and is cultivated in the eastern states of the USA, and in parts of the American West. In Britain, it is grown mainly in Norfolk, the Vale of Evesham and Essex. In the northern hemisphere, the season is astoundingly short, from as early in May as the weather allows, until the end of June. As soon as the first English asparagus appears, I order and eat substantially, for eating asparagus is one of life's joys.

It is also one of life's luxuries, as asparagus is very expensive. It takes two to three years before an asparagus bed bears fruit, and each spear has to be cut by hand. The bed, too, although once established and managed properly will last and improve for up to twenty years, cannot be used for anything else for the remaining ten months or so of the year (although it has elegant ferny leaves which would not look out of place in the flower garden).

Asparagus should be eaten as soon as possible to enjoy the best flavour. Wrinkled, dirty or dry spears can be old and woody, and always look for spears of the same length and thickness. It's cheaper usually to buy spears loose by the pound or kilo than to buy the bunches already tied. Fat white spears are popular in Europe and America; thinner green and purplish ones in Britain – where sprue, very thin green spears, are cheap(er) and just as delicious. Store in the fridge if you must.

To prepare asparagus, peel the stem thinly with a potato peeler. Cut off the white or brownish woody ends to make the spears the same size, and to fit your cooking pot – you

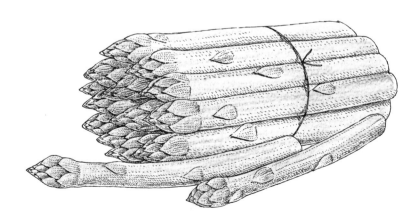

want the tougher stems to boil in the water, and the tender green tips to be *clear* of the water so that they steam and cook more gently. Lay the spears flat on a piece of string half-way up their stems, and gently but firmly tie them into a bundle with a firm knot. The number of spears can depend on their thickness and, of course, on the width of your pan. Special tall cylindrical asparagus pans are available, which make it all very easy, but they are an expensive item to have lurking at the back of the kitchen cupboard for so much of the year. You can improvise instead. A friend uses a flameproof enamel coffee pot in which the spears are held upright, or an ordinary large deep pan can hold the spears, with crumpled foil surrounding them to keep them upright like guardsmen. If the lid won't fit, fold a piece of foil gently around the tips and fasten to the saucepan to contain the steam. (Never throw asparagus water away, as it's full of goodness, and can be used to give flavour to a soup or stock.)

The freshest asparagus, to my mind, only needs to be boiled briefly, then eaten as is with melted butter – or Hollandaise, which is even more delicious. Cold cooked asparagus can be served with vinaigrette, a green or orange mayonnaise, or a béarnaise. Asparagus is also used in soups, quiches, soufflés, as an hors d'oeuvre or starter, as an accompanying vegetable (more common in the USA), and the tips look and taste delightful as a garnish.

A final thought, to justify that annual expense! Asparagus is a diuretic (thus very healthy according to Culpeper), is rich in Vitamin A as well as Vitamins B_1, B_2, and C, and is very low in calories (though, sadly, this is not true of its traditional accompaniments). Don't drink red wine with asparagus, as the traces of sulphur in the vegetable are enough to make the wine taste metallic.

ASPARAGUS SOUP

Basic recipe (see page 11)
2lb (900g) asparagus stalks, trimmed

Save the beautiful tips for another recipe, or for a garnish.

BOILED ASPARAGUS

For six people, two spears of asparagus each with some melted butter or, better still, some Hollandaise (see page 17), will serve as a delicious starter. (I have been known, though, to eat rather more than this on occasions!)

This recipe was tested using large cigar-sized asparagus – 'Evesham' – but if you find the thinner type, 'Formby', the timings below will be halved.

About 1¼lb (550g) asparagus, or 12 sticks
2 pints (a good litre) boiling water
4 teaspoons salt
2 teaspoons lemon juice

Twelve asparagus spears weighing this amount before preparation will leave you with 1lb (450g) after the woody ends have been cut off and the outer layer of skin removed with a potato peeler.

Tie the asparagus together in a bundle as described earlier, then put them, heads proudly up, into the boiling water in your asparagus or ordinary pan. Add salt and lemon juice and surround with crumpled foil if necessary. Bring back to the boil and cook for:
10 minutes – crisp
12 minutes – firm
15 minutes – soft

AUBERGINE

SOLANUM MELONGENA

BAKED ASPARAGUS

About 1¼lb (550g) asparagus
Butter
2 pints (a good litre) water
1 tablespoon olive oil
1 tablespoon white wine
1 teaspoon fresh lemon juice
4 black peppercorns
1 teaspoon salt

Prepare the asparagus as previously described, but don't tie with string. Lightly butter the base and sides of an earthenware or Pyrex casserole dish which will comfortably hold your asparagus lying down flat, gently overlapping if necessary.

In a separate saucepan bring the remaining ingredients to the boil. Pour this boiling mixture over the asparagus and cover with lid or foil. Bake in a preheated oven at 375°F/190°C/Gas 5 for:

    20 minutes – crisp
    25 minutes – firm
    30 minutes – soft
    Serve with Hollandaise (see page 17).

ARTICHOKE, see *GLOBE* and *JERUSALEM*

AUBERGINE IS THE FRENCH name for eggplant (as the vegetable is known in America), but it is an ancient name, originally deriving from the Sanskrit, *vatimgana*. Native to Asia, most particularly India (where it is known as brinjal), it has been adopted most enthusiastically into the cuisines of eastern Mediterranean countries. In India aubergines have been cultivated for over 4000 years; the Arabs have been eating them since the fourth century, and brought them to the west; and the Moors were thought to have introduced them to Europe, during their centuries of occupation of Spain. Grown as ornamental plants for some time in Europe, they were viewed with great suspicion; one English 'herball' of the late sixteenth century stated sourly that the people should avoid such foreign fruit, and eat only those which were home grown. The fact that aubergines were thought to cause epilepsy may

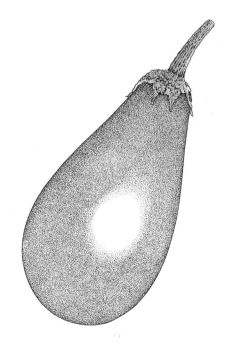

have had something to do with it! Thomas Jefferson introduced them to the United States, and early nineteenth-century American cookbooks have several recipes.

Aubergines, related to tomatoes, potatoes and peppers, are grown in warm countries throughout the world, but can only be grown under glass (unless in a very warm spot) in Britain. Mediterranean countries like Spain, Italy and Cyprus export large quantities. Although imported varieties are available throughout the year, they are best and cheapest in August and September. The harvesting time for home-grown aubergines is from July to early November.

Aubergines come in all shapes, sizes and colours. They can vary from the small round tomato or egg shape, to long cucumber shapes, and round footballs of up to 1 lb (450g) in weight. Size does not seem to affect flavour. The most commonly seen are purple-black in colour, but they can range through pale and dark green, yellow, violet and white.

When buying, look for an aubergine which is tight and shiny – like humans, a wrinkly skin

betokens age – and the peel, which does not need to be removed, contains much of the flavour. If not using straight away, store in the salad compartment of the fridge.

To prepare aubergines, wipe clean and cut off both ends. Depending on the recipe, cut in half, in slices or chunks (with a stainless steel knife, preferably, to lessen discoloration) and sprinkle with salt. Leave for up to 3 hours. This allows bitter juices to drain out, and also prevents them soaking up too much oil in cooking. Drain thoroughly and pat dry on kitchen paper.

Aubergines are always eaten cooked, and they do, undeniably, soak up a lot of fat – but they also soak up lots of spices and flavourings. They are delicious sliced, dipped in a light batter and deep-fried, and they are an essential part of many famous dishes: Provençal ratatouille, moussaka (which probably came from Turkey, but is now the most famous Greek dish), the *melanzane* dishes of southern Italy, Turkish *Imam bayildi* ('the Imam fainted' – from pleasure rather than from epilepsy, one hopes), and an aubergine dip from the Lebanon, known as poor man's caviar.

AUBERGINE SOUP

I wasn't convinced that this *would* make a soup until I cooked the following recipe. Don't be put off by the final colour as the taste is tantalising.

Basic recipe (see page 11)
1½lb (675g) aubergines, wiped and roughly diced
8oz (225g) potatoes, peeled and roughly diced

Garnish with toasted almonds or grated radishes. I served it with little round biscuits coated with a thin layer of cream cheese, and dotted with the relatively inexpensive red lumpfish roe. On another occasion, I was pretty liberal with some rather tired fresh dill just about to turn to seed in the herb garden, and the final taste was delicious.

DEEP-FRIED AUBERGINE

FOR 6 PEOPLE
1 aubergine, about 8–10oz (225–275g)
Salt
1 egg
2 tablespoons seasoned flour
Oil for deep-frying

Wipe the aubergine with a damp cloth, and top and tail. Slice diagonally into ¼ inch (5mm) slices and arrange flat on a baking tray. Sprinkle with salt and leave for 3 hours, turning half-way through this time. Transfer to kitchen paper and dry on both sides.

Lightly beat the egg in a bowl, and put the seasoned flour in another. Coat each slice of aubergine with the beaten egg, and then dip into the flour.

Fry for 4 minutes in preheated oil or the fryer, at 360°F/182°C. Transfer to kitchen paper and serve at once.

DEEP-FRIED AUBERGINE CHIPS

Aubergine can also be deep-fried in a tastier batter as chips – follow the recipe for deep-fried courgettes on page 69. But do remember to sprinkle with salt and allow to drain of liquid for at least a couple of hours before drying well and coating with batter.

SAVOURY AUBERGINE CASSEROLE

To ring the changes, you could add a little of your own curry powder mix – but not in such quantity that it takes over the dish.

FOR 6 PEOPLE
6oz (175g) aubergine, peeled
Salt
1 tablespoon oil
1oz (25g) butter
2oz (50g) onions, chopped
2 tablespoons celery, chopped
3 tomatoes, peeled, seeded and finely chopped

Cut the peeled aubergine into ¼ inch (5mm) cubes, and sprinkle with salt. Leave for 1 hour, and then dry on kitchen paper.

Heat oil and butter together then sauté the chopped onions until lightly golden. Add the aubergine cubes and cook for 10 minutes. Add the chopped celery and cook for 5 minutes before adding the diced tomatoes. Cook all together for a further 5 minutes. If you like, add some grated cheese or savoury cheese breadcrumbs (see page 19) just before serving.

BATAVIA, see ENDIVE
BEANS, see BROAD, FRENCH and RUNNER

26

BEANSPROUTS

PHASEOLUS AUREUS

THE BEANSPROUTS WE SEE MOST commonly are the germinated sprouts of the mung bean, known in China for some 3000 years. The mung bean is lighter than other pulses, and is often served as an invalid food in India, as it does not cause wind! They germinate easily, giving a sprout with a pleasant and crisp, if bland, flavour.

As far as health is concerned, beansprouts are a valuable source of nutrients. Pulses in general are good sources of protein when cooked unsprouted, but the process of germination, sprouting, more than doubles their content of some vitamins, C in particular. They also contain minerals and some protein.

In fact, many pulses and seeds can be sprouted like mung beans, and many have more distinctive flavours: soya beans (nourishing, but not very easy to sprout and taste 'beany'), wheat (tastes like corn), buckwheat, triticale, alfalfa, chick peas, and fenugreek (which has a distinctively curry-like flavour). Mustard and cress are the classic sprouting seeds, easy enough to be grown by even the smallest toddler, but tomato and potato seeds are poisonous, and should never be sprouted.

Mung beans – and others – can be bought from oriental and health-food shops, and are stocked by some supermarkets. They should be soaked first for about 3 hours in clean water – four cups of water to one cup seeds. They can then be put between blotting paper, tied in a cloth or towel, laid on flannel or – the most popular way – put in a glass jar to germinate. Choose a large clean jar and put in the beans (as they will increase in volume by up to ten times, make sure the jar is big enough, or use more than one). Fill with tepid water, and then cover the top of the jar with a piece of muslin (or doubled J-cloth), fastened with an elastic band. Turn the jar on its side over the sink so that all the water drips out, and then put the jar into a dry dark place. Repeat the soaking and draining procedure once a day, or more often in hot weather, perhaps. When the sprouts are ready, in about 3 days, remove carefully from the jar. They won't look the same as commercial sprouts which are grown in a way that straightens them – yours will be twisty and curly – but they'll taste the same.

Place in a bowl of cold water and stir around to free the husks. These should float to the surface, and you can tip them away.

Beansprouts are usually very lightly cooked in oriental recipes, often stir-fried. They could also be served raw in a salad, but as all sprouts contain a substance which can inhibit the digestion of protein, they should not be eaten raw in quantity. Even the quickest cooking can destroy this substance, so they could be happily stirred at the last moment into a hot consommé and, added to the Persian cucumber soup on page 71, they make a delightfully crunchy garnish.

BEETROOT

BETA VULGARIS

HE BEET OR BEETROOT THAT we know today developed from *Beta maritima*, a European seashore plant whose root was cultivated by German gardeners in the Middle Ages. But the Romans also knew the beetroot, growing it originally for its young leaves and only gradually recognising the value of the swollen root as a food. Red beets were at first regarded with great suspicion in Britain but have been a favourite since Tudor times.

There are four categories of beet: the table beetroot; spinach beet or chard; the sugar beet (developed by Napoleon and now one of the world's largest commercial crops); and the wonderfully named mangel-wurzel, which is used for cattle fodder. Beet grows best in temperate to cool regions, which is why it has become more prominent in the cuisines of northern Europe and North America. Maincrop beetroot is available all year round, as it stores well, but bunches of small globe beetroot available from June are a special treat. In fact, vegetable gardeners can thin the seedlings (the 'seeds' are actually a cluster, so several plants develop from one 'seed'), and use the fresh tender leaves plus the tiny roots to make a delicious salad. Beetroot are rich in sugar, potassium and other nutrients.

Globe or long-rooted beetroot are available, and they are best when young, before the flesh has a chance to become stringy. They are knobbly, and dark in colour, with bright red flesh when cooked. Golden beetroot appear spasmodically on the market, and have the advantage of not staining everything in sight with red juice.

For beetroot (a 'bossy' vegetable according to Jane Grigson) must be treated with the utmost care to prevent it 'bleeding' – which it can do profusely, staining work surfaces, pans, hands, accompanying vegetables, as well as leaching out flavour and goodness. The leaves must be twisted off gently, above the root, and the skin must not be broken or pierced in any way. To prepare for cooking, gently wash off surplus grit, and never cut off the ends.

Most beetroot are boiled (indeed many greengrocers sell them cooked), but they can also be baked, and eaten raw, grated. According to size, they take about 1 ½ hours to cook. When ready, they should be cooled quickly under cold water when the skins will slide off easily. The tops can be cooked like spinach.

Beetroot's rather earthy taste combines well with some of the strongest flavourings – with anchovies, oranges, capers, apples, mustard, horseradish, onions and garlic. (You *must* try the recipe with orange juice and walnut oil.) In the USA, beets with orange juice are Yale beets, and with a sweet-sour sauce Harvard beets. In Britain beetroot is generally a pickle or a constituent of a salad – for it is most commonly served cold. It is in Polish, Scandinavian and Russian cuisines that it is more extensively used, primarily in bortsch, a soup that can range from a pale pink consommé to a rich vegetable broth with reinforcements of meat and pulses. Beetroot is served with soured cream in Russia and Poland, and with herring around the coast of the North and Baltic seas.

BEETROOT SOUP

Basic recipe (see page 11), but using duck stock instead
of chicken
1½lb (675g) beetroot, peeled and diced
8oz (225g) potatoes, peeled and diced
Rind and juice of 2–3 oranges

My favourite herb with beetroot soup is thyme.

BEETROOT AND APPLE SOUP

Basic recipe (see page 11)
1lb (450g) beetroot, peeled and diced
1lb (450g) apples, wiped and cut into wedges

This is also a nice combination. When serving, hot *or* cold, add coarsely grated Granny Smith apples as a garnish.

GRATED BEETROOT FRIED WITH ORANGE AND WALNUT OIL

FOR 6 PEOPLE
10oz (275g) raw beetroot, peeled, topped and tailed
1 tablespoon walnut oil
Juice and rind of 1 orange

Grate the beetroot into a bowl. Heat the oil in an 8 inch (20cm) frying pan, then add the orange juice and rind. Add the grated beetroot and stir-fry, using a wooden spoon, for:
   4 minutes – crisp
   5 minutes – firm
   8 minutes – soft
   This is a simple dish to do while you are attending to the main course. Garnish with chopped mint which adds a little extra taste appeal. It is also extremely nice cooked crisp, then served cold in or as a salad.

BEETROOT, ONION AND CHEESE SAVOURY

This starter should be made in 5–6 inch (12–15cm) round Pyrex or porcelain dishes, one per person. I'm a great garlic lover, so I use a lot in the dishes at first, but each to his own taste.

29

PER PERSON
Garlic
Butter
2oz (50g) small beetroot, peeled and sliced into ⅛ inch
* (3mm) slices*
½oz (15g) onions, finely chopped
1oz (25g) Cheddar cheese, grated
1 tablespoon natural yoghurt

Rub the insides of the dishes with a peeled, lightly crushed garlic clove, then butter them. Preheat the oven to 350°F/180°C/Gas 4.
   In each dish, fan out the beetroot slices in circles, starting from the middle. Mix the onions and cheese together, and place on top of the sliced beetroot.
   Put dishes on a baking tray and bake in preheated oven for:
   15 minutes – crisp
   20 minutes – firm
   25 minutes – soft
   When serving, top each dish with a little lightly heated natural yoghurt, and garnish with chopped fresh herbs.

BROAD BEANS

VICIA FABA

STEAMED BEETROOT BALLS

FOR 6 PEOPLE
1 large raw beetroot, topped and tailed
2 pints (a good litre) boiling water
1 teaspoon salt

Peel the beetroot with a sharp, stainless steel knife, and then, using a Parisian scoop, cut out into balls, allowing six or approximately 1oz (25g) per person.

Place in a colander over a pan of salted boiling water, and steam:
  8 minutes – crisp
  10 minutes – firm
  15 minutes – soft

T HE BROAD BEAN, PROBABLY the daddy of them all, has been grown by man since prehistoric times. Originally native to North Africa – where a brown variety, *fuls*, is still grown – they were cultivated by the Ancient Egyptians and the Greeks. They were believed, however, by many to be unclean, the cause of insomnia and bad dreams, and Ancient Romans regarded them as harmful to the vision. In fact, even today, many Mediterranean peoples (and their descendants in many other countries) suffer from an allergy, favism, which causes vertigo, headaches and other symptoms, and which results directly from eating broad beans. The broad bean was the *only* bean grown in the Old World before Columbus discovered the New and with it other varieties such as the haricot, and was a staple food for peasants in many countries during the Middle Ages.

Broad beans are the first beans for picking in spring, and are available in Mediterranean climates from March, and usually from the end of May until the beginning of September in Britain. If very young (less than 3 inches or 8cm in length), both pods and beans may be eaten (they are often eaten raw in Italy to accompany *prosciutto*, and in Spain and Italy as a nibbler before a meal with wine and cheese), and if you've grown them yourself, the top 5 inches (12cm) can be plucked and cooked like spinach.

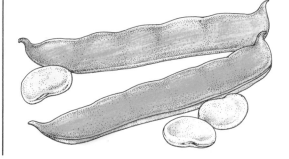

BELL PEPPER, see PEPPER
BORECOLE, see KALE

But the majority available from growers are larger and have a thick pod which is generally inedible and has to be discarded. The older the bean in the pod, the larger the black line or scar on it. In *Food in England*, Dorothy Hartley says when the scar becomes black, 'country people call them "blackspotted beans", and reckon them indigestible food, though good enough for a hungry plough-boy'! When older, not only the pod needs to be removed, but also the grey outer skin of the individual beans before further cooking. Dried, broad beans are a valuable source of protein.

Prepare broad beans according to their age. Some experts advise shelling them with gloves because the hands can be stained black. (I remember, when evacuated to a farm during the war, that the farmer's daughter attempted to remove a wart on her hand by rubbing it with a freshly picked, cut raw broad bean. The wart was still there after the season was over, but nettle stings were immediately cooled after rubbing with the white furry inside of the broad bean pod.)

When cooking broad beans, a sprig of fresh savory added to the water – as they do in France and Germany – enhances the flavour, although parsley seems to be the traditional flavouring for broad bean sauces in Britain. Cook older beans twice, once to remove the outer skin, then again, with oil or seasonings to serve. Use dried broad beans (after soaking for about 12 hours, changing the water at least twice), to flavour and add substance and goodness to winter soups, casseroles and stews. Broad beans are often cooked with a ham or bacon joint to soak up the flavour, and a tasty purée can be spread on hot toast and topped with scrambled egg. Broad beans (or chick peas) are the major ingredients of the Egyptian and Israeli Arab dish, *falafel*, fried rissoles, which are nourishing, cheap and tasty.

BROAD BEAN SOUP

Basic recipe (see page 11)
2lb (900g) broad beans, podded

If you like, throw in 1 tablespoon of fresh uncooked peas per portion just as you're serving. This provides texture and is an unusual combination.

Fresh sage is a delightful herb to use discreetly when making this soup.

BROAD BEAN LEMON SOUP

Basic recipe (see page 11)
2lb (900g) broad beans, podded
Juice and rind of 2 lemons

Add lemon juice and rind at the beginning of cooking.

BROAD BEAN HAZELNUT SOUP

Basic recipe (see page 11)
2lb (900g) broad beans, podded
4oz (100g) ground hazelnuts

Add the hazelnuts after liquidising the soup.

31

STEAMED BROAD BEANS

Without any doubt my favourite summer vegetable but, oh, so wasteful, and rather on the pricey side as out of 2lb (900g) of broad bean pods purchased from your greengrocer, you will only get about 8–12oz (225–350g) of actual beans. When these are cooked and then have their outside skin removed (if older), the final weight will be just about 4–6oz (100–175g). Yes, that reduction *is* drastic, isn't it – but well worth all the effort and trouble!

FOR 6 PEOPLE
2lb (900g) broad bean pods
1 pint (550ml) boiling water
1 teaspoon salt
4 rashers back bacon

Shell the broad beans, weigh them (see below), and place in a colander over the saucepan of boiling salted water. Put the lid on the pan, or cover firmly with foil.

If out of the initial 2lb (900g) you got 8oz (225g) young beans, cook:
   4 minutes – crisp
   5 minutes – firm
   6 minutes – soft
If out of the initial 2lb (900g) you got 12oz (350g) of older beans, cook:
   8 minutes – crisp
   10 minutes – firm
   12 minutes – soft
Take colander off the boiling water, and remove beans. If you have older beans, wait until they've cooled a bit, then hold each individual bean between your thumb and finger, and gently snap off the dark end. Carefully squeeze the bean, and the centre will pop out leaving the pale hard skin behind.

When you wish to serve cooked broad beans, young or old, finely dice the bacon and fry until crisp. Simply pour the diced bacon and fat over the cooked beans, and serve at once.

BROAD BEANS WITH FRENCH DRESSING

This is my very favourite way of serving steamed broad beans – as a cold starter course, on a bed of shredded lettuce and radishes. To this you can add fresh herbs to taste.

At the last minute pour over a slightly warmed French dressing (see page 18) and, better still, paint the base of your serving plate first with either hazelnut or walnut oil. And if you're really feeling like a beanfeast, scatter some crisply fried diced bacon with the fat over the beans just before serving.

BROAD BEANS WITH CHEESE SAUCE

Steam as above, and then fold into the sauce (see page 17).

BROAD BEANS WITH WINE SAUCE

Steam as above, and then fold into the sauce (see page 17).

PURÉE OF BROAD BEANS
(see also page 13)

FOR 6 PEOPLE
1lb (450g) broad beans, podded
1oz (25g) butter
¼ pint (150ml) single cream

Steam the beans to the soft stage (see above), dry over gentle heat with the butter, and then purée them with the cream. If they were getting past their prime, you'll be surprised at the effort then needed to get them through the sieve!

To make the dish go a little further, you can add to the sieved purée 4oz (100g) ground hazelnuts, 4oz (100g) Philadelphia cream cheese and 1 egg.

BROCCOLI

BRASSICA OLERACEA

OLD BROAD BEANS COOKED IN SWEET WHITE WINE

You could cook them in cider instead of the wine if you like.

FOR 6 PEOPLE
3lb (1.5kg) broad bean pods
Butter
¼ pint (150ml) sweet white wine

This quantity of bean pods will, when shelled, give you about 12–16oz (350–450g) beans.

Place in a buttered casserole and pour the wine over them. Cook in preheated oven at 350°F/180°C/Gas 4 for:
    20 minutes – crisp
    25 minutes – firm
    30 minutes – soft

BROCCOLI IS A BRASSICA, A form of cabbage (that most fruitful of plants, related to kale, Brussels sprouts, and cauliflower), and broccoli is obviously most closely related to the latter. Both broccoli and cauliflower are grown for their heads of immature flowers known as curds. The Romans knew broccoli – Apicius recorded it in *De Re Coquinaria* – and its Italian origin is obvious from the name, the plural of *broccolo*, cabbage sprout or head. The geographical origins of broccoli are debatable (thought to be Asia Minor and the eastern Mediterranean), but Italy has always been a major producer. Catherine de Medici is credited with having brought it to France from her native Tuscany when she married Henry II, and indeed Italian broccoli, or calabrese, is the commonest variety available today. Introduced to Britain in the eighteenth century, broccoli was also known then in the United States, but its culinary delights were ignored by American cooks until well into the twentieth century.

Broccoli is available in several types. It may be white, but is more usually green or purple. Some varieties produce a purple cauliflower-like head, others produce delicious little side shoots. Calabrese produces larger

central heads which, when cut, encourage the growth of side shoots. White and purple varieties of broccoli are available all year round; calabrese is best in July and August.

When buying, make sure the colour is good, the heads look small, fresh and tightly packed, and the stalks are brittle. Avoid limp leaves and yellowed curds. Look at the base of the stalks, and if they look dry or feel woody, don't buy.

To prepare broccoli, cut off the lower portion of the stalks and scrape. Remove any large wilted leaves, and soak in salted water with a little lemon juice for a short while to clean. Cook a large head like cauliflower – in florets or whole, in a minimum of water, or steam it. Smaller sprouts can be tied together in bunches like asparagus. Indeed broccoli is one of the many candidates for the title 'poor man's asparagus', and can be eaten in many of the same ways as asparagus – with melted butter, Hollandaise, mayonnaise or béarnaise.

Broccoli must never be over-cooked as it will be too soft and mushy. It should be crisp and bright green and, interestingly, it is one of the few western vegetables which has been adopted and used by Chinese chefs who stir-fry small florets to crisp, colourful and flavourful perfection. Always save the cooking water for soups, stocks or sauces, as it will contain some of the nutrients of the broccoli – Vitamin C and the rarer Vitamin A.

Broccoli is most often used as an accompanying vegetable, but it can also be served as an hors d'oeuvre, cold with a vinaigrette, as asparagus above, or in soups. Small florets can be dipped in a light batter and deep-fried, and sprinkled Italian style with Parmesan and/or buttered breadcrumbs; it can be served in a good cheese sauce like cauliflower; and it blends wonderfully in a traditional old English recipe with eggs, either scrambled or in an omelette.

BROCCOLI SOUP

As you will realise, to serve only the ends of this vegetable provides you with a lot of 'waste', but this can be made into a very wholesome soup.

If you do not wish to use it immediately, do remember that soups freeze well (see page 12).

Basic recipe (see page 11)
2lb (900g) broccoli stems, bases and outer leaves

Serve garnished with grated, rich-tasting Cheddar cheese.

STEAMED BROCCOLI HEADS

For six people, you will have to purchase at least 1lb (450g) of broccoli – try to get a head per person – from the greengrocer, as there is a bit of waste (but use it in the previous soup recipe). When cut to approximately 3 inch (8cm) lengths the individual portions will be just over 1 1/2oz (40g) each, so there is practically half wasted!

FOR 6 PEOPLE
At least 1lb (450g) broccoli
1 pint (550ml) boiling water
Salt and freshly ground pepper

Place the broccoli heads down flat on the base of the colander, and season with salt and freshly ground pepper. Place the colander over the boiling water – to which you've added 1 teaspoon salt – and put on the lid (or cover tightly with foil). Steam for:
    10 minutes – crisp
    12 minutes – firm
    15 minutes – soft

BOILED BROCCOLI

Once again about 1lb (450g) has to be purchased but as the cooking is more severe you can leave on a little extra stem – about 4 inches (10cm) in length is ideal.

FOR 6 PEOPLE
1lb (450g) broccoli
2 pints (a good litre) boiling water
1½ teaspoons salt

When the water, with added salt, is boiling well, drop the broccoli heads in and bring back to the boil. Cover with the lid, and cook for:
    8 minutes – crisp
    10 minutes – firm
    12 minutes – soft
    If you plan to serve this cold as a side dish, do make sure that you pour the French dressing of your choice (see page 18) over the broccoli while it is still hot, and *then* leave to cool.

BROCCOLI WITH TARRAGON CREAM

Boiled or steamed broccoli is transformed when you indulge in the luxury of topping it with a generous spoonful of tarragon cream (see page 18).

BROCCOLI WITH HOLLANDAISE

Or better still, with a lovely warm Hollandaise (see page 17).

BROCCOLI POLONAISE

Steamed or boiled broccoli is given an additional flavour if you simply scatter over savoury cheese breadcrumbs (see page 19) just as you are about to serve it. Toasted whole almonds are delicious too.

BROCCOLI FRIED WITH SESAME AND RASPBERRY

Use only the actual flower heads for this, which should weigh about 1oz (25g) each. The quoted quantity of 2–3oz (50–75g) per person is sufficient.

FOR 6 PEOPLE
12–18oz (350–500g) broccoli heads
3 tablespoons sesame oil with raspberry vinegar (see page 10)

Simply prepare and wash the heads and then wipe dry. Blanch for 1 minute in boiling water, then refresh under running cold water. Drain well.
    In a 10 inch (25cm) frying pan, heat the sesame oil and raspberry vinegar gently. Add the blanched drained broccoli, and stir-fry with a wooden spoon for:
    3 minutes – crisp
    4 minutes – firm
    5 minutes – soft

BROCCOLI FRIED IN BACON FAT

This is exactly the same as the previous recipe, but the blanched, drained broccoli heads are stir-fried in 3 tablespoons bacon fat instead of the sesame and raspberry mixture.
    Towards the end of cooking, generously grind some coriander seeds over the pan from your coriander mill.

BRUSSELS SPROUTS

BRASSICA OLERACEA GEMMIFERA

BAKED BROCCOLI WITH BACON

You will have to purchase about 2lb (900g) broccoli as this, when prepared, should give you six heads of about 4oz (100g) each.

FOR 6 PEOPLE
About 2lb (900g) broccoli
6 large rashers smoked middle bacon

Twirl a rasher of bacon round each broccoli stalk from the stem base end up towards the flower, and secure with a cocktail stick if necessary.

Place each wrapped stalk on to a piece of foil, wrap up fairly loosely, and place on a baking tray.

Preheat the oven to 400°F/200°C/Gas 6 and bake:
25 minutes – crisp
30 minutes – firm
40 minutes – soft
Take out of the foil and serve at once.

You could also remove the bacon-wrapped stalks from the foil, place back on the baking tray, then sprinkle liberally with grated cheese. Finish off very briefly under the grill.

SPROUTS ARE, OBVIOUSLY, A member of the cabbage family – looking like compact bright green cabbages in miniature. They are called Brussels sprouts because they are thought to have been first grown around that city in the thirteenth to fourteenth centuries. But their history is vague, as there are no culinary mentions to be found until, so Jane Grigson says, Eliza Acton's *Modern Cookery* of 1840. They had already been taken to America by Thomas Jefferson at the beginning of the nineteenth century, but the enthusiasm there for the vegetable seems to have been no greater – as it still is not, since Britain would appear to be the largest world consumer of the crop (although Spain and Italy are slowly beginning to appreciate them as a winter vegetable).

And Brussels sprouts are indubitably one of the most important of the winter vegetables in Britain, cropping from October until the end of February (early varieties can begin in late August), although it is generally thought that sprouts are sweeter when picked after the first frost. One almost feels winter is just round the corner when the first sprouts appear in the shops, and they are, of course, now the traditional British accompaniment to the Christmas turkey.

Brussels sprouts come from a plant with a stout firm stem which bears the individual sprout 'heads' up most of its height, and which is crowned at the top with a messy mass of crumpled leaves (which can be cooked like cabbage or greens). The most perfect sprouts should be small rather than large, a vivid green, and firm to the touch. Any sign of yellowing means they are slightly over the hill, but they can still be used for soups and purées. If leaves are loose and the sprout 'gives', it will be old and tasteless and good only for the compost heap. Try to buy and eat sprouts on the same day as only then can you guarantee freshness and their full content of Vitamin C.

To prepare Brussels sprouts, cut off a slice at the stalk end and remove coarse or dirty outer leaves. Leave to soak in slightly salted water for no longer than 10 minutes. Cut a small cross in the stalk to ensure this cooks at the same rate as the compact leaves.

Brussels sprouts should never really be cooked soft, unless you wish to make a purée. They are best when boiled for a minimum length of time, until still crisp – although many, of course, prefer their vegetables softer.

Mostly used as an accompanying vegetable, Brussels sprouts could also merit eating as a vegetable dish on their own, with a good cheese sauce, say, or a butter and herb sauce. They are also eaten as a soup (often with potatoes or other flavouring added to diminish the strong cabbagey flavour: hazelnuts, as in my recipe, are good), and a purée can form the basis of a delicious soufflé. One of the most popular recipes has chestnuts with the sprouts (why not try the more unusual *water* chestnuts) – and sprouts can also be eaten raw, sliced very thinly into winter salads.

BOILED OR STEAMED BRUSSELS SPROUTS

I find that five to six sprouts per person is an ample portion when being served with two other vegetables. When the outer leaves and stalks are cut off larger sprouts, you will be left with about 12–14oz (350–400g). The cute, small round ones don't need such rigorous trimming, so a smaller quantity will give about the same prepared weight.

FOR 6 PEOPLE
1½lb (675g) large or 1lb (450g) small sprouts
1 pint (550ml) boiling water
1 teaspoon salt

The base of each sprout should be just gently criss-cross cut, which allows this tougher part to cook in the same time as the lovely round vegetable itself.

Using boiling water with added salt, the following cooking times are relevant for both boiling and steaming:

Large			Small
10 minutes	–	crisp –	6–8 minutes
12 minutes	–	firm –	8–10 minutes
15 minutes	–	soft –	10–12 minutes

Personally, I prefer to boil sprouts initially for only 4 minutes before refreshing them under running cold water. I then leave them to one side, and as and when I wish to serve them, I stir-fry them quickly over a high heat in either bacon fat or a mixture of walnut oil and butter. Bacon bits are delicious, too, with Brussels or, if you want to, you can fry the sprouts off in herb butter, and garnish them with a very thin slice of fresh lemon.

FRIED BRUSSELS SPROUTS WITH CHESTNUTS

For a crunchier texture, and a more unusual flavour, try finely diced water chestnuts with the sprouts instead of the sweet chestnuts.

FOR 6 PEOPLE
1lb (450 g) Brussels sprouts
4 tablespoons bacon fat
8oz (225g) fresh chestnuts

Prepare sprouts as in the previous recipe, then add them to boiling salted water. Bring back to the boil, and simmer for 3–5 minutes only, according to their size. But do not overcook. Drain and return to low heat to dry out.

When you want to serve them, melt the bacon fat in a small frying pan, and toss the sprouts in the hot fat until they are browned on the outside.

Meanwhile place the chestnuts in a bowl and cover them with boiling water. Remove two at a time and, using a small sharp knife, remove the outer shell and the inner skin. It is quite a simple process, really, provided you work quickly and don't let the water go cold (otherwise you have to throw it out and repeat it all).

Chop the peeled chestnuts and mix them in with the browned sprouts and bacon fat. Serve as quickly as possible.

PURÉE OF BRUSSELS SPROUTS (see also page 13)

FOR 6 PEOPLE
1lb (450g) Brussels sprouts
1oz (25g) butter
1/4 pint (150ml) single cream

Prepare and cook the sprouts until very tender (about 10–15 minutes). Drain well, then return to the dried pan with the butter and dry out over a low heat.

Liquidise with the cream, and pass through a fine hair sieve into the buttered top of a double saucepan, to reheat when needed.

When reheating, you can tart up the basic purée in a variety of ways. You can lightly fry off small pieces of smoked bacon (about 4oz or 100g), dry them on kitchen paper, and sprinkle over the purée. A lemon twirl not only looks nice on top of this but the taste of the juice is interesting. You can incorporate about 4oz (100g) ground hazelnuts at the liquidising stage, or I have often tickled people's palates by sprinkling the purée with some toasted desiccated coconut and some very finely chopped red peppers.

BRUSSELS SPROUTS SOUP

Basic recipe (see page 11)
2lb (900g) prepared even-sized sprouts
4oz (100g) ground hazelnuts

Stir in the ground hazelnuts after the soup has been liquidised and sieved.

BUTTERNUT SQUASH, see
PUMPKIN AND SQUASH

CABBAGE

BRASSICA OLERACEA CAPITATA

ALL BRASSICAS – THE CABBAGE family, which includes Brussels sprouts, broccoli, cauliflower, collards, kale and even kohlrabi – are descended from the wild cabbage. This can often be found in waste places, usually as an escape, but still grows naturally wild in southern Britain, on the White Cliffs of Dover in particular. (The exceptions are the Chinese cabbages which are of a different genus – see page 64.) Cabbage – that most English and most maligned of vegetables – has been cultivated and eaten for thousands of years: sauerkraut or pickled cabbage was served to labourers working on the Great Wall of China in about 200 BC! The Ancient Greeks knew it (Pythagoras liked it, but he apparently was almost vegetarian anyway); the Romans prized it, according to Cato (who thought it the best vegetable of all); and the Celts and Saxons virtually lived on it, and valued it medicinally.

Thought by some to originate around the Mediterranean, it is more likely that it developed along the coasts of Britain and more northerly Europe, the cool moist climates which the present-day plant prefers. And this is undoubtedly why it is commoner in the cuisines of Britain, Holland, Scandinavia and Germany – although peasant soups featuring cabbage are eaten in southern France and in Portugal.

Cabbages are available all year round, and are classified according to the time of year. In Britain, spring cabbages are available in April and May, spring greens (picked before the heart has developed) from November to April, summer and autumn cabbages are available from June to October, and winter varieties from August to March. The tight-headed white cabbage, sometimes known as the Dutch white, is now grown in Britain as well, and is available from October to February, Savoy from August to May, and the magnificent red from August to January. The heads, too, can classify the cabbage, as they can be conical or round in shape, and range in colour from dark and light green to pink and purple.

Generally regarded as a boring vegetable – its name is associated in English with a boring, unadventurous person (although the nicer French use *mon petit chou* as a term of endearment) – cabbage is astoundingly versatile. Its reputation probably derives from the fact that the English have tended to cook it to death, and uninterestingly, but it can be baked, spiced,

39

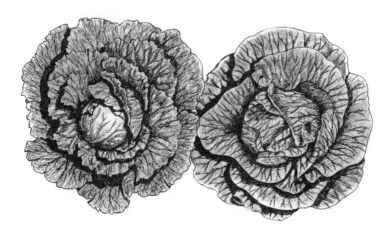

made into soup, pickled, creamed, stuffed – served in many different and delicious ways. It is also full of Vitamin C.

When buying cabbage, always look for brightness of colour (a pale green Savoy should be avoided at all costs), and crispness of leaves. Brown smudges, holes in leaves, and a browning stem are other pointers to age and poor quality.

To prepare, depending on the way in which it is to be used, cut off the bottom of the stem and any outer coarse leaves. If shredding, cut cabbage in quarters, and soak in cold, slightly salted water for no longer than 10 minutes. Cut out central cores, and then shred. If removing leaves to stuff, cut off bottom of core, and gently peel leaves away from head.

Cabbage should be cooked for the very shortest time if using as an accompanying vegetable; it should really still be crisp for texture, flavour and goodness. The leaves may be blanched before stuffing and then baking (like cabbage dolmas, for instance). A whole cabbage can be hollowed out for stuffing and then baked. Cabbage can be added to casseroles and soups, for long slow cooking – the *potées*, *garbures* and *soupes aux choux* of French peasant cookery – and it features cooked in the British bubble and squeak and the Irish colcannon. It can also be eaten raw, shredded or grated into winter salads, and is a major constituent of the salad coleslaw (from the Old English *cole*, Dutch *kool*, or German *Kohl*, all meaning cabbage). The classic European cabbage dish, however, is sauerkraut.

I haven't given any cabbage soup recipe, or any basic boiling or steaming recipes, as I think whole generations of people (well, Britons anyway) have been put off cabbage for ever by the school-dinner syndrome of a wet smelly mush. (Incidentally, it is the sulphur content of cabbage which is responsible for the unpleasant smell given off during cooking.)

CABBAGE WITH CIDER

FOR 6 PEOPLE
¼ pint (150ml) cider
12oz (350g) firm white cabbage, finely shredded
1 sharp eating apple

Put the cider into a saucepan, and bring to the boil. Add the shredded cabbage, cover with a lid, and cook:

    4 minutes – crisp
    5 minutes – firm
    10 minutes – soft

Stir after each 2 minutes of cooking time. Coarsely grate the apple cold into the cabbage just before serving.

CABBAGE WITH ORANGE

FOR 6 PEOPLE
Juice and rind of 1 large orange
12oz (350g) firm white cabbage, finely shredded
2oz (50g) flaked almonds, toasted

Cook cabbage as in the previous recipe, but use the orange juice instead of the cider. Garnish with the toasted almonds.

CABBAGE BOATS

I have specified a Savoy cabbage, but a white cabbage – or indeed any – can be used instead for this recipe. Serve a wedge per person as a supper dish with other vegetables.

FOR 6 PEOPLE
1 large firm Savoy cabbage
Oil (walnut, hazelnut or olive)
Sea salt and freshly ground black pepper

Remove the outer leaves from the cabbage, cut in half, then with a small sharp knife with a point, remove the main stalk.

Cut the half cabbages into 'melon-shaped' wedges, each one weighing about 3oz (75g). Paint the wedges on all sides with your favourite oil, then season with salt and pepper.

Wrap tightly with strong clingfilm, then poach in simmering water, uncovered, for:

7 minutes – crisp (but warm right through)
8 minutes – firm
10 minutes – soft

BACON CABBAGE BOATS

This, too, is a good supper dish.

FOR 6 PEOPLE
1 large firm cabbage
6oz (175g) cheese and herb pâté (see page 16)
6 rashers smoked bacon, derinded

Prepare and cut the cabbage as described in the previous recipe.

Spread the wedges with 1oz (25g) cheese and herb pâté, and then wrap each in a piece of bacon. Secure with a sharp wooden cocktail stick.

Wrap each wedge loosely in foil and place on a baking tray. Place in preheated oven at 375°F/190°C/Gas 5, and bake for:

20 minutes – crisp
25 minutes – firm
30 minutes – soft

STUFFED CABBAGE BOATS

FOR 6 PEOPLE
1 large firm cabbage
About 8–12oz (225–350g) mushroom pâté (see page 104)
At least 6 spring onion ends (leaves), blanched

Prepare cabbage as in cabbage boat recipe, but this time do *not* throw away the outside leaves. Blanch these whole (you'll need six) in boiling salted water for 2 minutes, until soft and pliable.

Separate out the layers of each individual wedge (it's fiddly, I warn you), and line each leaf layer with a thin layer of mushroom pâté. Then reconstruct each wedge again. Tie up with the blanched spring onion ends, then wrap each wedge in a blanched outside leaf so that the boat becomes a parcel.

Place on a buttered tray in a preheated oven at 375°F/190°C/Gas 5 and bake for:

20 minutes – crisp
25 minutes – firm
30 minutes – soft
Do *not* serve the outside leaves.

CABBAGE PLATTER

This is like a pizza for vegetarians, as it makes an excellent base for other cooked vegetables – fried grated carrots can be placed on top (see page 50), or two different puréed vegetables look very attractive. It's also delicious topped with the onion and blackcurrant sauce on page 111.

FOR 6 PEOPLE
1 large, firm cabbage
About 8 tablespoons oil (or bacon fat)

Remove outer leaves from cabbage, and then lay the round firm vegetable on its side. Using a very sharp, preferably saw-edged knife, cut into slices of about ½ inch (1cm) thickness, placing each one on a baking tray coated liberally with oil or bacon fat.

Paint each slice with more oil or bacon fat, cover the tray completely with foil, and place in a preheated oven at 375°F/190°C/Gas 5. Bake for:

20 minutes – crisp
22 minutes – firm
25 minutes – soft

BAKED CABBAGE WITH GARLIC AND JUNIPER

FOR 6 PEOPLE
2lb (900g) cabbage
8 juniper berries
2 large cloves garlic, peeled
$\frac{1}{2}$ teaspoon sea salt
2 tablespoons olive oil

Remove the outer leaves and cut the cabbage into four. Cut out the firm hard stalk from each quarter, and slice the cabbage very finely using a sharp, stainless steel knife.

In a pestle and mortar (or liquidiser) pound (or blend) the berries with the garlic and sea salt, until you get a smooth paste.

Just cover the bottom of a 9 pint (5 litre) saucepan with the olive oil, and heat through until beginning to smoke. Put in the juniper/garlic mixture, and stir with a wooden spoon. Add the finely grated cabbage, and stir-fry for several minutes until the cabbage is well coated with oil. Remove to a casserole dish and bake in a preheated oven at 425°F/220°C/Gas 7 for about 15 minutes.

If you like very crisp vegetables, just stir-fry in the saucepan for about 3 minutes – the flavour will be imparted to the cabbage by then, and as the vegetable is so finely chopped, it will have heated through.

You can also bake cabbage similarly, but with the rind and juice of 2 lemons, 2–4 sprigs of chopped fresh mint, and lots of freshly ground black pepper instead of the garlic and juniper berries.

BAKED SAVOURY CABBAGE

FOR 6 × 3 INCH (8CM) RAMEKINS
Melted butter
Salt and freshly ground black pepper
4oz (100g) firm white cabbage, very finely shredded
2oz (50g) red peppers, finely diced
7$\frac{1}{2}$ tablespoons natural yoghurt
6 tablespoons farmhouse Cheddar cheese, grated

Grease the ramekins with melted butter, and season well with salt and pepper.

Mix together the shredded cabbage and finely diced peppers, and divide between the ramekins. Add to each ramekin 1$\frac{1}{4}$ tablespoons of the yoghurt, then top with 1 tablespoon of grated cheese.

Place ramekins in a bain marie (a roasting tray half-filled with hot water) and cook in preheated oven at 300°F/150°C/Gas 2 for:
20 minutes – crisp
25 minutes – firm
30 minutes – soft
This dish is rather juicy when cooked, but very nice and tasty as a vegetable accompaniment!

BACON WALNUT CABBAGE

FOR 6 PEOPLE
2 tablespoons bacon fat
12oz (350g) firm white cabbage, finely shredded
1 heaped tablespoon chopped walnuts
2 teaspoons mint, finely chopped (if available)

Heat the bacon fat in a large frying pan and, when hot, add the finely shredded cabbage. Stir-fry, using a wooden spoon, for:
3 minutes – crisp
5 minutes – firm
8 minutes – soft
Serve garnished with chopped walnuts and mint.

42

STUFFED CABBAGE

This makes a delicious supper dish. Use the scooped out cabbage shreds in a soup or another appropriate dish.

FOR 6 PEOPLE
1 large cabbage, about 2lb (900g)
6oz (175g) red cabbage, finely shredded
2 oranges
¼ teaspoon freshly grated nutmeg
Sea salt and freshly ground pepper
2oz (50g) butter

Remove outer leaves and cut off the base so that the cabbage will stand easily and freely. Using a sharp, pointed, small stainless steel knife, carefully scoop out the middle – from the top – until you are left with a 'bowl' (about 9oz or 250g comes out).

In this 'bowl' place the shredded red cabbage mixed with the fresh segments from the oranges, plus the rind and juice with the grated nutmeg. Season with salt and pepper, and top with the knob of butter.

Place the stuffed cabbage on a large piece of foil, bring up the four corners to the top and tie or press together securely to resemble Dick Whittington's bag of goodies. Place on a baking grid in a roasting tray half full of boiling water, and cook in a preheated oven at 375°F/190°C/Gas 5 for:
   1 hour – crisp
   1¼ hours – firm
   1½ hours – soft
Serve the cabbage cut into wedges. You could also add chopped nuts, diced red peppers, celery and apple to the filling if you like.

SPICED RED CABBAGE WITH APPLES AND ORANGE

FOR 6 PEOPLE
2lb (900g) red cabbage, finely shredded
4oz (100g) butter, melted
1lb (450g) Granny Smith apples, peeled, cored and
   sliced
8oz (225g) onions, finely chopped
Freshly ground black pepper
Juice and finely grated rind of 2 oranges
2 cloves garlic
¼ teaspoon each powdered nutmeg, allspice,
   cinnamon, thyme, and caraway seeds
½ pint (300ml) red wine
2 tablespoons wine vinegar
2 tablespoons brown sugar

Make sure you remove all the inside cabbage stalk before shredding the cabbage, then toss it in the melted butter, making sure all the leaves are coated evenly. Put a ½ inch (1cm) layer of the cabbage into the base of a heat- and oven-proof casserole dish large enough, eventually, to take all the cabbage in layers.

Then sprinkle on some of the apples, and some of the onions. Give this layer a generous coating of black pepper, and a little of the orange rind. Repeat this layering process over and over again until you have reached the top of the casserole, and you have none of the ingredients left.

Liquidise together the garlic, spices, wine and wine vinegar with the orange juice and sugar. Pour this over the top of the dish. Bring to the boil on top of the stove, then bake in the preheated oven at 375°F/190°C/Gas 5, for 20 minutes.

It's delicious the next day too!

43

NORWEGIAN RED CABBAGE

FOR 6 PEOPLE
1 large red cabbage
2oz (50g) butter
1 teaspoon salt
8fl. oz (225ml) soured cream
1 teaspoon caraway seeds
Freshly ground black pepper

Shred the cabbage finely, then cook with a little boiling water, the butter and salt until barely tender, about 8–10 minutes.

Drain well and blend in the soured cream and the caraway seeds. Season with pepper and heat gently for 5–8 minutes.

CALABRESE, see BROCCOLI
CAPSICUM, see PEPPER

CARROTS

DAUCUS CAROTA

ONE OF THE WORLD'S MOST important root vegetables, carrots have a long history of cultivation. Thought to have originated in Asia (coming to Europe via North Africa, Spain, then France), they have been eaten for some 2000 years. The Romans ate them, but they didn't appear in Britain until about the reign of Charles I, when they were considered so fashionably exotic that court ladies would wear the feathery leaves as decorations on their gowns (the tops that children grow in saucers are decorative in themselves, and they can also be used in flower arrangements). Carrots were purple and yellow in those days, and it is believed the Dutch produced the present bright orange varieties in the Middle Ages. In Tudor times, sweet carrot puddings were popular, made with dried fruits and spices, and boiled beef and carrots is a dish redolent of Olde England.

Carrots contain Vitamin A; and a juice made from carrots is the wine of vegetarians and health fanatics (but although good in modest quantities, it could be dangerous in excess).

Eating carrots has long been associated with an increased ability to see in the dark, and with curlier hair (or is that crusts?) – but the night vision 'acquired' by the bomber pilots in the Second World War was probably due more to the invention of radar than to the statutory issue of carrots!

Carrots have been used medicinally for centuries. John Wesley in 1785 asserted that to 'live a fortnight on boiled carrots only' was a cure for asthma. In the spa, Vichy, carrots boiled in Vichy water were prescribed to cure eating excesses and digestive problems, and are still thought to be curative.

Carrots are a member of the umbellifer family – along with both types of fennel, parsnips, the Queen Anne's lace of the flower garden (a common roadside weed, the wild carrot, in the USA, and brought to the New World by English colonists), anise, chervil and parsley. In fact, carrots cooked with their herbal relatives are particularly delicious. Another umbellifer, alarmingly, is hemlock – that with which Socrates disposed of himself.

45

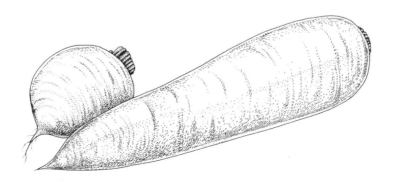

Carrots are available in Britain throughout the year, but varieties are dependent on the seasons. Young slender carrots with their foliage intact are usually sold in bunches. When buying, look for fresh leaves and a healthy colour. Avoid pitted, bruised and broken carrots. Maincrop carrots are larger and coarser, sold without the leaves, and by weight. Many older carrots have a woody core. For the home-grower of carrots, the best English ones are those from seeds sown in February, planted out in March, and harvested at the end of May.

To prepare carrots, always remember that most of the vitamins are near the skin (as with most vegetables, in fact), so they should never be peeled unless absolutely necessary. Scrub both old and new well with a brush under cold water, and slice or cut to suit the recipe. If you are hygiene-conscious, you can peel the skin away, but your taste buds will have been deprived of a sheer joy in my opinion, especially with new carrots. And try to peel old carrots *after* cooking if you must. Rarely do carrot tops seem to be eaten – although I like to leave an inch or so on baby carrots for serving – but they can be used happily in the stock pot.

Carrots have come to be a 'foundation' vegetable (rather like onions), used in stews, casseroles and as a base for roast and baked meats with other roots (and help to make a particularly rich brown gravy). They are also a common accompanying vegetable – boiled, steamed or occasionally baked or roasted – and make delicious soups as you will see from the soup variations on the following pages. Some of my favourite methods of cooking them are in mixed vegetable dishes (see pages 143 and 144).

Carrots, of course, are also eaten raw – in slivers for dunking into dips (good for teething toddlers, too, apparently), and grated into salads. The Chinese carve wonderful decorative follies out of them for garnishes; our own piece of carrot peel, held together by a toothpick and placed in iced water to hold its shape, pales (literally) in comparison.

Carrots also feature, perhaps surprisingly, in many sweet dishes. Next to sugar beet, though, carrots have the highest sugar content, and were used in the Second World War instead of sugar in tarts or cakes when sugar was unavailable or rationed. Carrots appear in carrot cakes and the Indian fudge, halva; they are often used as an economy measure in Xmas puddings instead of some of the more expensive dried fruit. I use them in *my* Xmas puds – 1oz (25g) per pudding – purely because it keeps them moist. In *Food*, Waverley Root dismisses other carrot uses: 'England and the US make jam from carrots, rarely, and also produce carrot "wine" (even more rarely, thank God)'!

CARROT SOUP

Basic recipe (see page 11)
2lb (900g) carrots, topped, tailed and scrubbed

CARROT AND CORIANDER SOUP

Basic recipe (see page 11)
2lb (900g) prepared carrots
2 tablespoons whole coriander seeds

Add coriander at the beginning of cooking.

CARROT AND GINGER SOUP

Basic recipe (see page 11)
2lb (900g) prepared carrots
4 whole pieces ginger in syrup

Add ginger at the beginning of cooking.

CARROT AND APPLE SOUP

Basic recipe (see page 11)
1½lb (675g) prepared carrots
8oz (225g) sharp apples, roughly chopped

Add the apples, skin, core and all, at the beginning of cooking.

CARROT AND ORANGE SOUP

Basic recipe (see page 11)
2lb (900g) prepared carrots
Juice and rind of 2 oranges

CARROT AND SPINACH SOUP

Basic recipe (see page 11)
2lb (900g) prepared carrots
Spinach purée (see page 131)

When serving, add 1 tablespoon of spinach purée per plate, as a garnish.

BOILED NEW BABY CARROTS

What a joy it is to see on the market the lovely baby, new season carrots with their beautiful green feathery tops. They are often rather mucky, but believe you me, where there is muck there is a truly sweet, buttery flavour. Bunches usually have about fourteen to eighteen carrots in them and weigh, with the tops on, about 1–1¼lb (450–550g) – approximately a third of the bought weight is the bushy tops (which can be stored for the stock pot).

FOR 6 PEOPLE
1 bunch new carrots, about 4 inches (10cm) in length, with feathery tops (about 14–18 carrots)
1 pint (550ml) boiling water
1 teaspoon salt

Wash the carrots really well after cutting off the very thin trailing bottoms, and nip off the green tops down to about 1 inch (2cm) – these will look attractive on the dinner plate.
    Put the prepared carrots in the boiling salted water, and bring back to the boil. Cook for:
    6 minutes – crisp
    7 minutes – firm
    8 minutes – soft
    Serve immediately.

STEAMED NEW BABY CARROTS

FOR 6 PEOPLE
1 bunch new carrots (as above)
2 pints (a good litre) boiling water
2 teaspoons salt

Prepare the carrots as in the previous recipe, then place them in a colander over the saucepan of boiling salted water. Cover with a lid (or foil) and steam for the same amount of time as above.

BOILED MAINCROP CARROTS

This quantity of carrots will serve six people with two other accompanying vegetables.

FOR 6 PEOPLE
1 lb (450g) large maincrop carrots
1 pint (550ml) boiling water
2 tablespoons sugar
1 teaspoon salt

Peel the carrots and top and tail them. Slice them into circles of 1/4 inch (5mm) thickness. (There will be about 4oz or 100g of waste.)
   Put the carrots into the boiling water with the sugar and salt, and bring back to the boil (about 1 1/2 minutes). Cook for:
   3 minutes – crisp
   5 minutes – firm
   7 minutes – soft

STEAMED MAINCROP CARROTS

Prepare the same quantity of carrots as above and put them in a colander over the boiling water. Add the sugar to the carrots themselves, and the salt to the water. Cover with a lid (or foil) and steam for:
   5 minutes – crisp
   8 minutes – firm
   12 minutes – soft

GLAZED CARROTS WITH CARAWAY AND LEMON

FOR 6 PEOPLE
1 lb (450g) large maincrop carrots
1 teaspoon sea salt
2oz (50g) butter
1 teaspoon caraway seeds, finely ground in pestle and mortar
Juice and rind of 1 small lemon

The preparation of the carrots is important, as after peeling they should (in fact must) be cut into equal-sized pieces, thin circles of about 1/8 inch (3mm) thick.
   Add the sea salt to a pan of cold water and, when boiling, add the carrots. When the water comes back to the boil, cook for only 3 minutes. Strain and cool under running cold water.
   Just before serving, melt the butter and reheat the carrots in this, scattering over them the ground caraway and lemon juice and rind. This takes only a few minutes.

CARROTS GLAZED WITH THYME

Boil 1 lb (450g) carrots as in the previous recipe then, when you wish to serve them, fry off in 2oz (50g) butter into which you have sprinkled 1 teaspoon fresh thyme leaves.
   A teaspoon of fresh lemon juice can also be added, and I occasionally add a level tablespoon of soft brown sugar to the butter when finishing off to give caramelised thyme/lemon carrots.

CARROTS GLAZED WITH MARJORAM

Follow the recipe for glazed carrots with caraway and lemon, but use 1 level teaspoon of chopped fresh marjoram instead of caraway, and for the lemon juice substitute orange. With the sugar as well, it really is delicious!

CARROTS GLAZED WITH FRESH LIME

Follow the recipe above for caraway and lemon, but when finishing off, add juice and rind of 1 fresh lime to the butter (*no* sugar). Garnish with chopped parsley or fresh mint.

CARROTS GLAZED WITH CORIANDER

Cook your carrots as for the caraway and lemon recipe (above). Generously grind on whole coriander as you would black pepper while glazing with the butter, or, better still, add 3 tablespoons finely chopped fresh coriander.

CARROTS GLAZED WITH PERNOD

Cook the carrots as for the caraway and lemon recipe (above), then when reheating, sprinkle with a touch of Pernod, as if shaking vinegar on your bag of chips.

CARROTS MASHED WITH BLACK PEPPER AND ORANGE

FOR 6 PEOPLE
1½lb (675g) large maincrop carrots
1oz (25g) butter, softened
Rind and juice of 1 orange
Salt and freshly ground black pepper

After peeling, topping and tailing, you should be left with about 1lb (450g) in weight. Cut in circles as in the basic boiling recipe (see page 48), and cook to the *soft* stage, for about 7–8 minutes after coming back to the boil. Drain well and put the carrots back over a low heat to dry out.

Put the cooked carrots into a glass Pyrex bowl and add the very soft butter and the orange rind.

Using a small, sharp pointed kitchen knife, simply, quickly and deftly cut and chop away until you have mashed carrots. (You *can* use a masher, but I like the texture produced by cutting.)

Now, according to your personal taste, add freshly ground black pepper along with about 1 tablespoon of the orange juice. Put the bowl back over a saucepan of water, and cover with either a butter wrapper or greaseproof paper, and simple reheat when needed – which will take about 8–10 minutes.

CARROTS MASHED WITH BLACK PEPPER AND HORSERADISH

Follow the previous recipe, but add 1 tablespoon horseradish cream to the carrots when starting to 'mash' them, and omit the orange juice and rind.

PURÉE OF CARROTS (see also page 13)

FOR 6 PEOPLE
1lb (450g) large maincrop carrots
1oz (25g) butter
¼ pint (150ml) single cream

Prepare the carrots in the usual way, then cut into thin circles as in the basic recipe (see page 11). Boil or steam until soft, about 8–12 minutes, depending on the process used. Strain, and put back in the saucepan with the butter over a low heat to dry out.

Liquidise with the cream and, if you like, to add a special flavour, mix in 1 tablespoon of ground coriander. Then sieve as usual for a fine texture.

49

GRATED CARROTS WITH ORANGE AND WALNUT OIL

12oz (350g) large maincrop carrots, peeled and grated
Grated rind of 2 oranges
1½ tablespoons walnut oil

Put the grated carrots and orange rind in a bowl and leave for at least 2 hours, covered, to allow the flavours to combine.

Line the frying pan (an 11 inch or 28cm one is best) with the walnut oil, smearing it all over the base, and put over heat. When the oil starts to smoke, stir in the carrots, and simply stir-fry, using a wooden spoon, for 3–4 minutes. (Use only the recommended amount of oil as too much walnut taste will overpower the carrot and orange.)

This is also lovely cold, with freshly ground black pepper.

FRIED GRATED CARROTS WITH RADISHES

FOR 6 PEOPLE
12oz (350g) large maincrop carrots, peeled and grated
4oz (100g) radishes, topped, tailed and grated
2 tablespoons olive oil
1oz (25g) butter
Chopped parsley or chives

Combine the grated carrots and radishes in a bowl, and cover with clingfilm until required.

Melt the oil and butter together, then stir-fry the carrot mixture, using a wooden spoon, over a high heat for 3–4 minutes. Sprinkle generously with chopped parsley or chives.

To make the dish even more delicious, you could also add 2 tablespoons of chopped fresh mint.

DEEP-FRIED CARROTS

FOR 6 PEOPLE
1lb (450g) large maincrop carrots, peeled, topped and
  tailed
Milk
4oz (100g) seasoned flour
Oil for deep-frying
Chopped chives
Sea salt

Cut the carrots into 2 inch (5cm) pieces. Stand these on their ends and cut down into slices of about ¼ inch (5mm) thick, and then these slices in ¼ inch (5mm) chips.

Coat with milk, then strain. Cover with seasoned flour, then put back into strainer to shake off excess flour.

Deep-fry at 360°F/182°C for 3 minutes. Remove to kitchen paper to drain, and serve immediately with chopped chives and sea salt.

CAULIFLOWER

BRASSICA OLERACEA BOTRYTIS

YET ANOTHER MEMBER OF THE prolific cabbage family ('nothing but cabbage with a college education', Mark Twain), cauliflower is thought to have originated in the Middle East, coming into Europe in the thirteenth to fourteenth centuries. The Romans grew a flowering cabbage, but that could have been broccoli, rather than the modern cauliflower as we know it. Cauliflowers were known in Elizabethan England, coming from Spain, and as the word *chou-fleur* did not exist in French until the early seventeenth century, the French were not much in advance of the Americans – for cauliflowers have been grown on Long Island for over 200 years.

Cauliflowers (the name coming from the Old English *coleflower*, or cabbage flower, just like the French), are available all the year round. They are the most difficult of the brassicas to grow successfully in Britain, but modern methods – and a prolific crop from Cyprus –

ensures that year-round supply. When buying cauliflowers, look for a creamy to white compact head without loose, brown, grey or damaged curds. The leaves should be crisp and fresh in colour, and the vegetable should smell pleasant. Jane Grigson puts it perfectly: 'If the cauliflower looks back at you with a vigorous air, buy it.'

Cauliflower is a healthy vegetable, but must always – as should *all* vegetables – be used when as fresh as possible. I clearly recall being brought one day a cauliflower that a friend had picked at dawn. The florets still twinkled diamond-like with the morning dew. We steamed it for lunch and ate it outside on the patio with some heated garlic butter poured over the four quarters. In so doing we were able to take full advantage of its high content of phosphorus, calcium, folic acid (Vitamin B complex) as well as the usual vegetable nutrients! But, sadly, seldom can we be fortunate enough to get one so young and fresh.

51

To prepare cauliflower, cut off the outer leaves – these can be cooked like cabbage (for that basically is what they are: the Chinese use them, but then they use anything, even chicken feet!), and they have a slightly sweeter taste than cabbage – and cut out any superficially stained curds. Plunge head down into lots of salted cold water for about 30 minutes to remove any insect life.

Depending on the recipe, leave the head whole – in which case you may want to cut a cross into the stem – or divide into florets, which will cook more quickly (you could divide into florets *after* cooking whole if you like). If a cauliflower doesn't fit your pot, but stands proud of the top, cover with foil. Many people say the stem should be boiled in the water while the top is steamed out of the water. This is certainly what I was taught, but I have found if the slightest bit of soil or dirt is left in the cauliflower that this comes to the top and stains the curds; so I always place my cauliflower in head first, with the stalk sticking up. A little lemon juice in the water can help preserve and intensify the white colour.

Cauliflower features in many classic dishes, especially in a gratin or cheese sauce in Britain. This can make a good and satisfying light main course – like my buttery lunch above – but it is also served as an accompanying vegetable, particularly good with beef. Cooked, cauliflower can be topped with toasted flaked almonds, with buttered breadcrumbs, with chopped hard-boiled eggs, or with a 'meringue' topping and baked. It can be served cold, with mayonnaise or vinaigrette; it can be puréed or creamed, stir-fried in tiny florets, or made into a tasty soup. The florets can be deep-fried as fritters, and raw can be added to salads or used as a crudité for dips. Cauliflower is also a common pickle and chutney ingredient.

CAULIFLOWER SOUP

Basic recipe (see page 11)
2lb (900g) cauliflower

A touch of nutmeg will always enhance a cauliflower soup, and toasted pine kernels make an attractive and tasty garnish.

CAULIFLOWER CHEESE SOUP

Basic recipe (see page 11)
2lb (900g) cauliflower
4oz (100g) strong Cheddar cheese, grated

Add the cheese when reheating the soup.

STEAMED WHOLE CAULIFLOWER WITH TOASTED ALMONDS

Without any doubt this is a superb way to cook fresh white young cauliflower.

FOR 6 PEOPLE
1 cauliflower, about 1¾lb (800g)
2 pints (a good litre) boiling water
2 teaspoons salt
2oz (50g) butter, melted
2oz (50g) flaked almonds, toasted

Remove the outer hard stalk of the cauliflower and then, using a sharp pointed knife, make a V incision in the stalk, removing as much as possible of the core.

Fit a colander or steamer snugly over the large saucepan of boiling water, and add the salt to the water. Place the cauliflower *head down* on the holey bottom of the steamer, and cover with the lid (or foil). Turn heat down a little, and steam for:
    10 minutes – crisp
    12 minutes – firm
    15 minutes – soft
Cut the steamed cauliflower into wedges and coat with the melted butter. Sprinkle with the toasted almond flakes.

52

CAULIFLOWER WITH CHEESE SAUCE

Cook the cauliflower as above to the crisp stage, then coat with cheese sauce (see page 17).

CAULIFLOWER WITH MUSHROOM SAUCE

Steam the cauliflower as above, then coat with the mushroom sauce (see page 17).

CAULIFLOWER WITH HOLLANDAISE

This is the most luxurious and delicious of the lot. Steam as above, and serve coated with the Hollandaise (see page 17).

CAULIFLOWER PURÉE (see also page 13)

This is delicious on its own, merely with a little nutmeg, say, but it can also be topped with, or mixed with, any of the ingredients listed below.

FOR 6 PEOPLE
1 large cauliflower, about 1 1/2lb (675g) in weight, trimmed
3 pints (1.7 litres) boiling water
Salt
1 1/2oz (40g) butter
1/4 pint (150ml) single cream
Freshly ground black pepper

The cauliflower should be cooked slowly *head down* in the boiling water (with 2 teaspoons salt added) for about 12 minutes, until *soft*.

Drain, cut into eight pieces, removing as much stalk as possible, and return to the pan with butter to dry out. Purée with the cream in the food processor. Pass through a sieve and spoon into six buttered and lightly seasoned ramekins.

Now add, mix in, top or whatever, using some of the suggestions below, and leave until you wish to reheat and serve.

To reheat, put the individual dishes into a bain marie and place in the oven at 350°F/180°C/Gas 4 for 15 minutes.

WITH GRATED CHEESE

53

Put 2oz (50g) grated Cheddar cheese on top and, after reheating, flash under the grill at the last minute to brown.

WITH CHOPPED WALNUTS

Put 2oz (50g) chopped walnuts on top after reheating.

WITH FRESH THYME

Mix 1 teaspoon chopped thyme into each purée before reheating.

WITH NUTMEG AND DICED GINGER

Use about 1 teaspoon crystallised or preserved ginger, and a pinch of freshly grated nutmeg. Mix in before reheating.

STIR-FRIED CAULIFLOWER WITH CORIANDER

FOR 6 PEOPLE
1 large cauliflower
Salt
1 tablespoon olive oil
1oz (25g) butter
Ground coriander seeds

Cut away the individual florets from the hard centre of the cauliflower. You will need about 12oz (350g) for six people.

Place these in a saucepan full of simmering water with 2 teaspoons salt added, and bring back to the boil. Cook for only 4 minutes. Strain immediately and dry on kitchen paper.

When you wish to cook them further, just before serving, smear the base of the frying pan with the olive oil and butter, heat, and stir-fry the florets, using a wooden spoon, for:

2 minutes – crisp
3 minutes – firm
4 minutes – soft

Generously grind coriander from your mill over the cauliflower, and serve immediately.

If you like bacon fat, use that instead of the olive oil and butter.

CAULIFLOWER STIR-FRIED IN SESAME AND RASPBERRY

Prepare and cook the cauliflower exactly as in the previous recipe, but stir-fry in the sesame oil with raspberry vinegar mixture (see page 10). You'll need about 3 tablespoons.

Do be careful, though, to make sure that you transfer the cooked florets to clean kitchen paper which will absorb any surplus sesame oil. If you dish this out on to the individual guests' plates without draining, the sesame oil soon finds its way into the other vegetables, and tends to 'take over'.

54

CELERIAC

APIUM GRAVEOLENS RAPACEUM

ALSO KNOWN AS TURNIP-rooted celery (exactly what it is, celery persuaded to become a turnip!), celeriac was developed in Renaissance times by European gardeners. It was not known in Britain until about 1723 when a garden designer and seedsman introduced it, and named it, the seeds coming from Alexandria. Only now, some 250 years later, is it becoming familiar in Britain, although it has always been a popular winter vegetable in Europe.

Its season stretches roughly from October to March. It varies in size from that of a large cooking apple to that of a coconut, and has a brown fibrous skin, and creamy white flesh with a pronounced celery aroma and flavour. Younger roots of about 1lb (450g) in weight are best; older and larger roots can be woody or hollow. It often comes with the leaves still

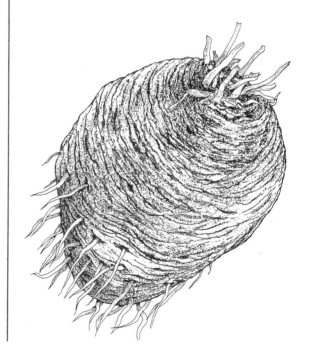

attached; these are not eaten as they are bitter, but they make an excellent flavouring for soups and sauces, and on the Continent are an essential part of a bouquet garni.

When buying, try to choose the smoothest celeriac you can to prevent waste: the skin is thick and needs to be peeled deeply to get rid of knobbles. It should be firm with no sign of mushy flesh. To prepare, cut first into pieces so that you can see what you're doing when peeling. Drop peeled pieces into acidulated water (water with a little vinegar or lemon juice) to prevent discoloration.

Celeriac is often served raw, grated into salads; it is marinated and served in a mustardy French dressing or mayonnaise for a classic French hors d'oeuvre, rémoulade. But it is most often cooked: in a purée, often with potato; as a soup; sliced and fried in breadcrumbs as 'steaks'; and served au gratin – and I think you'll find a good few ideas in the following pages.

CELERIAC SOUP

Basic recipe (see page 11)
2lb (900g) celeriac, peeled
Juice and rind of 2 oranges

Add the juice and rind at the initial cooking stage, and garnish with fresh mint leaves if you have them to hand.

BOILED DICED CELERIAC

1lb (450g) of celeriac, when topped, tailed and peeled will give you about 12oz (350g).

FOR 6 PEOPLE
1lb (450g) celeriac
2 pints (a good litre) boiling water
1 teaspoon salt

Peel the celeriac and top and tail, then cut into ¼ inch (5mm) cubes.

With the salted water simmering, add the cubes of celeriac and bring back to the boil. Cover with a lid, and boil swiftly for:
    3 minutes – crisp
    4 minutes – firm
    6 minutes – soft
    Drain well.

DICED CELERIAC WITH LEMON AND THYME

Follow the previous recipe, but when strained of water, return to low heat to dry out quickly. Then stir-fry for 2–3 minutes, using a wooden spoon, with 1 tablespoon fresh lemon juice mixed with 1 teaspoon finely chopped fresh thyme.

DICED CELERIAC WITH HONEY

Prepare and cook exactly as in boiled diced celeriac but, when cooked, at the end simply stir in 2 tablespoons of clear runny honey.

DICED CELERIAC WITH GRATED APPLES AND GARDEN PEAS

Follow the recipe for boiled diced celeriac, but at the end, when drying out, add an apple that has been grated with its skin on, and 3 tablespoons of raw fresh garden peas to give a little colour and crunchiness. Grated fresh horseradish along with finely grated salad radishes can also be added to give colour as well as tang!

DICED CELERIAC WITH CHEESE AND CHIVES

Follow the recipe for boiled diced celeriac, but bring back to the boil for only 2 minutes, and then strain and refresh under running cold water.

Put into six buttered ramekin dishes, and top each with a tablespoon of grated cheese mixed with finely cut fresh chives.

Reheat when needed in a bain marie in an oven at 350°F/180°C/Gas 4 for about 15 minutes. Finish off under the grill quickly, so that the cheese bubbles.

CELERIAC PURÉE
(see also page 13)

Prepare and cook celeriac as in the recipe for boiled diced celeriac, but to the soft stage. Dry out with 1oz (25g) butter over a low heat, then purée with ¼ pint (150ml) single cream, and sieve.

When serving, after reheating in a double saucepan, sprinkle each portion with a teaspoon of toasted desiccated or grated coconut, or toasted pine kernels.

CELERIAC CROQUETTES

FOR 6 PEOPLE
1 lb (450g) celeriac
3oz (75g) butter
2 eggs
Seasoned flour
4oz (100g) breadcrumbs (or grated coconut)
Salt and freshly ground black pepper
2 tablespoons oil

Prepare the celeriac as usual, cube, then cook to the soft stage as on page 55 (about 6 minutes). Drain well and return to the saucepan with 1oz (25g) of the butter and a beaten egg. Cook over a high heat for a minute. Remove from heat and chop finely.

The consistency should be pretty thick, as you want now to shape the mixture (when cooled, of course) into six sausages, about 2 inches (5cm) long, and 1 inch (3cm) round.

Roll the sausages in the seasoned flour and then in the remaining lightly beaten egg. Turn into the breadcrumbs (or the coconut, which is particularly delicious) which have been seasoned with a little salt and pepper. Leave to chill until firm, about 1 hour at least.

Place the oil and remaining butter in a frying pan, heat, and fry the croquettes for 8–10 minutes. You could also deep-fry them, at 360°F/182°C for 8 minutes.

CELERIAC AND COURGETTE CAKE

FOR 6 PEOPLE
4oz (100g) celeriac, peeled and grated
4oz (100g) courgettes, wiped and grated
6oz (175g) potato, cooked and mashed
Salt and freshly ground pepper
Seasoned flour
Oil
Butter

Mix the vegetables together, and season with salt and pepper. Press in a suitable frying pan, so that the mixture becomes 'cake'-shaped. Shake seasoned flour over and chill well (about 1 hour). Put a plate over the frying pan and invert the 'cake' on to it. Sprinkle with seasoned flour.

Melt about 1 tablespoon oil with 1oz (25g) butter in the frying pan, and slide in the cake. Fry for 4–5 minutes then turn over to do the other side (use the plate again, and more oil and butter if necessary) for another 4–5 minutes. Cut into wedges to serve.

Another way of doing this dish is to double up on the fat and oil, melt them together in the frying pan, then place six egg cutters in the pan. Pile the mixture into these and fry for 4 minutes. Slowly slide the cutters off the small 'cakes' and, using a palette knife, turn the cakes over to brown on the other side.

PAN-FRIED CELERIAC BALLS

When you top, tail and peel the celeriac, you will have about 1 ½lb (675g) left.

FOR 6 PEOPLE
2lb (900g) celeriac
2 tablespoons dripping
Sea salt

Using a Parisian scoop, scoop out the peeled celeriac into balls. (Use what is left either for grated celeriac or celeriac purée, or add to a soup.)

In a 10 inch (25cm) frying pan, melt the dripping (or some butter and oil, but the dripping certainly enhances the final flavour). Add the balls and stir-fry, using a wooden spoon, for:
  3 minutes – crisp
  4 minutes – firm
  5 minutes – soft
Drain on kitchen paper, sprinkle with sea salt, and serve immediately.

If left to go cold, these celeriac balls are delicious on cocktail sticks with cubes of cheese or ham, and served as cocktail canapés garnished with parsley sprigs.

GRATED CELERIAC WITH HORSERADISH

FOR 6 PEOPLE
1lb (450g) celeriac, topped, tailed and peeled
Lemon juice
1 tablespoon olive oil
1oz (25g) butter
½ tablespoon horseradish sauce

Use the coarse grater and grate the celeriac. (If doing this early on in the day, sprinkle with lemon juice, put in a bowl covered with clingfilm and leave in the fridge.)

When you wish to cook, melt the olive oil and butter together in a frying pan, and bring to a high heat. Add the grated celeriac and stir-fry quickly for 3 minutes, stirring the horseradish sauce in at the end.

Another flavour which would go well with the celeriac is that of fresh salad radishes. Stir in about 3oz (75g) grated radish at the end of stir-frying instead of the horseradish.

CELERIAC CHIPS

FOR 6 PEOPLE
10oz (275g) celeriac, peeled
Oil for deep-frying
Sea salt
Freshly chopped parsley

Cut the celeriac into ¼ inch (5mm) 'chips'. Pat dry. Fry off in preheated fryer or oil at 325°F/163°C for 2 minutes, then remove from fryer.

When you wish to serve, fry off once again at 360°F/182°C then quickly turn out on to kitchen paper, and sprinkle generously with sea salt and freshly chopped parsley. Serve immediately.

Quite nice for cocktail parties, providing you have ample paper napkins to pass around!

CELERY

APIUM GRAVEOLENS DULCE

CELERY HAS BEEN CULTIVATED for centuries: the Egyptians apparently grew and ate it; the Greeks grew it and used the seeds medicinally; the Romans both ate it and *wore* it – they believed wreaths of celery could protect them from hangovers! Thereafter it seems to have reverted to the wild, and it is not until the 1640s that it made its appearance in Britain from Italy.

The plant is native to Europe, but is also grown in the USA. It is available more or less throughout the year. It appears pale and green in supermarkets in plastic sleeves, and in the home-harvesting season, from better greengrocers, as a white head with black soil still adhering to it. No real need to say which I think is better: the plastic can make the celery sweat, especially in hot weather, and this makes

it become slightly soft, which is no good for man nor beast as the crisper the celery the tastier it will be; and who could mind scrubbing earth off the stalks – a minor chore when one thinks of the deliciousness to come. Unfortunately long gone are the days of the celery men at northern markets (the one I remember wore a khaki tropical suit and an old-fashioned pith helmet, minus the back-neck flap) – as well as the noble trade of 'celery washer' (it's probably all done by machine now), washing and packing for market, and tying together with gold or green withies (*much* better than polythene).

The average shop-bought head of celery weighs approximately 2¼lb (about 1kg), and when buying, always try to feel the head for firmness. Choose a thick, plump base, and smooth stalks. The leaves, if they're still on – and they ought to be – should be fresh and lively

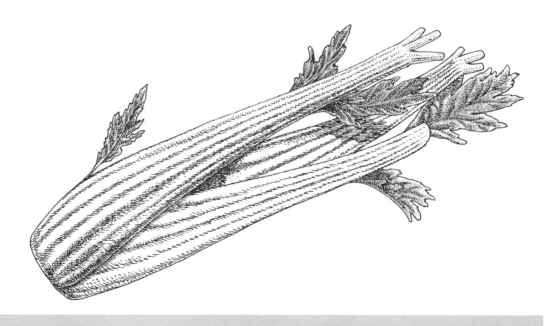

looking. When you get the celery home, cut off the root base and, depending on ultimate usage, take off the individual stalks and wash separately, or wash as well as you can keeping the head together. Never soak in water for any length of time as this, too, has a softening effect. Store always in a cool dark place, or in the salad drawer of the fridge.

If necessary, remove any damaged, coarse or browny outer stalks, but don't throw them away: they can be used in the stock pot along with the root base, or stewed slowly in a pan with water or stock, the flavoured liquid to be used in other soups, stocks and sauces. You may need to string the celery, an easy process, but use these too. Try not to waste the leaves either: they make as good a flavouring ingredient as the stalks, and my grandmother used to dry and crumble them and keep as a dried herb in a small jar, handy for seasoning meats, fish and other vegetables. The leaves could also be deep-fried, like parsley sprigs, as a tasty garnish.

Celery is usually thought of first as a flavouring, and secondly as a cold, uncooked, salad vegetable, and I must admit that I like it best raw, dipped into sea salt, and eaten just as it is (an entirely British taste, apparently). It goes wonderfully with the cheese board too, chops up into salads, makes a 'container' for canapés, and what would we do at Miller Howe without our celery twirl garnishes? But it can be cooked as a vegetable in its own right, braised, baked or stir-fried (never quick boil or high bake it, as it needs slow cooking), or made into a variety of delicious soups.

A few final thoughts. Celery seeds crushed with salt make celery salt (delicious in cheese pastry), and, according to Dorothy Hartley, as well as being full of Vitamin C, celery is a 'sovereign cure for rheumatism'.

CREAM OF CELERY SOUP

Basic recipe (see page 11)
1½lb (675g) celery, washed and trimmed
8oz (225g) potatoes, peeled

CELERY AND FENNEL SOUP

Basic recipe (see page 11)
1lb (450g) celery, washed and trimmed
1lb (450g) fennel, washed and trimmed

CELERY AND DILL SOUP

Basic recipe (see page 11)
2lb (900g) celery, washed and trimmed
2 tablespoons dill seeds

Add the seeds at the beginning of cooking.

BAKED SAVOURY CELERY

FOR 6 × 3 INCH (8CM) RAMEKINS
Melted butter
Salt and freshly ground black pepper
4oz (100g) celery, finely diced
2oz (50g) red pepper, finely diced
7½ tablespoons natural yoghurt
6 tablespoons Cheddar cheese, grated

Grease the ramekins with melted butter, and season well.

Mix the celery and red pepper dice together and divide between the ramekins. Add 1¼ tablespoons yoghurt to each ramekin then top with 1 tablespoon of the grated cheese.

Place ramekins in a bain marie and bake in a preheated oven at 300°F/150°C/Gas 2 for:
  30 minutes – crisp
  40 minutes – firm
  45 minutes – soft

BAKED CELERY WITH ONIONS AND PEPPER

Use 4 inches (10cm) from the base of the celery head for this, keeping the thinner and tasty tops for other cooking – salads, casseroles, plain with cheese, for canapés – or for the deep-fried strips (see page 61). It's a good side vegetable.

FOR 4 PEOPLE
1 head celery
4oz (100g) onions, finely chopped
3oz (75g) butter
8 tablespoons red pepper, finely diced
4 tablespoons sherry
Salt and freshly ground black pepper

Cut the washed base bulb into four wedges, which should weigh approximately 3oz (75g) each, having removed any nasty outside stalks, and the actual base root.

In the meantime, fry off the finely chopped onions in 1oz (25g) of the butter, and leave to drain on kitchen paper.

Cut out four 10 inch (25cm) squares of foil and, dull side up, put ½oz (15g) of the remaining butter on each. On top of this put a wedge of celery, cover with a quarter of the onions, and a quarter of the red pepper. Add 1 tablespoon sherry per foil square (pull the sides up a little first), salt and freshly ground black pepper, then make up into 'Cornish pasty' shaped parcels.

When you wish to cook, preheat the oven to 375°F/190°C/Gas 5 and put the parcels on a cooling rack in a bain marie. Place in the oven and cook for:
    30 minutes – crisp
    35 minutes – firm
    40 minutes – soft

CELERY BAKED WITH YOGHURT, APPLE AND RED PEPPER

Once again, only 4 inches (10cm) of the base of the head of celery is used, but this time only two portions are obtained. It's obviously rather more substantial, so could be served as a starter.

FOR 2 PEOPLE
1oz (25g) butter
1 head celery
4 tablespoons natural yoghurt
2 tablespoons apple (Granny Smith preferably), finely diced
4 tablespoons red pepper, finely diced
Salt and freshly ground black pepper

Spread the butter on the dull sides of two squares of foil, about 10 inches (25cm), and place the halves of celery on top. Pull the sides of the squares up slightly, then cover each half of celery with 2 tablespoons yoghurt, 1 tablespoon finely diced apple and 2 tablespoons red pepper. Season, then fold into a 'Cornish pasty' shape.

Bake in preheated oven – at 300°F/150°C/Gas 2 – on a rack in a bain marie, for:
    45 minutes – crisp
    55 minutes – firm
    60 minutes – soft

STIR-FRIED CELERY WITH SESAME-RASPBERRY SAUCE

FOR 6 PEOPLE
1lb (450g) prepared celery stalks
5 tablespoons sesame oil with raspberry vinegar (see page 10)
3 tablespoons stock (see page 11)
2 tablespoons soya sauce
3 cloves garlic, made into a paste with ½ teaspoon salt

Cut the celery crosswise in to ¼ inch (5mm) slices.
For the sauce, bring all remaining ingredients

CHICORY

CICHORIUM INTYBUS

together in a small saucepan, and cook for 5 minutes. It makes about ¼ pint (150ml).

When you wish to cook the dish, simply stir the celery into the sauce and simmer for:

5 minutes – crisp
8 minutes – firm
15 minutes – soft

LIGHTLY CURRIED, DEEP-FRIED CELERY STRIPS

FOR 6 PEOPLE
14–16oz (400–450g) celery stalks (or tops of stalks)
Milk
3oz (75g) plain flour
4 teaspoons curry powder of choice
Oil for deep-frying

For this you can make use of the top parts of the celery as well. Cut each stalk into 2 inch (5cm) pieces, and then into ¼ inch (5mm) thick strips. Soak in cold milk until you want to fry them.

Put the plain flour, mixed with the curry powder, on a flat baking tray. Drain the celery strips in a sieve (the milk can be used for a sauce later), and then decant into the curry/flour mixture. Mix to coat by hand, then put the strips back into the sieve to shake off surplus flour.

In your preheated fryer or pan of oil, at 360°F/182°C, fry off the strips for 4 minutes, using the handle of a wooden spoon to stop them clogging together. Transfer to kitchen paper to drain, and serve immediately, preferably with sea salt.

CHARD, see SPINACH

 CHICORY IS A MEMBER OF A WIDE family, which is partly why there is so much confusion about the name. For what the British and Belgians call chicory, the Americans and French call Belgian endive; what we call endive, the Americans and French call chicory! Looking at it from the British point of view, both endive and chicory are similar plants, one (chicory) being *Cichorium intybus*, the other (endive) being *Cichorium endivia*: the white compact head called chicory in Britain (called by the Belgians *witloof* or white leaf, which name, if adopted, would probably solve all the problems!) is the cultivated and forced leaf as opposed to the natural leaf of its relation, which is the endive (well, broadly speaking, anyway).

Chicory is the long silvery-white tightly folded leaf vegetable, often known in Belgium as goat's beard as well (just have a look and you'll

61

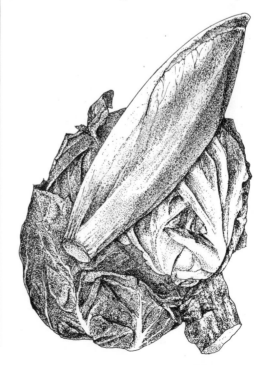

see the resemblance). It is native to Europe and Western Asia, but is also grown in the USA. It was first formally cultivated and forced to produce the white chicons (as they are known) about the mid to late nineteenth century by a Belgian gardener, thus the Belgian connection. Indeed, the majority of the crop still comes from Belgium. It is available and at its best from autumn to spring.

Chicory should be chosen for firmly packed, white leaves. Avoid any with yellow curling leaves and tops which are turning green – this betokens age. The chicons vary considerably in size, but the average head weighs about 5oz (150g). Chicory always comes wrapped in dark blue or purple paper which, I presume, is to keep out the light and preserve the blanched white colour. Keep wrapped in the paper when you get it home, or store in the dark.

When preparing chicory, cut off the thick root base, and remove any outer damaged leaves. Any cut surfaces will discolour, so use swiftly. Don't leave soaking in water as this intensifies the chicory's natural bitterness.

Chicory is a welcome addition raw to a salad, as it is bitter and crunchy, and combines particularly well with citrus fruits. It can also be steamed or braised and served with melted butter, and a variety of white sauces. Many of the following foil-baked recipes can be enhanced by coating with a tablespoon of tomato provençale (see page 140) when serving.

There is yet another chicory, the Magdeburg chicory, which has long roots which are dried and ground to add to coffee – not now for economy, but for the taste, and much appreciated in France. And to confuse matters even further, there is one variety of chicory for forcing and blanching, 'Sugar Loaf', of which the 'natural' leaves can be eaten by gardeners in summer – just like endive!

STEAMED CHICORY

The average weight of a chicon or head is usually 5oz (150g) which will give you about ½–1oz (15–25g) waste when the outer leaves are removed, and the base of the stalk is nicked off.

FOR 6 PEOPLE
3 heads chicory
2 pints (a good litre) boiling water
Salt and freshly ground black pepper
Oil

Cut each head of chicory into quarters lengthwise.

In a large saucepan, bring the water to the boil, with 1 teaspoon salt, then place the quarters of chicory in a colander. Paint lightly with oil, and season too (a little lemon juice is nice). Place the colander over the boiling water and cover with a lid. Steam for:

    4 minutes – crisp
    5 minutes – firm
    6 minutes – soft

At the crisp and firm stages, the actual core base could be a little tough, so remove this before serving, *but* the lovely leaf ends will be to your liking!

CHICORY BRAISED IN ORANGE JUICE

FOR 6 PEOPLE
3 heads chicory
2 large oranges
Butter
Salt and freshly ground black pepper

Cut each head of chicory in half lengthwise. Grate the rind off the oranges and squeeze the juice.

Lightly butter the base of a Pyrex dish, and season liberally. Place the chicory in the dish, cover with the orange juice and rind, and the lid (or foil). Place in a preheated oven at 375°F/190°C/Gas 5, and bake for:

    15 minutes – crisp
    20 minutes – firm
    25 minutes – soft

BAKED CHICORY WITH STAR ANISE

Whole chicory heads do look nicer than pieces when actually served, but they are quite filling.

FOR 6 PEOPLE
6 heads chicory
6oz (175g) butter
12 whole star anise
Salt and freshly ground black pepper
6 tablespoons white wine

Remove any stained outer leaves from the chicory, and nick off the firm root end.

Cut six pieces of foil measuring 8 × 10 inches (20 × 25cm), and on to each put ½oz (15g) butter and on this 1 star anise. Lay the whole chicory down on top, and season with salt and pepper. Put a further ½oz (15g) butter on top, with another star anise. Pull up the sides of the foil slightly before adding 1 tablespoon white wine to each foil package, then fold up completely and press firmly together.

Preheat oven to 375°F/190°C/Gas 5, and place packages on a cooling rack over hot water in a bain marie. Bake for:
15 minutes – crisp
20 minutes – firm
25 minutes – soft

BAKED CHICORY WITH CHEESE AND HERB PÂTÉ

Follow the method and timing exactly as in the previous star anise recipe, but use 1oz (25g) cheese and herb pâté (see page 16) beneath each head of chicory and 1oz (25g) on top instead of the butter (a total of 12oz or 350g). Omit the star anise, and add the white wine to each foil package.

BAKED CHICORY WITH ORANGE

Follow the method and timing exactly as for baked chicory with star anise, omitting the star anise and using the 6oz (175g) butter. Substitute the juice and rind of 2 oranges for the white wine.

BAKED CHICORY WITH GARLIC

63

Follow the method and timing exactly as for baked chicory with star anise, but first, using a sharp pointed knife, make little incisions near the base and half-way up each head of chicory. Insert into each incision a half clove of garlic (you'll need, therefore, 6 cloves in all). Omit the star anise, of course, and use the butter and white wine as in the original recipe.

CHILLI PEPPER, see PEPPER
CHINESE ARTICHOKE, see
JERUSALEM ARTICHOKE

CHINESE LEAF

BRASSICA PEKINENSIS

THIS IS ALSO KNOWN AS Chinese cabbage and *pe-tsai* (white vegetable), and comes originally from eastern Asia, northern China in particular. Although eaten in the Far East since as long ago as the fifth century AD, it was completely unknown in Europe before the twentieth century, and it is only since Israel started to export their crop to the UK in the early 1970s, that it has become truly familiar.

As its name suggests, it *is* a cabbage, and can be cooked as such, but it is milder in flavour, and doesn't contain the sulphurous fumes. It looks rather like a cross between a heavy and ribby Cos lettuce, and a head of celery; it also resembles Swiss chard. As with any brassica, avoid any outer wilting or yellowish leaves.

It can be prepared in a variety of ways. Cut off the root end and either separate and wash the leaves, or just cut off the quantity you need from the head and return the rest to the salad drawer of the fridge. In general, the delicate leafier tops could be used raw in salads, and the thicker ribs towards the base will cook well – but all can be used either raw or cooked.

The spinach recipes on pages 131 and 132 are all good for this vegetable – but watch it carefully, it's delicate. It could always be quickly stir-fried, by itself, in a good oil like sesame, or with an interesting flavouring, like freshly grated ginger; a little soya sauce added at the end gives a Chinese flavour; or you could add some dry cooking sherry.

I have also briefly cooked it, shredded, in a little boiling leftover consommé, and garnished the bowl with finely chopped spring onions.

A little freshly ground nutmeg makes a lot of difference in many of the recipes.

COLLARDS, see KALE
CORN ON THE COB, see
SWEETCORN

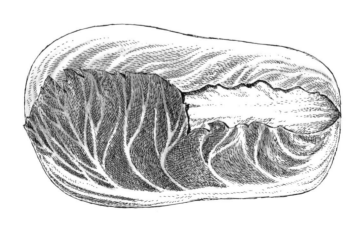

COURGETTES

CUCURBITA PEPO

OURGETTES, CLOSELY RELATED to marrow, squash and pumpkin, are a member of the *Cucurbitaceae* family, which also includes cucumbers, gherkins and melons. Courgettes are a distinct variety of vegetable marrow, specially developed and grown, and harvested early, when only about 4–6 inches (10–15cm) long. They are a fairly recent vegetable to Britain and America, coming from Italy – where they are *zucchini*, the name by which they are known in America – and were not known at all in a 'separate' sense before the Second World War. In fact, as Jane Grigson says – and few food writers would disagree – courgettes were almost the 'creation' of Elizabeth David in her first book, on Mediterranean food, published in 1950.

Courgettes can be successfully home grown, when they can be picked even younger – at about 2–3 inches (5–8cm). In fact they grow so quickly that it is quite difficult, unless you're very vigilant, to catch them before they start becoming – literally – baby marrows. Most shop-bought courgettes will be larger, and are at their best during the summer months, although they can on the whole be bought throughout the year. Still try to buy the smallest, though, when they look like short thick cigars. Look for straight, firm and light green courgettes and, if you can, *feel* them: although greengrocers wouldn't approve, a courgette skin that a fingernail can press through quickly with ease, is a little over the hill. Try to use on the day of purchase, and if impossible, store in the salad drawer of the fridge.

There is no need to peel courgettes, or to remove the seeds – as you would with its larger relation, the marrow. Wash swiftly in cold water, then cut off a short slice at each end. The smallest courgettes often don't need to have anything done to them at all, but depending on the recipe, larger ones should be chopped, halved or sliced. They can be 'degorged' like aubergines: slice them, sprinkle with salt, and

65

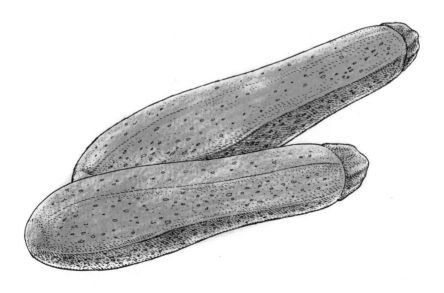

leave in a colander so that the water (which can be bitter) can drain out. Dry thoroughly on kitchen paper before cooking. This also prevents them soaking up too much oil in cooking, like aubergines.

Courgettes are incredibly versatile. Small ones can be cooked whole, or grated or sliced raw into a salad. Larger ones can be sliced and fried, grilled, coated in fritter batter and deep-fried, or halved, stuffed and baked. When used as a vegetable in casseroles they have a tenderising power, and easily absorb other flavours in your recipe. They are an essential ingredient in ratatouille (see page 119). A Mexican dish has them grated into a pancake batter, and then fried.

The flowers of both marrow and courgette can be cooked and eaten. On a couple of memorable occasions in Florence, I've eaten them. The first time, the flowers were battered and then deep-fried, and to this day I don't know whether it was the flavouring in the batter or the taste of the flower pollen, but I've never been able to recreate the taste or root out a remotely similar recipe from any of my hundreds of cookbooks. The other time, which even today I can see, smell and taste mentally, was when I was served courgette flowers finely chopped with basil, then fried and placed in scooped-out beefsteak tomatoes topped with buttered eggs. Anton Mosimann of The Dorchester Hotel serves steamed stuffed courgette flowers still attached to the courgette.

COURGETTE SOUP

Basic recipe (see page 11)
2lb (900g) courgettes, wiped, topped and tailed

Garnish with freshly deep-fried courgette circles (see page 69) – delicious!

COURGETTE AND FENNEL SOUP

Basic recipe (see page 11)
1lb (450g) courgettes, wiped, topped and tailed
1lb (450g) fennel, washed and trimmed

COURGETTE AND ROSEMARY SOUP

Basic recipe (see page 11)
2lb (900g) courgettes, wiped, topped and tailed
1–2 tablespoons fresh rosemary

COURGETTES WITH MARSALA

FOR 6 PEOPLE
12oz (350g) courgettes
2 tablespoons oil
1oz (25g) butter, softened
Salt and freshly ground black pepper
2 tablespoons Marsala
Toasted almond flakes

Wipe each courgette with a damp cloth, cut off the top and tail, then score six channels lengthwise with a scorer. Cut crosswise into 1/4 inch (5mm) slices.

In a frying pan, 10 inch (25cm) preferably, bring the oil and soft butter to smoking point. Add the courgettes, swiftly season with salt and black pepper, and stir-fry for only 2 minutes, using a wooden spoon.

Turn the heat up to full, add the Marsala, and stir in. Serve immediately with toasted almond flakes.

Sherry – sweet or dry to personal taste – could be used instead of the Marsala.

GRATED COURGETTES WITH FRESH LIME

FOR 4–6 PEOPLE
1lb (450g) courgettes, wiped, topped and tailed
Juice and grated rind of 1 lime
1oz (50g) butter

Grate the courgettes finely, and mix with the grated rind and juice of the lime. Leave to marinate for most of the day.

When you wish to serve them, all you do is toss the grated courgettes in the heated butter for about 4 minutes. Serve immediately.

GRATED COURGETTES WITH ORANGE

Exactly the same as the above, but substitute the juice and rind of 2 oranges for the lime.

GRATED COURGETTES WITH LEMON

Use the juice and grated rind of 1 large lemon instead of the lime.

COURGETTES BRAISED WITH ORANGE

FOR 6 PEOPLE
12oz (350g) courgettes (see below for sizes)
Juice and grated rind of 1 orange
Butter

Top and tail the courgettes, and wipe clean with a damp cloth. Score four or five channels lengthwise with a scorer.

Place in a buttered Pyrex dish and cover with the juice and rind of the orange. Preheat the oven to 350°F/180°C/Gas 4, and bake the courgettes for:

Length	Width	Time	Texture
5 inches	½ inch	25 minutes	crisp
(12cm)	(1cm)	30 minutes	firm
		45 minutes	soft
6 inches	¾ inch	30 minutes	crisp
(15cm)	(2cm)	40 minutes	firm
		50 minutes	soft
7 inches	1 inch	35 minutes	crisp
(18cm)	(3cm)	45 minutes	firm
		55 minutes	soft

COURGETTES BAKED IN HONEY AND SOYA SAUCE

This dish can be made using whole small courgettes, or larger courgettes which have been evenly sliced.

FOR 6 PEOPLE
1lb (450g) courgettes, wiped, topped and tailed
Butter
FOR WHOLE COURGETTES
2 dessertspoons runny honey
2 teaspoons soya sauce
FOR SLICED COURGETTES
1 dessertspoon runny honey
1 teaspoon soya sauce

Prepare the courgettes according to size, and lightly butter a suitable baking dish. Preheat oven to 375°F/190°C/Gas 5.

Mix the honey and soya sauce together and put into the baking dish with the courgettes. Mix to coat. Cover with a lid (or foil) and bake for:

Whole			Sliced
25 minutes	–	crisp –	15 minutes
30 minutes	–	firm –	20 minutes
35 minutes	–	soft –	25 minutes

COURGETTES BAKED IN HONEY AND RASPBERRY VINEGAR

Prepare and cook the courgettes exactly as before, but using raspberry vinegar instead of the soya sauce.

BAKED COURGETTE CUPS

This isn't a favourite way of cooking courgettes, but it does look good at a dinner party. It can be prepared in the morning, and then simply cooked through just prior to serving, so it has its advantages – and is also an ideal way of making use of larger courgettes.

FOR 6 PEOPLE
At least 4 large courgettes (but see method)
1 pint (550ml) boiling water
1 teaspoon salt
At least 6oz (175g) filling of choice – mushroom pâté, tomato concasse, or savoury ham filling (see pages 104, 138 and 19)

Fairly fattish courgettes are needed, and you simply wipe the skin clean, remove top and tail, then cut into approximately 1½ inch (4cm) sections. Using a Parisian scoop, gently, but positively, remove the inside in order to form a cup-like shell – obviously not going right through. Have two per person. (Use the leftover courgette flesh for another recipe – in soup, or pan-fried, or in the stock pot.)

Blanch the courgette cups in the boiling salted water for only 2 minutes, and immediately refresh under cold running water. Put to one side, on kitchen paper, to drain.

Fill with mushroom pâté, or other filling of choice, and when you wish to serve, place on a greased baking sheet in a preheated oven at 375°F/190°C/Gas 5 and bake for 8–10 minutes. Serve immediately.

SAVOURY STUFFED COURGETTES

This is used as an accompanying vegetable, but one whole courgette per person (with an increase in filling, too, naturally) makes a nice starter or supper dish.

FOR 6 PEOPLE
3 large courgettes, weighing about 8oz (225g) each
4oz (100g) Cheddar cheese, grated
2oz (50g) celeriac, coarsely grated
1oz (25g) red pepper, finely chopped
1 tablespoon natural yoghurt
1 dessertspoon tomato purée
Salt and freshly ground black pepper
1 egg, lightly beaten
4oz (100g) butter, softened

Wipe the courgettes with a damp cloth, cut off the ends, and then cut lengthwise in two. Scoop out two-thirds of the flesh carefully (put it in the stock pot). Preheat the oven to 375°F/190°C/Gas 5.

For the filling, mix the cheese, celeriac, pepper, yoghurt and tomato purée together. Lightly season with salt and freshly ground black pepper, and then add the egg to bind, with half the butter. Mix it all together to a paste consistency, and then, using a teaspoon, fill the courgette halves with the mixture, piling up if necessary.

Break up the remaining butter and place in blobs all over the base of a dish which will take the six courgette halves comfortably. Place the stuffed courgettes in the dish, and cover with foil or a lid. Bake for 10 minutes, then remove cover, and bake for a further 10 minutes to brown.

DEEP-FRIED COURGETTES

As chips or ¼ inch (5mm) circles, this is without any doubt my favourite way of cooking courgettes. (Aubergines can also be prepared this way.)

FOR 6 PEOPLE
1lb (450g) courgettes
Oil for deep-frying
BATTER
4oz (100g) plain flour, sieved
1 teaspoon salt
2 eggs, separated
¼ pint (150ml) beer
2 tablespoons olive oil

The batter should be made first thing in the morning so that the gluten can expand. Put the sieved plain flour into a bowl along with the salt. Beat the egg yolks with the beer and olive oil, and slowly combine with the flour, preferably using an electric hand beater. When satisfied that your mixture is lovely and smooth, put it to one side, cover with clingfilm, and leave in a warm spot until you wish to use it.

This batter, when tested, easily coated nine courgettes about 5 inches (12cm) long. Simply trim the ends off the courgettes and either cut them lengthwise into chips or score them about five times lengthwise and then slice into ¼ inch (5mm) circles. Put into a sieve, sprinkle with extra salt, and let the chips or slices stand for at least 30 minutes to remove some of the excess liquid. Drain, rinse – to remove salt – and pat perfectly dry on kitchen paper or a teatowel.

When you are ready to fry off the courgettes, heat the pan of oil or the deep-fryer to 365°F/185°C. Beat the egg whites until stiff, and fold into the batter mixture. Dip the chips or circles in the batter so that they are coated. Fry *a few at a time* only, so that the temperature of the oil is not reduced too much, and for just 2 minutes. Remove to kitchen paper and keep warm in a low oven until all are cooked.

COURGETTES IN CHEESE CUSTARD

This custard can also be baked in individual ramekins and served as a starter.

FOR 4–6 PEOPLE
1lb (450g) courgettes
1–2 tablespoons olive oil
1 medium onion, finely chopped
1 clove garlic, crushed
2 eggs plus 1 egg yolk
½ pint (300ml) double cream
4oz (100g) Cheddar cheese, grated
Fresh parsley, marjoram, basil or tarragon
Salt and freshly ground black pepper
1oz (25g) butter

Wipe the courgettes, top and tail them, then slice thickly. Fry off in the olive oil very briefly. Remove and drain well on kitchen paper whilst frying off the onion with the garlic in remaining oil (or a little extra, if necessary). Drain these as well.

Make a custard by beating the eggs and egg yolk into the cream, before adding the cheese, herbs and seasonings to taste.

Butter a medium-sized ovenproof casserole and line with about ½ inch (1cm) of the custard. Bake this in a preheated oven at 350°F/180°C/Gas 4 for about 8 minutes. Then arrange the onions and courgettes on top, and put in the rest of the custard. Cook at the same temperature for a further 20–30 minutes until set. Serve in spoonfuls.

CUCUMBER

CUCUMIS SATIVUS

ANOTHER MEMBER OF THE squash and gourd family, cucumbers are related to pumpkins, melons, courgettes etc. They are one of the oldest vegetables, having been cultivated for about 4000 years: they were grown by the Sumerians, rate mention in the Old Testament, and were popular with the Romans – the Emperor Tiberius is widely acclaimed as being the instigator of the 'frame' in which to cultivate the year-long supply he demanded. In Britain they were grown in the fourteenth century, but only gained real popularity in the sixteenth. Dr Johnson was famously rude about them, saying they should be sliced, dressed with a pepper vinegar and then thrown away 'as good for nothing'; but Mrs Beeton used them extensively in cold dishes.

Christopher Columbus introduced the cucumber – thought to originate in India – to the New World, through Haiti, and they apparently became very popular with the Pueblo Indians! Nowadays, they are grown throughout the world (even in the Sahara), and throughout the year – although generally speaking, they're best in late summer.

There are two basic types of cucumber (although a glance at the displays in ethnic shops will reveal many odd shapes and colours): the familiar, long, thin green hot-house or frame cucumber; and the shorter, thicker, rough-skinned ridge cucumber (so called, not for its ridged skin, but because it used to be grown on raised ridges of soil). The former must, in Great Britain and similar climates, be grown under glass; the latter can be successfully – and more easily – grown outside. There are white varieties of cucumber popular on the Continent, and an apple cucumber is occasionally seen – which is yellow and shaped like an apple (needless to say). Gherkins are a type of ridge cucumber, grown and picked small for pickling.

Choose your cucumbers as you would any other similar vegetable: the colour must be good, the skin plump and healthy (that you can't press a fingernail into easily). It must be firm, not slushy or wrinkled. Cucumbers, being about 96 per cent water, don't contain very much else, but there is some Vitamin A and C content when eaten very fresh. They are thought by some to be indigestible; to 'not agree with them', and indeed can cause wind – though I've never noticed any such effect. . . . They're apparently a natural diuretic, and are used a lot in natural beauty recipes – slices as refreshing

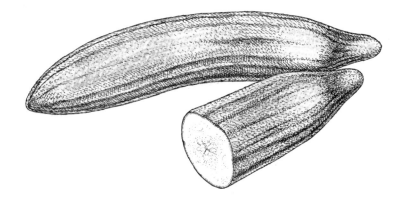

eye pads, as a tonic when rubbed over the skin, and as a soother for sunburn. To carry on in the same vein, the English herbalist, Gerard, said cucumbers cooked with mutton and mixed with oatmeal were a cure for 'red and shining fierie noses' . . . well!

Cucumbers don't need much preparation for eating. The skin can be bitter, but peeled cucumber looks and tastes rather bland. Cut channels down the side with a scorer to lessen skin content, if you like – and they'll look more attractive when sliced to boot. The ends are cut off – these can be bitter, too – but, unless the cucumbers are quite mature and large, the seeds (the indigestible part, perhaps?) don't need to be removed. Some say they should be salted and left to drain like courgettes, but I don't feel this is necessary. But use cucumbers as soon as possible; they don't like hanging around, and don't like the cold of the fridge.

I really only like cucumbers raw – in salads, sandwiches, as a crudité for dipping into a dip – but they can be cooked as a vegetable. They make a good container, as in one of the following recipes, for a tasty stuffing, and they can be made into soups or sauces (particularly good with poached salmon, chicken or oily fish). They pickle extremely well, in pieces, or whole as gherkins.

But it is raw that they excel. The French eat them with salted whipped cream; the North Europeans combine them with soured cream; and many cuisines ally them with yoghurt: the Indian raita – which so usefully cools the curry-heated mouth and throat – as well as the Turkish caçik and the Greek zaziki. They combine well with strawberries – in Elona salad – with dill, with sorrel, with tomatoes (think about the Spanish chilled soup, gazpacho).

I like them because they're so refreshing – and they're *not* fattening!

PERSIAN CUCUMBER SOUP

FOR 6 PEOPLE
2 tablespoons raisins
1 tablespoon cooking brandy
1 cucumber
½ pint (300ml) single cream
½ pint (300ml) natural yoghurt
2 cloves garlic, crushed
1 tablespoon tarragon vinegar
1 tablespoon fresh mint, finely chopped
1 tablespoon cocktail gherkins, finely chopped
2 hard-boiled eggs, finely chopped

The day before you intend serving the soup, leave the raisins soaking in the cooking brandy – overnight, or for at least 12 hours.

Wash and dry the cucumber and grate it coarsely. Stir together all the ingredients in a large container, and leave to chill for as long as possible.

Serve in chilled soup bowls and garnish with fresh herb sprigs – dill or fennel would be lovely.

CUCUMBER BALLS

As an accompaniment to salmon or many fish dishes, this rather 'upmarket' way of cooking cucumber is delicious.

Simply peel the cucumber and, using a very small Parisian scoop, make balls which should be blanched momentarily then immediately put under cold running water and left to one side.

Mix into a reduced double cream sauce (see page 18) at the last minute with the merest touch of freshly ground nutmeg.

71

DANDELION

TARAXACUM OFFICINALIS

RIDGE CUCUMBER CUPS

Ridge cucumbers are the ones used mostly for pickling and chutneys, but I take a certain pleasure in their ugly appearance and often use them as 'containers', like courgettes, for stuffings such as mushroom pâté.

Wipe the skins of about 6 ridge cucumbers of 4–6oz (100–175g) each in weight, and top and tail. Cut into approximately 1½ inch (4cm) sections – you want two 'cups' per person, so the number of cucumbers you buy will depend on their size.

Thereafter, make into cups, blanch, fill and bake exactly as courgette cups (see page 68).

'**D**ANDELION?' SAY YOU – THE man must be scraping the bottom of the barrel to get a D entry in his book! And indeed it is, to many, the most objectionable and persistent of garden weeds, although it has a long and worthy history as a food plant. It was thought to be one of the 'bitter herbs' mentioned in the Old Testament; medieval vegetable gardens would contain a row or two of dandelion plants, mulched and blanched to a great size; and John Evelyn the diarist (1620–1706) mentions it as good for eating. Medicinally, dandelions have been used since the tenth century, and I suppose this is based on their not inconsiderable reputation as a diuretic, most clearly seen in the French name *pissenlit* (a name echoed – and worse! – in many British local names for the plant).

The dandelion is related to wild chicory – that which, when cultivated, forced and blanched, gives us the white chicons – and its roots are used in much the same way as chicory roots, dried and ground as a coffee substitute. The taste is thought by many to be indistinguishable from real coffee, but is probably valued most in times of stringency, and because it doesn't contain caffeine like real coffee (dandelion coffee can be bought in health-food shops). The roots can also be

CURLY KALE, see KALE
CUSTARD MARROW, see PUMPKIN
AND SQUASH

ENDIVE

CICHORIUM ENDIVIA

cooked and eaten, a popular vegetable in Japan.

The flower buds can be fried in butter, the flowers themselves make a wine (which apparently tastes like a mild retsina), as well as beer, teas and tisanes. Dandelion flower honey is a speciality, and in Russia the white milky substance contained in the root, rather like latex, is used to make a synthetic rubber!

So, as you can see, the dandelion is not just the scourge of gardeners, but is eminently useful as well. But it is the leaves which are most eaten, and dandelions – the name from the French *dent-de-lion*, lion's teeth (probably from the toothed leaves) – are actually cultivated commercially in France. The leaves, full of vitamins and minerals, were recommended for eating during the Second World War by the British 'Radio Doctor', but we still do not seem to partake as much as the French. They are eaten in the American South with other wild leaves, as something called poke salad, and further north, in areas where Dutch and other northern European immigrants have settled.

The leaves of dandelions, whether cultivated or wild, are best in spring, before the flower buds have formed, and when very young – the older they get, the more bitter they get. Many gardeners blanch them, by growing under flowerpots, heaped over with compost or manure: this lightens the leaf colour and renders them less bitter. They can be cooked like spinach, in butter, or made into a soup; but are best – young, tasty and peppery – in salads with other salad leaves, with tomatoes, cress, chives or parsley, and with tasty dressings. The classic French dish is *Salade de pissenlits au lard*: dandelion leaves with crispy bacon bits, and the bacon fat poured over.

EGGPLANT, see AUBERGINE

THIS IS THE CURLY, MOP-HEADED winter vegetable which is known as chicory in France and the USA (see under the heading Chicory for a more detailed examination of this confusion). Anyway, it is as ancient as white chicory (they're closely related) and is thought to be one of the 'bitter herbs' of the Book of Exodus. It comes from northern China and southern Asia, and has been cultivated in Europe since about the end of the thirteenth century. It is a useful winter vegetable, available until late in the season after other greens have disappeared.

There are two basic types of endive – the very curly, thin-leaved one, and the broader-leaved Batavian endive, often just called Batavia or escarole. Both are bitter in taste – a bitterness that is reduced by blanching, as with chicory. And the newly fashionable 'red lettuce', radicchio, from Italy, is also a close relation to both endive and chicory (*radicchio* is an alternative Italian word for chicory).

FENNEL

FOENICULUM VULGARE DULCE

74

When buying endive, look for dry firm heads, with no sign of greasiness on the base. The outer leaves will be dark green in colour, and the centre should be yellow to white (this is achieved by putting an old dinner plate or flowerpot over the centre of the plant while growing, to cut out the light and thus blanch it). To prepare for eating, cut off any outer damaged leaves – those which are unblanched are much coarser – trim off the root base, and wash well. Drain and dry, and separate into individual spears with leaves and a little white stem if using in a salad. If you intend to cook the endive, leave it whole after washing, or cut larger ones in half.

Endive is usually used raw in salads, where its bitter crunchiness is welcome when mixed with other salad leaves. A Catalonian recipe uses a hot chilli dressing, and strong dressings do tend to be better than mild. Radicchio leaves are ideal as a garnish, and indeed the colour fades to a murky brown if cooked. Endive can also be cooked, though, as a vegetable, and served with a variety of sauces: I like it simply poached, or better still steamed, and then served lukewarm with a tangy French dressing. But I rarely serve it at Miller Howe as, to be perfectly honest, it is not popular as a cooked vegetable.

I'M ASHAMED TO SAY I HAD NOT realised that there were two varieties of fennel! I grandly asked the gardener at Miller Howe to plant some fennel in the garden so that we could have lashings of the green feathery herb for flavouring and garnishing as well as the plump bulbs for serving as a vegetable. Plant the bought seeds he duly did, and up sprouted stalks and feathery herb, but not a bulb in sight! So now I know, although they're closely related, they *are* different! Florence fennel or finocchio, the *bulb*, is a sub-species, a cultivated form, of the herb fennel – which grows wild over much of Europe, including Britain, and in California.

The herb fennel (*Foeniculum vulgare officinalis*) has been grown for centuries – the Romans cultivated it for its seeds and edible shoots; the Anglo-Saxons used it both in cookery and medicine; and it was much used in eighteenth-century English cookery. The bulbous fennel was one of the many plants with which Thomas Jefferson experimented in his Virginia garden in the 1820s, and it comes now mainly from Italy (obvious from both its names), in whose cuisine it features most.

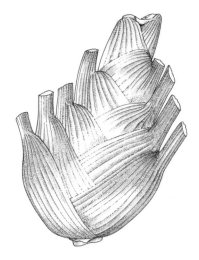

ESCAROLE, see ENDIVE
FAVA BEANS, see BROAD BEANS

Florence fennel is grown for its bulb-like swollen leaf base which tastes of aniseed. Choose well-rounded roots, of a pale green to white colour – the plant should be blanched, so never buy any which are a darker, deeper green. To prepare it for eating, remove the outer coarser leaves, and cut off the bulb base. The average bulb weighs about 12–14oz (350–400g), and after trimming, will be about 8oz (225g). Cut off the top stalks but always use the waste in the stock pot; keep the feathery leaves, too, for garnishes and sauces as they're a good substitute for the herb fennel. When fennel is to be eaten raw, slice the trimmed head across thinly, and then separate into thin strips (keep in iced water if not using straight away). If planning to cook fennel, cut the trimmed head into halves or quarters, or leave whole, depending on size.

Fennel is most delicious raw in salads, with its pungent aniseed flavour and celery-like texture. It goes well with a strong-flavoured olive oil dressing or a garlicky mayonnaise. But it can be cooked in a variety of interesting ways, when the flavour is less pronounced. It is boiled, steamed or braised, and goes particularly well with a Parmesan cheese and butter sauce. It can be sliced and briefly cooked in butter, and is a good tasty accompaniment to fresh pasta.

The herb fennel is particularly associated in culinary terms with oily fish – perhaps because of the plant's affinity with coastal habitats, and because it has a reputation as a digestive (fennel seeds are included in the mixture chewed to aid digestion and sweeten breath after Indian meals) – and in many Mediterranean countries, fish are grilled over dried fennel twigs and charcoal. The bulb fennel is thought to possess some of these digestive qualities too, and cooked, it can be helped along with a drop of Pastis or Pernod, to emphasise the healthy aspects and taste!

FENNEL SOUP

Basic recipe (see page 11)
2lb (900g) fennel, washed and trimmed

FENNEL AND COURGETTE SOUP

Basic recipe (see page 11)
1lb (450g) fennel, washed and trimmed
1lb (450g) courgettes, wiped, topped and tailed

75

FENNEL AND ALMOND SOUP

Basic recipe (see page 11)
2lb (900g) fennel, washed and trimmed
4oz (100g) ground almonds

Stir the ground almonds into the soup after sieving.

BOILED FENNEL

FOR 6 PEOPLE
1 large fennel bulb, about 12–14oz (350–400g)
2 pints (a good litre) boiling water
1 teaspoon salt

Prepare the fennel, removing the outer discoloured leaves, and the base, then cut into ¼ inch (5mm) cubes.

Plunge the cubes into the boiling salted water, bring back to the boil, and cook for:
4 minutes – crisp
5 minutes – firm
7 minutes – soft

STEAMED FENNEL

The same quantities are used for six people, and the fennel should be prepared in exactly the same way as the previous recipe. Put the fennel cubes in a colander over the saucepan of boiling salted water, cover with a lid (or foil) and bring back to the boil. Cook for:

    5 minutes – crisp
    6 minutes – firm
    10 minutes – soft

STEAMED WHOLE FENNEL

FOR 6 PEOPLE
1 large fennel bulb, about 12–14oz (350–400g)
2 pints (a good litre) boiling water
1 teaspoon salt

Trim the fennel and place, with the green feathery trimmings from the tops, on the base of a colander. Put this over the pan of boiling salted water and cover with the lid (or foil). Steam for:

    30 minutes – crisp
    40 minutes – firm
    45 minutes – soft

When cooked, remove from the colander, cut into six pieces, and serve with a sauce – Hollandaise or cheese are good (see page 17).

BAKED FENNEL QUARTERS

FOR 4 PEOPLE
1 large fennel bulb, about 12–14oz (350–400g)
2oz (50g) butter

Remove any stained outer pieces of the fennel bulb, as well as the feathery tops. Wash and then cut into quarters of about 2oz (50g) each.

Have ready four pieces of foil, measuring approximately 9 × 7 inches (23 × 18cm), and put a ½oz (15g) knob of butter on each piece. Place a fennel quarter, along with any green feathery bits (which provide so much flavour) on top of the butter, and fold the foil round into compact parcels.

Place on a cooling rack over a roasting tray with hot water in the base. Bake in the preheated oven at 400°F/200°C/Gas 6 for:

    15 minutes – crisp
    20 minutes – firm
    25 minutes – soft

This recipe can be varied in a number of different ways. You could add ½oz (15g) finely grated Cheddar cheese to each parcel. Or, instead of the butter, you could add 1 tablespoon of natural yoghurt to each parcel. Or, the grated rind and juice of an orange would also add an interesting flavour.

FRENCH BEANS

PHASEOLUS VULGARIS

FRENCH BEANS ARE A DWARF variety of green bean, also known as haricots verts, kidney beans, dwarf beans, and snap or string beans in the USA. They were unknown in the Old World before Columbus discovered America, and were introduced to Britain during the reign of Elizabeth I – along with the potato and sweetcorn, both New World basics.

Green beans are all very similar, but the French variety – named, although it is originally South American, because of its popularity in France – is a young small pod which usually has no strings (as opposed to the runner bean, which is longer, larger and *has* to be de-stringed). Green beans are eaten pod and all, and if left to mature will produce the haricot bean which is dried for the protein-rich pulse of the winter. Green, the beans and pods contain worthy amounts of Vitamin C.

French beans include a number of types, ranging from almost flat pods of up to 7 inches (18cm) long, to shorter and plumper pods. Home-grown beans are available, young, crisp and mid-green in colour, from July to October, but imported varieties, usually from Kenya, are available throughout the year. These Kenyan varieties are what I call matchstick – they're thinner, shorter, and a joy to serve and eat. Yellow and white varieties are also sometimes available. When buying, try to snap one in half without the greengrocer seeing, and if it snaps crisp and clean it is fresh (obviously the origin of one of the American names). If you can't use them all on the day of purchase, and they begin to wilt, revive them in a closed plastic bag in the chilling compartment of the fridge.

When preparing for cooking, very young French beans – and the matchstick ones – only need topping and tailing, but maturer beans will need more painstaking effort: after topping and tailing, the thinnest, merest sliver should be cut off each side. From 12oz (350g) beans, you will be left with about 8oz (225g) after trimming.

When cooking, the simplest methods – quick boiling and steaming – are the best. Leave the lid off the pan when boiling, which helps to preserve the bright green colour. If when cooking, you plan to cook more than you need immediately, put the remaining French beans into iced water to preserve their colour. If using in a salad, do not dress until about to serve, as they lose colour and their crisp texture.

Cold in a good dressing, young French beans taste and look wonderful; garnished with toasted almonds or fried crispy bacon chunks they are even better. Stir-fried in garlicky butter, they are magnificent; with a little double cream and lemon juice they are incomparable. I *like* French beans!

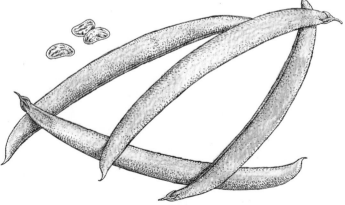

BOILED OR STEAMED FRENCH BEANS

FOR 6 PEOPLE
12oz (350g) French beans, topped and tailed
1 pint (550ml) boiling water
1 teaspoon salt

Plunge the beans into the boiling salted water, or place in a colander *over* the boiling water. Bring back to the boil and cook for:
    5 minutes – crisp
    8 minutes – firm
    10 minutes – soft
    Season with lots of freshly ground black pepper, and serve at once.

MATCHSTICK FRENCH BEANS

These thin French beans are about 4–5 inches (10–12cm) long, and all you have to do when preparing them is cut off their tops and tails. As there is literally *no* waste, you will be able to give 6 people an ample portion by buying only 8oz (225g). Makes up for their cost!

FOR 6 PEOPLE
8oz (225g) thin French beans
1 pint (550ml) boiling water
1 teaspoon salt

Plunge the beans into the boiling salted water and bring back to the boil. Cook for only:
    2 minutes – crisp
    4 minutes – firm
    6 minutes – soft
    Personally, I prefer to cook them for the 2 minutes, strain and refresh them under cold running water, and then fry them off immediately in a mixture of walnut oil and butter with a liberal sprinkling of freshly ground black pepper.
    They can also be steamed over boiling salted water. They are cooked for:
    4 minutes – crisp
    6 minutes – firm
    8 minutes – soft

STEAMED FRENCH BEAN PARCELS

FOR 6 PEOPLE
About 12–16oz (350–450g) matchstick French beans
6 long thin strips of leek or chives, blanched
1 pint (550ml) boiling water
1 teaspoon salt

Allow about 10 beans per person (about 2oz or 50g after preparation). Tie the beans into neat parcels with the blanched strips of leek or chives. Place in a colander over the pan of boiling salted water, and bring the water back to the boil. Cook:
    6 minutes – crisp
    8 minutes – firm
    10 minutes – soft

FRENCH BEAN SALAD

Use matchstick French beans for this if you can, and I 'cook' them for an even shorter time as I love the crunchiness.

FOR 6 PEOPLE
8oz (225g) small French beans, topped and tailed
1 pint (550ml) boiling water
Salt and freshly ground black pepper
DRESSING
4 tablespoons olive oil
2 tablespoons white wine
1 teaspoon white wine vinegar
A little castor sugar

Place the beans in the boiling water with 1 teaspoon salt, and bring back to the boil. Drain off the water immediately, and refresh the beans under very cold water. Leave to drain and cool thoroughly.
    Arrange the beans decoratively on a serving platter or on individual plates. (If you have time, layering them up at right angles to each other, building them up into a trellis shape, looks good.) Leave to one side, and just before serving, season generously with the pepper.
    Make the dressing in the blender and pour over the beans at the very last minute.

78

GARLIC

ALLIUM SATIVUM

O F THE SAME GENUS AS LEEKS and onions – the lily family – garlic is thought to be native to Central Asia. It is now grown all over the world, with supplies coming into Britain from Italy, Spain and France; it is grown in the USA, in California, Texas and Louisiana, but is also imported. Garlic is an ancient vegetable: the pyramid builders in Egypt were given a clove of garlic every day to keep them healthy, and its lovers and haters have proliferated ever since. Historically, garlic seems to have been used more as a 'folk' medicine than as a culinary flavouring: in *New England Cookery* (1808), Lucy Emerson wrote primly that 'gar-licks though used by the French, are better adapted to medicine than cookery', and it is perhaps only in the last fifty years that British and American cooks have come to appreciate the plant for its flavouring powers.

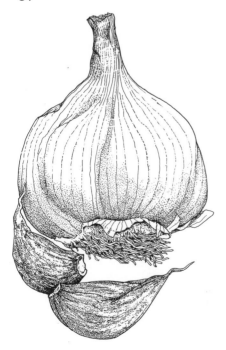

Its medicinal properties, though, are undisputed. Culpeper said that garlic opened the lungs and gave relief from asthma, and indeed garlic is excreted through the lungs, which could be beneficial to lung disorders. Garlic also contains substances which delay blood clotting, and may reduce the risk of heart attacks. The juice of garlic is a strong antiseptic, and was used as such by the French army, deprived of conventional medicine, during the First World War. With so many benefits, no wonder the folk tales attribute to garlic the ability to ward off the evil eye and keep vampires at bay!

Garlic comes in various types, and in various colours, but in general we see the white-, pink- or purple-skinned, with small to medium cloves on the bulbs. (For goodness' sake, do remember that a *clove* is just one of the many oval pieces which form the bulb or head: I once had a furious letter from a buyer of *Entertaining with Tovey* who said her cheese and herb pâté had been a complete disaster. She had used two whole *bulbs* instead of two *cloves*, and I didn't wonder that her guests left early and her husband wouldn't speak to her.)

In early summer, garlic is fresh and large, and quite difficult to peel; later on the heads will have dried out a bit. Always carefully buy bulbs that you can *feel*, otherwise the cloves may have dried out too much. Keep it in a dry, dark place.

I am a compulsive 'kitchen-gadget-shop ogler' as I simply cannot walk by one. Invariably I find something new which I cannot live without, or can't understand how I lived without until now. But I give full marks to the purveyors of garlic presses for being utterly useless objects (which should immediately be given to your next bring-and-buy sale). They simply produce a few drips of garlic juice and some stringy pieces. For me the only way to squeeze garlic is as follows.

79

At home I have a 'garlic board' measuring 6 × 4 inches (15 × 10cm) which has been faithfully in use now for fourteen years; when I want to locate it, I simply take a great sniff! I remove the skin of the garlic clove and place it flat on the board and then, using a round-edged sharp knife, simply hack away removing little by little on to half a teaspoon of soft runny salt. The salt helps make the garlic mushy and paste-like, which is the consistency you are looking for when adding garlic to a dish.

Garlic is used so extensively as a flavouring in so many cuisines that I have not bothered to reproduce any standard recipes – delicious as they may be – such as aïoli, bagna cauda or garlic soup; garlic butter you will find in the introductory chapter, and garlic flavouring occurs in many of the recipes throughout the book. What I have done is use garlic as a vegetable – or garnish really – which to some may be the height of olfactory and culinary horror; for garlic *aficionados* it will be a *must*!

The following recipes will accompany grilled meat, especially lamb – steaks or chops – beautifully, and the flavour and after-effects won't be too strong because the cloves are cooked whole. (But, just in case, if you chew on cardamom seeds after eating garlic, the smell on the breath will be neutralised.)

BOILED GARLIC CLOVES

FOR 6 PEOPLE
5–6oz (150–175g) whole garlic
¼ pint (150ml) milk

This quantity of whole garlic should produce about 24 cloves, which should be topped, tailed and skinned. Place in a saucepan and cover with the cold milk. Bring to the boil and simmer for:
    4 minutes – crisp
    5 minutes – firm
    6 minutes – soft
    (Use the milk from this and the next recipe for mildly garlic-flavoured sauces, or for adding to a soup.)

SHALLOW-FRIED GARLIC CLOVES

FOR 6 PEOPLE
5–6oz (150–175g) whole garlic
¼ pint (150ml) milk
2oz (50g) dripping

Top, tail and skin the cloves (about 24), and then simply cover with the milk. Leave for 24 hours. Strain, and dry the cloves on kitchen paper.

In a small frying pan, melt the dripping, add the cloves, and cook for:
    4 minutes – crisp
    5 minutes – firm
    10 minutes – soft

DEEP-FRIED GARLIC CLOVES

FOR 6 PEOPLE
5–6oz (150–175g) whole garlic
Oil for deep-frying

Simply top, tail and skin the cloves of garlic (about 24 in all), and then heat the oil in pan or deep fryer to 365°F/185°C. Fry for:
    2 minutes – crisp
    3 minutes – firm
    5 minutes – soft

GLOBE ARTICHOKE

CYNARA SCOLYMUS

THOUGHT TO HAVE COME originally from North Africa (its name is derived from the Arabic, *al-karsufa*), the globe artichoke is a member of the thistle family, is related to the cardoon, and has been cultivated in Europe for thousands of years. The Romans and Greeks enjoyed them, and Elizabethan England was reintroduced to their joys by Italian imports. Catherine de Medici, who took them with her from Italy to France, was considered rather fast by the French court when she ate them (to bursting point, apparently), as they were considered to be an aphrodisiac. Italy remains the major producer, followed by France, and California supplies the majority of the American crop. Funnily enough, despite being popular until the end of the nineteenth century, in Britain at least they seemed to disappear until about the 1960s. A Scottish friend, coming to London in 1967, had to be shown, to her acute

embarrassment, how to eat them at a posh dinner party. (Perhaps that's why they fell from favour – they *are* a lot of work.)

But they are also one of the most elegant and delicious of vegetables, and make an ideal starter, either hot or cold. The part eaten is the young, immature flower head: the base of the leaves is scraped off with the teeth, and the *fond* (bottom or heart) is separated from the leaves and the 'choke', and eaten with a knife and fork. The hairy fronds of the inedible central choke eventually become the purple thistle flower; once this starts to turn purple, the artichoke is inedible.

They are best young – as with nearly all vegetables – and the lucky Italians, Spanish and southern French can eat very young small artichokes in spring, before the chokes have developed, raw and whole. A further part of the home-grown artichoke can be eaten: before a three- or four-year-old plant (its maximum productive life span) is thrown away, its stems – or chards – can be blanched to eat, raw or cooked, like celery. The gardener can also benefit from the foliage itself: the plant looks wonderful in the herbaceous border.

When buying artichokes, look for crisp, not too brown leaves, with a slight bloom on them. Before cooking, plunge them head down into salted water to remove any dirt or insect life. Remove the stem, and any untidy bottom leaves. Many people believe in cutting off the tops of the leaves, but I can't for the life of me imagine why, other than for visual neatness (and who wants neat food?). Any cut edges should immediately be rubbed with lemon juice to lessen discoloration, or store the prepared heads in acidulated water until ready for cooking.

Cook in lots of boiling salted water – with vinegar or lemon juice added if you like – for 30–50 minutes, depending on size. (Never cook

81

HOP SHOOTS

HUMULUS LUPULUS

82

in iron or aluminium pots as they can discolour.) Test when the cooking time is nearly up: if a leaf comes away easily, the artichoke is cooked.

I like artichokes best as a starter, when I can take off the leaves one by one, dip them hot into melted (or lemon) butter or Hollandaise, or cold into vinaigrette, with the anticipation of the delicious *fond* to come. (Always remember to provide a spare plate for the discarded, tooth-marked leaves, and finger bowls for messy hands.) Cooked artichokes can also be stuffed, after the hairy choke has been scraped away, with a variety of fillings – mushroom pâté (page 104) would be good. The hearts themselves can be used in other ways, in salads, with antipasto, fried in butter, in quiches, and in purées (Jane Grigson writes of French babies being weaned on artichoke purée: I can only echo her comment: Lucky babies'!) If only cooking the artichokes for the hearts, waste not, want not, and scrape off the leaf flesh to add to the dressing or mayonnaise.

EVERYONE KNOWS THAT HOPS are used in the making of beer, but fewer people are aware that hops can also be eaten. Hop shoots were a vegetable and salad plant in Pliny's Rome and, as hops grow wild enthusiastically and chokingly, they were probably used as a vegetable in their native Europe long before the flower began to be used in brewing. It was Flemish settlers who planted the hop gardens of Kent in the sixteenth century, and interestingly, it is still the Belgians who make most use of the shoots as a vegetable (and brew a lot of beer too).

They are only available from early March until May, and if you live near an accommodating hop-grower, do try them. They should just be rinsed, tied together like asparagus, then boiled in salted acidulated water for a few minutes. They're eaten like asparagus, too, with melted butter or Hollandaise. They can be chopped with butter as a sauce, are served with cream or eggs in Belgium, in a risotto in Venice, and can be added to a soup.

GOOD KING HENRY, see SPINACH
GUMBO, see OKRA

HORSERADISH

COCHLEARIA ARMORACIA

HORSERADISH, THE MOST pungent of all cultivated roots, is a native of south-eastern Europe, and grows wild in Britain, all over mainland Europe, North America and New Zealand. It has an ancient history, as the Egyptians and Romans – both famed for their liking for strong tastes – grew it. Pliny thought it a very healthful plant and, indeed, it is good for the stomach (although my Nan said it gave her indigestion), it is antiscorbutic (prevents scurvy!), and is good for blocked sinuses and noses, and for the common cold. The juice mixed with the yolk of an egg makes a good embrocation apparently – all that heat *must* be good!

Horseradish is more of a condiment than a vegetable in its own right, so really I'm just trying to expand the H entry. But it's interesting, I think. The horseradish plant – the leaves are of no food value – has invasive tendencies, so take care when planting and digging up the roots. It grows everywhere on waste ground, and is generally ignored, so roots can probably be dug up quite happily. In fact, Richard Mabey in *Food for Free* says that 'British Rail could probably pay off their deficit if they cropped the plants growing along their cuttings'!

Wash the roots well and peel, then grate – preferably in the open air as it will make you weep more copiously than the very strongest onion. Serve the grated root directly on roast beef – it's the classic British beef accompaniment – or mix it with cream, yoghurt or soured cream to make a sauce. It's also used as an accompaniment for some smoked fish dishes, and in pickles. I've tried frying grated horseradish with sweet fruits, but can't say the results have been particularly pleasing. It loses its pungency quickly when grated – or cooked – but can be stored in vinegar in a screw-top jar (in fact makes a good hot vinegar). Good and different ways to serve it are mixed with grated cooked beetroot, or with mashed turnip or swede.

83

JERUSALEM ARTICHOKE

HELIANTHUS TUBEROSUS

84

THESE ROOT TUBERS ARE NATIVE to North America (greatly prized by the Red Indians), and were introduced to Europe in the early seventeenth century. They were named artichokes not because they're related to the globe, but because their flavour was likened to that of the globe artichoke heart (not *at all* similar, in my opinion). The Jerusalem part is a corruption of the Italian word *girasole*, sunflower, or 'turning in the sun', as the Jerusalem artichoke is related to the sunflower. They are available from October to March.

They're easy to grow, so it's odd that they seem to be less than popular, but the neglect may be due to the fact that they are quite difficult and fiddly to prepare because of their knobbles. When buying, therefore, try to choose the biggest – about 4 × 2 inches (10 × 5cm) – and smoothest, which will save time and trouble, and always buy a little more than you need, to allow for the inevitable wastage (use the knobbles in the stock pot).

The skins should be white or purplish, and avoid any which are too dirty. Scrub the artichokes well, and if they're smooth, you *can* peel them thinly, but I think the best flavour is near the skin, and would always advise you to cook them with the skins *on*. They may not look too attractive, but they taste much more delicious. Drop peeled artichokes immediately into acidulated water to prevent discoloration, and then boil or steam. Keep the water in which they've boiled as this will be full of flavour and can be used as the basis for a soup or sauce (in fact it sometimes sets to a jelly when cold).

Jerusalem artichokes have a very distinct, unusual flavour, which I find a delight. They make a wonderful soup – Palestine soup is a classic, re-emphasising the mistaken Jerusalem connection; lovely smooth creamy purées can go with beef or poultry; chips or fritters are crunchy on the outside, soft within; a soufflé is delicate. They can be roasted like potatoes and they can be eaten raw when young and tender, when the flesh tastes sweet and nutty. Try to cook them with other vegetables which aren't too strong in flavour – leeks as opposed to onions, for instance.

They are believed by some to cause wind, and I heard an even worse story of 'digestive' trouble. Somebody bought some Jerusalem artichokes – or so she thought – from the greengrocer, took them home and cooked them – and was very surprised (if not ill) with the result. She had been sold fresh root ginger, which is rather similar in size and shape – so beware!

There is another root artichoke – the Chinese artichoke – which is related to the dead nettle. It is also a white elongated tuber, and can be prepared in similar ways to Jerusalem artichokes. I've never seen them, so can't swear to this.

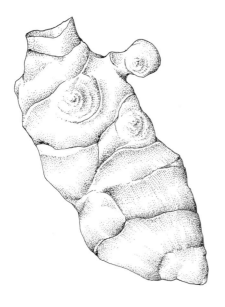

JERUSALEM ARTICHOKE SOUP

Basic recipe (see page 11)
2lb (900g) Jerusalem artichokes, scrubbed

BOILED OR STEAMED JERUSALEM ARTICHOKES

FOR 6 PEOPLE
12oz (350g) Jerusalem artichokes
1 pint (550ml) boiling water
1 teaspoon salt

Using a 'kitchen greenie' (those scourers for removing stains on your saucepans that you sometimes – ever so rarely – burn), or a cheap nail-brush specially for vegetable cleaning, scrub the artichokes well. Cut them into ½ inch (1cm) cubes and either plunge them into or steam them over the boiling salted water for:
>   4 minutes – crisp
>   5 minutes – firm
>   6 minutes – soft

JERUSALEM ARTICHOKES FRIED WITH BACON, ONION AND GARLIC

FOR 6 PEOPLE
1 tablespoon oil
4oz (100g) bacon, derinded and diced
4oz (100g) onion, finely chopped
2 cloves garlic, crushed
12oz (350g) Jerusalem artichokes, scrubbed and diced

Bring the oil to smoking point in the frying pan and add the finely diced bacon and onion along with the crushed garlic. Cook for 4 minutes until slightly golden and the flavours have blended.
    Add the Jerusalem artichokes and stir-fry for:
>   8 minutes – crisp
>   10 minutes – firm
>   12 minutes – soft

JERUSALEM ARTICHOKES WITH CREAM AND CHEESE

FOR 6 PEOPLE
2 cloves garlic
1oz (25g) butter
12oz (350g) Jerusalem artichokes, well scrubbed or
    peeled
½ pint (300ml) cold milk
Salt and freshly ground black pepper
Generous pinch freshly grated nutmeg
½ pint (300ml) double cream
2oz (50g) Cheddar cheese, finely grated

Peel the garlic, gently bruise it, and then rub all over the inside of a 2 pint (1 litre) casserole dish quite briskly to get a good garlicky flavour. Butter the inside of the dish.
    Cut the prepared artichokes into slices of about ¼ inch (5mm) thick. Bring the cold milk up to the boil with the salt, pepper and nutmeg, and when boiling, add the vegetable slices and cook for 10 minutes, simmering slowly.
    Drain the artichoke slices well (the milk could be used in a soup or sauce), and then bring the double cream mixed with the cheese up to the boil.
    Fan the par-cooked artichoke slices over the base of your dish and then pour the cream cheese mixture over them. Bake in the preheated oven at 350°F/180°C/Gas 4 for:
>   10 minutes – crisp
>   12 minutes – firm
>   15 minutes – soft

KALE

BRASSICA OLERACEA ACEPHALA

SAVOURY JERUSALEM ARTICHOKES

FOR 6 PEOPLE
3oz (75g) bacon, finely chopped
4oz (100g) onion, finely chopped
2 tablespoons cooking oil
12oz (350g) Jerusalem artichokes, scrubbed and cut
*   into 1/4 inch (5mm) cubes*
6 teaspoons pine kernels, toasted
4 tomatoes, skinned, seeded and chopped
9 tablespoons double cream

Fry off the bacon and onion in the oil until golden, and then transfer to a bowl. Add the cubed artichokes to the frying pan with the pine kernels and tomatoes, and simply mix to coat with the remaining oil. Transfer immediately to the bowl.

Put the double cream in the frying pan to deglaze it, then transfer to the bowl and mix together well with vegetables and bacon. Spoon out into lightly buttered individual ramekin dishes then bake in a bain marie in the preheated oven set at 350°F/180°C/ Gas 4.

They will take only about 20 minutes to cook to the crisp stage. I then usually top them with grated cheese or savoury cheese breadcrumbs (see page 19) and finish off under the grill.

KALE IS CLOSELY RELATED TO the wild cabbage which produced all the brassica cousins – the cabbages, Brussels sprouts, broccoli etc. It is a non-heading cabbage, however, and there are three principal types which can be eaten: the curly or Scottish kale, the plain-leaved kale, and rape kale. It has been cultivated for about 2000 years, and is most useful in that it is hardy, and a source of greens in the winter months – from early January to late April – when other greens are scarce. It has an extremely strong flavour, and the leaves are coarse, which is why there are probably more cattle and sheep sustained by kale than there are people! But kale is rich in iron, Vitamin C and calcium – so eat up your greens, they really *are* good for you!

KOHLRABI

BRASSICA OLERACEA CAULORAPA

It has long been cultivated in northern Europe, where it played an important part in keeping the peasants alive at the end of winter: the Danes and Germans eat it; the Portuguese use it as well as cabbage in their thick peasant soup caldo verde; and the Scots are perhaps the principal kale eaters: their kale brose – a cow cheek, kale and oatmeal soup/gruel – is thick and sustaining, and to be asked to 'kale' in the old days was to be asked to 'sup'. (The word kale comes from the Old English, *cole*, cabbage.)

Kale is a decorative plant, particularly the curly variety which is the most commonly seen, and the best to eat. (Apparently the Japanese plant kale along streets as decorative garden borders!) The youngest plants should always be used (older are fit only for the sheep), and look for fresh, bright green and really crisp leaves, with no sign of wilting or yellowing.

To prepare kale, separate leaves from the stems, and remove the pale-green or white mid-ribs. Wash thoroughly in cold water. Shred leaves just before – or after – cooking. Again the simplest methods are best – braising or steaming – but kale can be made into a soup, into potato and kale cakes like bubble and squeak – or indeed colcannon (which is often known as kailkenny). The strong flavour of kale goes well with fatty or smoked meats like pork or bacon (how the Danes and Germans serve it) and, interestingly, the collards of the American South, which are very similar to kale, are also cooked in a traditional dish with pork. Really fresh, fresh raw kale, the tenderest of leaves, can be used raw in a winter salad – dressed with a peppery lemon dressing and garnished with chopped hard-boiled eggs.

YET ANOTHER CABBAGE relative, in which the stem has swollen into a turnip shape. Although most often likened to a turnip – and they *do* taste similar, and indeed kohlrabi is often called cabbage-turnip – it is definitely not a root vegetable, as the swelling forms just above ground level. It is a native of the East, and has been adopted primarily by countries east of Germany, being popular in the European mainland and the Orient, but less so in Britain and the USA – although it is eaten in the southern states of America, as well as in many parts of Africa. Israel now grows a substantial crop. They were first grown in Britain to a significant level in the early nineteenth century, but were mainly fed to cattle. Mrs Beeton, however, was enthusiastic about them in the mid nineteenth century, saying they were 'wholesome, nutritious and very palatable'. In the hundred years or so since then, we seem to

have entirely neglected those encouraging
words.

Kohlrabi looks, to me, rather like my
junior-school drawings of German land-mines,
with all the spiky shoots sticking out of it. It is
basically a green or purple ball with blue-green
leaves at the top of stalks coming from the ball
itself. Most greengrocers trim off the root,
stalks and leaves, but if you can, buy with the
leaves on as they're a pointer to freshness (they
can also be cooked, if very young, like spinach,
but they don't tempt me – unless with loads of
black pepper and more than a hint of
horseradish). Choose (or pick if you grow them:
they grow in ten to twelve weeks from sowing)
small ones the size of golf to tennis balls rather
than larger (which will be tough and woody).
The best are available from July to December,
although they store well, so can be found up to
April.

To prepare kohlrabi, cut off stalk and root
ends, and scrub well. Peel before cooking if you
like – rather deeply – or after blanching. Place in
boiling water, bring back to the boil, and cook
for 2 minutes before submerging in cold water.
The skin will come off easily, and the cooking
time in subsequent recipes will not be affected.

They can be cooked simply – braised, boiled
or steamed – as well as stir-fried or simmered in
butter or sauces. They are good with
Hollandaise, and they can be hollowed out,
stuffed, and simmered in stock until tender.
They are then good served with a savoury
tomato or lemon sauce. Kohlrabi is often served
cold with mayonnaise as a starter in France, and
in Russia, with lashings of soured cream, it
accompanies those thick, rather dry slices of
smoked sausage. It can also be eaten raw in
salads, finely chopped in julienne strips like
celeriac, or grated and tossed in French
dressing.

BOILED KOHLRABI

FOR 6 PEOPLE
About 1 lb (450g) kohlrabi
1 pint (550ml) boiling water
1 teaspoon salt

Trim and peel the round bulbous pieces, and then cut
into ¼ inch (5mm) cubes – they will weigh about
9–10oz (250–275g). Place the cubes in the pan of
boiling salted water, bring back to the boil, and cook
for:
    2 minutes – crisp
    4 minutes – firm
    8 minutes – soft

STEAMED KOHLRABI

Prepare as in the previous recipe, then put in a
colander over the boiling salted water. Cover with
the lid (or foil) and steam for:
    5 minutes – crisp
    7 minutes – firm
   12 minutes – soft
Steaming gives a better finished look.

BAKED KOHLRABI WITH CREAM
AND CHEESE

FOR 6 PEOPLE
1 lb (450g) kohlrabi
Butter
4 tablespoons onion, finely diced
½ pint (300ml) double cream
3oz (75g) Cheddar cheese, finely grated

Trim and peel the kohlrabi, and then cut in half. Slice
into slices about ⅛ inch (3mm) thick. Butter the base
of a round 8 inch (20cm) Pyrex dish, and then make
circles of the kohlrabi half moons, building up into
layers.

Cover with the finely diced onion and the double
cream mixed with the cheese. Bake in the preheated

oven at 375°F/190°C/Gas 5 for 30 minutes. The kohlrabi will be crisp, succulent, luxurious and (I'm afraid) very fattening!

GRATED KOHLRABI FRIED WITH GINGER

FOR 6 PEOPLE
1lb (450g) kohlrabi
1½oz (40g) preserved ginger, finely chopped
1 tablespoon olive oil
1oz (25g) butter

Trim and finely peel the kohlrabi and then grate on the coarse side of the grater. You should have about 9–10oz (250–275g) in weight. Mix the grated kohlrabi with the finely diced ginger (and a little of the juice will do no harm), and leave for as long as you like (well, a few hours).

When ready to serve, simply heat the oil and butter together in a frying pan, add the kohlrabi and ginger, and stir-fry, with a wooden spoon, for 4 minutes. Serve immediately.

DEEP-FRIED KOHLRABI MATCHSTICKS

FOR 6 PEOPLE
10–12oz (275–350g) kohlrabi
Seasoned flour
Oil for deep-frying

Trim and peel the kohlrabi, then slice thinly. In weight you will need about 1oz (25g) per person for a good portion, and after the preparation this should be about what you're left with. Then, painstakingly, cut your thin slices into matchsticks.

Dry the matchsticks on kitchen paper, and preheat the deep fryer or oil to 365°F/185°C. *Just before* you intend cooking, shake the matchsticks in seasoned flour (easy in a paper or plastic bag), and transfer to a sieve and shake to get rid of excess flour. Deep-fry for:
4 minutes – crisp
6 minutes – firm
Surely you don't want them *soft*!

LADIES' FINGERS, see OKRA

LEEK

ALLIUM PORRUM

LEEKS ARE THOUGHT TO HAVE been cultivated in the Mediterranean (curious, as it is such a hardy vegetable) since prehistoric times. The emperor Nero apparently prized them highly (he ate them to improve his singing voice), and the Romans probably introduced them to Britain. They became so popular – and ultimately so common, in both senses of the word – that there are a number of derogatory phrases referring to the worthlessness of the leek – 'as green as a leek', or 'not worth a leek'. However, the leek was also raised to the heights in being adopted by the Welsh as their national emblem: a reference to the fact that St David distinguished his own men from the enemy in battle by the leeks in their hats. Leeks were so prolific in Saxon times that the kitchen garden was often known as the *leac tun* (leek enclosure), and from this derives the name of several British towns and villages today

(Leighton obviously originated as a vegetable patch!). The leek fell again from grace until about the middle of this century, partly because of fears (as Jane Grigson suggests from her reading of Mrs Beeton) that leeks smelled too strong on the breath. (What did Mrs B. think of garlic? Oh yes, 'but unless very sparingly used, the flavour is disagreeable to the English palate'.) The leek does not seem to enjoy *any* sort of popularity in the United States.

However belittled the leek may have been in centuries past, the fact remains that it is perhaps the most subtly flavoured of all the onion family. It has a distinguished history in both haute and peasant cuisines – there are many classical French dishes using *poireaux*, everyone knows the famous Vichyssoise soup (haute although using the humble potato and leek), and the leek is an essential ingredient in many national British soups, notably the Scottish cock-a-leekie.

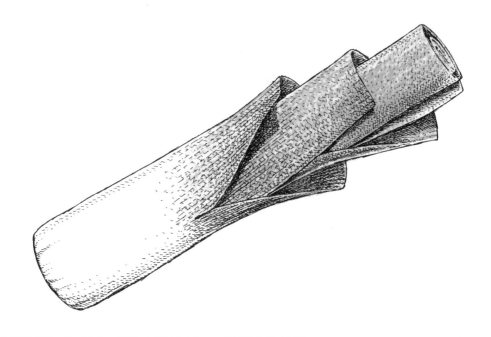

90

Leeks are thought of as a winter vegetable – widely available in Britain from September to mid April – but in fact can usually be obtained at any time of year. Out of season, however, they require more careful cooking, as they are often rather bitter and woody, and can have a tough central core. Always try to buy thin leeks – they are more tender, and younger – with a large proportion of white. Look for leaves that are fresh and unwilted, and it will ease preparation if they are not too dirty.

They need to be washed carefully as the leaves can hide an excessive amount of grit (they are earthed up to make them white). The easiest way is to trim off the green coarse leaves and the root end, split them in half, and stand upright in a large jug of cold salted water. If you want to serve them whole, trim root and leaf ends, and soak briefly in plenty of cold salted water in the sink or in a bowl: burrow in immediately by hand, attempting to clean away any dirt or soil, and make tiny slits up the sides if you can still see dirt lurking under the outer white layer. *Don't* leave them too long in the water though, and never throw away the trimmings which are just as full of flavour and goodness as the white parts: use them in the stock pot, or as part of a bouquet garni, where a green leek leaf is traditionally tied around the other ingredients.

Leeks can be used in flans or quiches, can be stuffed if slightly larger, and can be made into delicious soups. They are another contender for the title of 'poor man's asparagus', and can also be served in a variety of tasty sauces. They're delicious in a supper dish with sweetcorn and red pepper (see page 136). Cold, they make a good starter in a vinaigrette, and very young tender leeks can be sliced thinly, raw, into a salad.

LEEK SOUP

Basic recipe (see page 11)
2lb (900g) leeks, washed and trimmed

LEEK AND POTATO SOUP

Basic recipe (see page 11)
1lb (450g) leeks, washed and trimmed
1lb (450g) potatoes, peeled

Garnish this with walnut butter (see pages 15–16) and plenty of fresh finely chopped chives.

POACHED LEEKS

These can be served either hot or cold. Leeks vary so much in size and thickness, but I always endeavour to buy them the size of Blackpool rock, about 1 inch (3cm) in diameter, and up to 6 inches (15cm) of white from the base.

FOR 6 PEOPLE
1½lb (675g) leeks (or 6 leeks)
½ pint (300ml) white wine
2 tablespoons olive oil
2 teaspoons white wine vinegar
Salt and freshly ground black pepper

Trim the leeks, and cut in half if large, after which you should be left with about just over 1lb (about 500g) in weight. Place the leeks in an ovenproof dish or baking tray that will take them side by side, lying down flat.

Mix together in a saucepan the white wine, olive oil, wine vinegar, ½ teaspoon salt and some black pepper, and bring to the boil. Pour over the leeks then cover the dish with a lid (or foil) and bake in a preheated oven at 350°F/180°C/Gas 4 for:
    45 minutes – crisp
    55 minutes – firm
    60 minutes – soft

91

COLD POACHED LEEKS WITH SAVOURY YOGHURT

This starter recipe is only suitable for tender young leeks; larger ones would be on the tough side.

FOR 6 PEOPLE
6 leeks, poached (see previous recipe)
6 lettuce leaves
6 tablespoons raw carrot, finely grated
SAUCE
¼ pint (150ml) natural yoghurt
¼ pint (150ml) double cream
1 tablespoon tomato sauce
1 teaspoon English mustard
1 teaspoon wine vinegar
1 tablespoon chopped mixed herbs of choice
1 tablespoon castor sugar

Mix together thoroughly all the sauce ingredients.

Simply place each leek on a lettuce leaf, on individual small plates, and coat with the sauce, using 2 tablespoons on each leek. Garnish each one with a tablespoon of the finely grated carrot to which you have added the merest touch of castor sugar.

LEEKS BAKED IN CHEESE PASTRY

Serve hot or cold, as a starter or light lunch, and this is also an unusual idea for picnics.

FOR 6 PEOPLE
6 leeks, poached (see page 91)
1 batch cheese pastry (see page 14)

Follow the recipe for poached leeks, and cook until crisp, for 45 minutes. Remove from oven and allow to cool.

Then roll out the cheese pastry to ¼ inch (5mm) thick, and cut out triangles with a base a little longer than the leeks.

Place the leeks about ½ inch (1cm) up from the long bases of the triangles, and gently roll up until the pastry looks rather like a croissant. Put in the fridge to chill, and preheat the oven to 375°F/190°C/Gas 5.

On a greased baking sheet, bake the leeks for 15–20 minutes.

SLICED LEEKS COOKED IN YOGHURT

FOR 6 PEOPLE
1lb (450g) leeks
1oz (25g) butter, softened
Freshly ground black pepper
½ pint (300ml) natural yoghurt
2 teaspoons cornflour

When the leeks are topped, tailed, and outer leaves removed, they will weigh approximately about 10oz (275g). Lay each leek down flat on the chopping board and cut through its breadth with a sharp knife into ⅛ inch (3mm) thick circles – they must be extremely fine. Put into a bowl or sink full of cold water, and with your fingers break the circles up into individual rings. Put into a strainer to remove surplus water, and then dry on kitchen paper or a clean tea towel.

Scatter the sliced leeks over a 9 inch (23cm) round or 8 inch (20cm) oval Pyrex dish, which has been greased with the soft butter. Sprinkle liberally with freshly ground black pepper.

Add the yoghurt to the leeks, mixing in the cornflour as well (to prevent the yoghurt curdling). Place in a preheated oven at 300°F/150°C/Gas 2, and bake for:
25 minutes – crisp
30 minutes – firm
35 minutes – soft

SLICED LEEKS COOKED IN WHITE WINE

FOR 6 PEOPLE
1 lb (450g) leeks
¼ pint (150ml) white wine
1 teaspoon salt
1 oz (25g) butter
Toasted almond flakes
Chopped parsley

Prepare the leeks and slice them as in the previous recipe.

In a 9 inch (23cm) saucepan, place the white wine, salt and butter. Heat to melt the butter and then bring to the boil. Place the sliced leeks in this and, when it comes back to the boil, stirring with a wooden spoon, cook for:
   1 minute – crisp
   3 minutes – firm
   5 minutes – soft
   Serve at once, garnished with toasted almond flakes and chopped parsley.

SLICED LEEKS COOKED IN NOILLY PRAT

A more 'upmarket' way of serving the leeks, and a trifle extravagant. . . . Follow the above recipe, but only use 2½ fl. oz (75ml) Noilly Prat (*half* the wine quantity) with the butter etc. *No* garnishing is required.

SLICED LEEKS COOKED IN ORANGE JUICE

Follow the recipe for sliced leeks cooked in white wine, but use the juice and rind of 1 orange instead of the wine, with the butter. Serve garnished with either an orange twirl or orange segment.

LEEKS AND MUSHROOMS IN BACON FAT WITH CROÛTONS

FOR 6 PEOPLE
1 lb (450g) leeks
4oz (100g) mushroom stalks
1 thick slice white bread
2 cloves garlic crushed with 1 teaspoon salt (optional)
3 tablespoons bacon fat

93

Trim and wash the leeks, and cut into ⅛ inch (3mm) circles. You will need about 8oz (225g) mushrooms to get 4oz (100g) stalks (reserve the caps for finer dishes). Cut the stalks into ¼ inch (5mm) pieces.

Remove the crusts from the bread, and then cut bread into small ¼ inch (5mm) cubes. Scatter them on a baking tray and leave for a few hours to dry. Fry the croûtons in the bacon fat until brown – this usually takes about 5 minutes – turning occasionally with a wooden spoon. (If you like – and it tastes wonderful – crush the garlic with the salt and add to the croûtons in the frying pan.) Remove croûtons from the frying pan and leave in a warm place.

Fry off the mushroom stalks in the balance of the bacon fat, for 4 minutes, and then add more fat if necessary. Add the prepared sliced leeks, and cook for:
   5 minutes – crisp
   6 minutes – firm
   Serve at once, mixed with the croûtons, and garnish if you like with chopped parsley and finely diced red peppers.

LEEKS, SPRING ONIONS AND PEAS WITH TOMATO CONCASSE

FOR 6 PEOPLE
1lb (450g) leeks
6 spring onions
1oz (25g) butter
1 tablespoon olive oil
4oz (100g) frozen peas
6oz (175g) tomato concasse (see page 138)

Trim, wash and dice the leeks. Peel and trim the spring onions and cut into small pieces.

Melt the butter and oil in a frying pan, add the diced leeks and spring onions, and stir-fry, using a wooden spoon, for:
    5 minutes – crisp
    6 minutes – firm
    8 minutes – soft
Meanwhile, simply pop the peas into boiling, salted water, bring back to the boil, and cook for 3 minutes. Strain, and return briefly to the heat to dry off.

Mix the peas with the leeks and spring onions, and serve at once, topped with warmed tomato concasse.

DEEP-FRIED CURRIED LEEK ROUNDS

These are scrumptious as snacks to have with pre-dinner drinks. Rather messy, I must admit, as your hands do become a trifle greasy, but they're definitely moreish! They are also good sprinkled on top of biscuits thinly smeared with anchovy paste, or scattered over a grilled trout or fillet of plaice.

Simply slice the leeks into thin rings as described on page 92 and dry well before popping into cold milk. Put into a sieve to shake off surplus milk, then coat with lightly curried seasoned flour – a rough guide is 1 teaspoon of curry powder to 4 tablespoons of flour, but experiment to see what you like best. Preheat the deep-fryer or oil to 360°F/182°C, and fry leek rings for 1½ minutes. Drain well.

LEEKS COOKED WITH BACON AND CHEESE

This dish can be prepared in the morning, and then baked and flashed under the grill at (almost) the last minute.

FOR 6 PEOPLE
6 leeks, poached (see page 91)
6 rashers smoked bacon, derinded
3oz (75g) Cheddar cheese, grated

Cook the leeks as in the poaching recipe for 45 minutes until crisp, and then remove from the oven. Allow to cool.

Wrap each leek in a slice of smoked bacon, return to the cooking dish, and preheat the oven to 400°F/200°C/Gas 6. Bake for:
    10 minutes – crisp
    15 minutes – firm
    18 minutes – soft
Remove from the oven and sprinkle the grated cheese on top. Flash under the grill to brown, and serve at once. Super!

LETTUCE

LACTUCA SATIVA

THE ORIGINS OF LETTUCE GO back far into time: it was eaten by the Persian kings, by the Ancient Egyptians, and by the Greeks and Romans (who probably taught the wild stalky variety to form heads). It is thought to have originated in Asia Minor, but spread north and west from the Mediterranean. Columbus introduced it to America (which now must wear the crown as the major world consumer of lettuce), and Catherine Parr, the happily surviving wife of Henry VIII, would send to Holland for her supplies, as the home market – which only started in earnest in the fifteenth century – was obviously not adequate.

Lettuces, vaguely related to the daisy family, contain some Vitamin C when eaten very fresh, and have traces of Vitamin A and calcium. Less well known are their narcotic properties. The Flopsy Bunnies did not fall asleep unaided, as the juice of lettuce actually does contain traces of an alkaloid similar to that found in the opium poppy, and is one of the oldest known soporifics. It was used medicinally thus by the Greeks, and was at one time given to patients in a cake, along with poppy seeds, before and after surgical operations.

Lettuces come in all shapes and sizes, and fall into two main groups. The Cos lettuce is believed to come from the Greek island of Kos, hence its name, and travelled northwards via the Romans – hence (probably) its French and American name of Romaine. These are crisp-leaved, elongated lettuces. The other main type is the cabbage lettuce, which grouping is further sub-divided into smooth-leaved globular butterheads (the type we see most commonly) and the crisp-leaved, crisp-hearted lettuces, which include the Iceberg and Webb's Wonderful. There are also non-hearting lettuces known as 'leaf', 'loose leaf' or 'loose head', which include the attractive oak leaf lettuce.

The colour, shape and texture of a lettuce's leaves can depend on where it was grown, in what kind of soil – and, as always, on how far and how long it has travelled to get to you. A lettuce that droops, wilts or has a browny stem

or outside leaves, is well past its best. Lettuces, to take full advantage of the few nutritional properties they possess, should be eaten at the earliest opportunity. They don't take too kindly to the refrigerator, although some people swear by the virtues of a closed plastic bag in the salad drawer for crisping-up purposes. I find that they can keep for several days in a saucepan with a tight lid, or wrapped in newspaper in a cool place.

Lettuces are normally used in salads (although they can be cooked, as in the following recipes), and must be carefully and lovingly prepared. Break off the bottom of the softer-leaved varieties, and of Cos, and remove any coarse outer leaves. Wash if absolutely necessary – but then you must dry meticulously, on a clean cloth, or swing about outside in a special salad whirler/drier.

To prepare lettuce for a salad, break or tear individual leaves into pieces or shreds – but this must be done very shortly before you wish to eat it. Never *cut* lettuce as this bruises the leaves and turns them dark at the edges and ultimately a bit slimy. With Iceberg lettuces, you could, at a pinch, cut off the proportion you need immediately, but the remainder must be used up very swiftly. Far better to painstakingly remove the individual leaves and tear as above. Never dress a salad until the very last minute.

Lettuce and lettuce salads reach their heights in America, from whence we have the magnificent, all-American favourite, the Chef's Salad (salad greens, chicken, cheese, ham, celery, and hard-boiled eggs); the Waldorf Salad (with Cos, celery, apple, walnuts and

mayonnaise); and the Caesar Salad (Cos, garlic croûtons, eggs and Parmesan cheese). There are any number of combinations and computations – among them the Provençal Salade Niçoise, which has a lettuce leaf base then tomatoes, French beans, tuna fish and black olives. And don't forget the virtues of other salad leafed plants like endive, dandelion leaves, spinach or watercress in a salad – they add variety, colour and texture – as well as the less familiar such as corn salad, radicchio, celtuce (a hybrid of celery and lettuce), salad burnet, sorrel and leafy herbs.

Lettuce leaves are also useful, shredded, as a garnish, and I always, but always, include a lettuce leaf or two, painted with a little walnut oil, in a sandwich. In rationed post-war Britain, I remember the 'treat' of sugar wrapped in a lettuce leaf (the thought appalls me now).

But cooked lettuce dishes, particularly if you grow your own, and have plenty, are pleasant. They make a soup which I must admit I find a bit tasteless. (You could use bolted, shot or cleaned outer leaves for this: weigh out 2lb or 900g, and follow the basic recipe on page 11.) Lettuces can be braised, stewed, stuffed, and individual leaves can be a wrapping round fish (or *over* fish, as good as foil, to prevent browning when baked in the oven), around mousselines or any filling, rather like the vine-leaf dolmas. Lettuces can be shredded and cooked then made into a delicate soufflé, and the hearts are delicious with peas in the classic *petits pois à la française*. Lettuce *stalks* (would you believe) from bolted lettuce can be braised as a vegetable, or made into a preserve rather like root ginger.

BOILED LETTUCE QUARTERS

Only really to be done when you have a surplus of lettuce – and it can make a change from endless summer salads.

FOR 6 PEOPLE
1 large hearted lettuce
2 pints (a good litre) boiling water
Salt and freshly ground black pepper

Discard the outer leaves of the lettuce, and trim the bottom. Cut the lettuce into wedges, each weighing approximately 4oz (100g), and season well. Wrap well in strong clingfilm, making sure that the ends are tightly tied, like a boiled sweet wrapper (or you can place the wedge diagonally across a large square of film, bring up all the four corners to the centre, and tie securely).

Simply submerge the parcels in the boiling water to which you've added 1 teaspoon salt, bring back to the boil, and cook for:
    4 minutes – crisp
    6 minutes – firm
    8 minutes – soft

BAKED LETTUCE

FOR 6 PEOPLE
1 large Webb's Wonderful lettuce
Butter
Seasoning (see method)

A full-grown Webb's Wonderful lettuce is about 2lb (900g), and when you've trimmed it and cut off the outer leaves, will weigh in at about 1 1/4lb (550g).

Preheat the oven to 350°F/180°C/Gas 4. Lightly butter a piece of foil of about 20 × 18 inches (50 × 45cm), and season it well. Salt and pepper, of course, but some fenugreek seeds go well, or powdered cumin. A little white wine is nice too!

Simply fold up the foil around the lettuce and seasoning, rather like a football, then place in a roasting tin. Pour a little boiling water in the base

and bake for:
    40 minutes – crisp
    45 minutes – firm
    50 minutes – soft
    I must admit that it doesn't look very appetising on the outside when you open the foil, but when cut into four, six or eight wedges, the centre is very attractive, and it has an unusual taste.

97

FRIED LETTUCE WITH NUTS AND PINEAPPLE

FOR 6 PEOPLE
1 tablespoon walnut oil
1oz (25g) butter
At least 6oz (175g) lettuce, shredded finely
3oz (75g) fresh pineapple, finely diced
2oz (50g) toasted nuts, coarsely chopped

Gently heat the oil and butter in a 9 inch (23cm) frying pan. Stir-fry the lettuce, with a wooden spoon, for:
    3 minutes – crisp
    4–5 minutes – a little softer
    Immediately add very finely diced pineapple and nuts, and serve as quickly as you can. This dish looks *revolting* when cold, and doesn't taste too good either!

MANGE-TOUT PEAS

PISUM SATIVUM SACCHARATUM

ALSO KNOWN AS SUGAR PEAS, Chinese peas and snow peas, mange-touts (meaning, literally, 'eat-all') are, obviously, members of the pea family. The pea or garden pea has been around for centuries, and it is thought that the mange-tout – a variety of pea grown for its edible pod, and picked very young before the peas can develop – has been cultivated in Europe since the seventeenth century. Gerard in his *Herball* said it was good to eat 'cods [pods] and all the rest'. It has only quite recently, however, come back to favour, appearing as a fairly expensive delicacy in spring and early summer. They are as easy to grow at home as garden peas.

The pods can be eaten because, unlike garden peas, they have no tough inner, parchmenty skin. Look for fresh bright pods, with only the faintest hint of a line of peas forming under the skin. They should really be flat. Wash them briefly, then top and tail like French beans. They can be prepared several hours before you need to cook them, and provided they are lovely and young, it is a relatively simple task, one to do sitting out in the sunny garden, perhaps.

Normally, the thin small mange-touts simply need topping and tailing, and the slightly stringy edge removed. The tougher of the two (*if* they are tough) is invariably found on the side on which the minute peas are nestling. If right-handed, hold the flower or growing end of the mange-tout between the thumb and first finger of your left hand. Gently snap off the end, and slowly pull the string off, going down past the little peas to the opposite end. Try to remove coarse string, if any, on the other edge. Place in a bowl and when they are all prepared, put half a dozen ice cubes on top, and put in the fridge until you require to cook them. Cooking must always be done at the very last minute, just as you're about to dish up the main course.

They are best cooked simply, by steaming, until crisp to firm. They can be eaten like asparagus, in the hand and dipped into melted butter or Hollandaise. Popular with Chinese chefs, they are wonderful stir-fried, and they can be simmered briefly with cream. They can make a soup, but this seems rather a waste of their shape and texture.

98

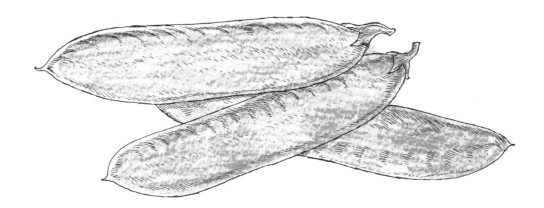

STEAMED MANGE-TOUTS

FOR 6 PEOPLE
10oz (275g) mange-touts
2 pints (a good litre) boiling water
2 tablespoons sugar
1 teaspoon mustard powder

Top, tail and string the mange-touts, and chill until needed.

Add the sugar and mustard powder to the boiling water, and then place the colander with the mange-touts on top. Cover with a lid (or foil), and steam for:

    3 minutes – crisp
    4 minutes – firm
    6 minutes – soft

STIR-FRIED MANGE-TOUTS

FOR 6 PEOPLE
10oz (275g) mange-touts
1 tablespoon olive oil
1oz (25g) butter
Salt and freshly ground black pepper

Prepare the mange-touts as above, and then chill. Just before cooking, dry them off thoroughly on kitchen paper.

Heat the oil and butter together in a frying pan or wok, and then stir-fry, using a wooden spoon, for:

    2 minutes – crisp
    3 minutes – firm
    4 minutes – soft

Season with salt and pepper (and with a little soya sauce if you want them to have a vaguely Chinese flavour).

OLDER MANGE-TOUTS

With all vegetables, there is always a time when the garden coughs up its last seasonal supply. At this time, mange-touts are slightly thicker than early in the season, and certainly not as sweet or succulent.

I find I have to top and tail them, and quite often I take a knife to the two edges (as if preparing runner beans). I then place each mange-tout flat on a cutting board, at a 90 degree angle from me, and then cut through it at 45 degrees in 1/8 inch (3mm) widths.

I place them in a bowl in the fridge (without water or ice) and leave to chill, and then cook as in the previous recipes – steamed or stir-fried – but obviously for slightly longer. I then sometimes top them with a spoonful of natural yoghurt.

99

MARROW

CUCURBITA PEPO OVIFERA

T HE MARROW OR VEGETABLE marrow – a close relation of the courgette (which is its baby brother), the squash and pumpkin etc – is one of the oldest vegetables in the world, having been grown in the Americas for thousands of years. These edible gourds were cultivated by Indians long before the arrival of Columbus in the New World, and it was not until at least the sixteenth century that the vegetable marrow reached Europe and Britain – since when the British have made it a firm favourite, have grown it to astronomical sizes for village shows, and have boiled it to a tasteless mush.

Marrow *is* in fact fairly tasteless when large – not surprising, as up to 90 per cent of it is water – and so should really only be eaten when no more than 12 inches (30cm) long, before the seeds have fully developed and the fibres become coarse and stringy. Marrows can be plain green, or green with yellow stripes, and should be firm and heavy, with no wrinkling around the growing stalk end. The fingernail test (hidden from the greengrocer) could be applied to determine age, but size is really the ultimate judge. Store in a cool, dry place, and use within three days.

To prepare young, tender marrows, simply wash, top and tail, and cut (no need to peel) as your recipe dictates, rather like courgettes. If they are older, thus larger, wash, cut in half or into rings, then remove the seeds and fibrous parts. Remove the skin, obviously, if cooking as a vegetable, purée, or soup, but stuffed marrow should retain its skin. Often a larger marrow can benefit from salting and draining, as with aubergines and courgettes.

Try always to cook in a minimum of water so that the taste (such as it is) is retained, and the excess water of the vegetable can evaporate – but I think frying and baking are better methods. Marrows need good, strong, accompanying flavourings to offset the blandness – tomatoes, garlic, onions, cheese etc – and your most flavourful stuffing should be used for the baked marrow recipe. Marrow can also be used in jams, pickles and chutneys, and the flowers, like those of courgettes, can be battered and deep-fried, or stuffed and steamed.

MARROW SOUP

Basic recipe (see page 11)
2lb (900g) marrow flesh

I like to add some ginger (root or preserved) or curry powder when cooking, as they're needed to improve the rather bland taste. Serve garnished with *raw* grated courgettes, which is different, and the crunchiness is tempting.

BAKED STUFFED MARROW

This is a super family dish for a cold evening. Serve it as it comes from the oven, but it is enhanced if you make a good strong cheese sauce (with an added touch of malt vinegar to give it a good bite!). Try to choose a marrow that is straight like a Swiss roll, rather than curved, for this recipe.

FOR 6 PEOPLE
1 marrow, about 2½–3lb (1–1.5kg)
1¼–1½lb (550–675g) stuffing of choice (see page 19)

Wipe the marrow, then cut off both ends. With a long-handled spoon start scooping out all the seeds, fibres and flesh, reaching in almost to the other end of the marrow, until you have a fair sized hole the length of the marrow. (From the above weight of marrow there will be about 12oz or 350g of waste.)

Force the stuffing of your choice into the scooped-out hole, then wrap the marrow in buttered greaseproof paper and then again in foil.

Preheat oven to 375°F/190°C/Gas 5. Place the foil package in a roasting tray, with boiling water in the base, and bake for:
1 hour 20 minutes – crisp
1 hour 30 minutes – firm
1 hour 45 minutes – soft

BAKED MARROW ROUNDS

These look nice in the middle of a vegetarian main course meal with grated cheese and raw carrot piled in the centre hole to look like a small pyramid. They're good for supper with other vegetables.

FOR 6 PEOPLE
1 marrow, about 2½–3lb (1–1.5kg)
Butter and/or oil

Simple wipe the outside of the marrow clean with a damp cloth and then slice through into rings, 1 inch (3cm) thick. Scoop out the seeds and fibres and a little of the inner flesh, then place on well buttered trays. Paint with further butter – or an oil if you like.

Preheat the oven to 375°F/190°C/Gas 5, and bake for:
15 minutes – crisp
17 minutes – firm
18–20 minutes – soft

DEEP-FRIED MARROW BALLS

FOR 6 PEOPLE
1 marrow, about 1lb (450g)
Seasoned flour

Allowing for six marrow balls each, you will have to start off with this size of marrow to allow for wastage.

Simple peel the marrow with a potato peeler and then scoop out the balls with a Parisian scoop. *Do not* cut the marrow in half, remove seeds and *then* start to make the balls, as this is very, very wasteful indeed!

Preheat the deep fryer or oil to 360°F/182°C. Toss the balls in seasoned flour (add a little curry powder – or better still, cinnamon – for flavouring as well as the usual salt and pepper), then deep-fry for:
4 minutes – crisp
5 minutes – firm
6 minutes – soft

MUSHROOMS

PSALLIOTA CAMPESTRIS

PAN-FRIED MARROW BALLS

If you don't want to deep-fry, the marrow balls as above – coated in seasoned flour – can be pan-fried in 2 tablespoons oil and 1oz (25g) butter for 3 minutes. Serve *immediately* garnished with chopped parsley or herbs.

MUSHROOMS HAVE BEEN known as food for centuries. They were encouraged to grow, if not actually cultivated, by the Romans and Greeks, and the matsutake and shii-take of Japan were perhaps the original cultivated mushrooms, dating back to the first century AD. The word mushroom is generally applied to edible fungi, but of the many thousands of species throughout the world, less than half are, in fact, mushrooms. Edible wild mushrooms have long been a delicacy in Europe, but in the UK and in the USA, we allow ourselves to be truly under-privileged, and only one mushroom is commonly eaten: the cultivated mushroom, closely related to the wild field mushroom (*Agaricus campestris*). This was developed by the French in the late nineteenth century (perhaps so that everyone else would eat them, leaving the French to their splendid truffles, ceps, morels and girolles!); they produced a sterilised spawn which enabled a consistent and therefore commercial crop to be grown.

The British didn't much like mushrooms at first, and were highly suspicious of them in the Middle Ages, and perhaps still are . . . the tendency of the mushroom to grow in the dark and on rich, manured soil, gives them a faintly evil aura, and their (thankfully) less frequent tendencies towards being hallucinogenic and poisonous, may explain why we never seem to take full advantage of the wild fungi growing free and delicious in fields and woods. Dorothy Hartley in *Food in England* describes beautifully the difference between the wild and the cultivated, which latter 'are a good useful mushroom for cooking and flavouring, but lack the delicacy of the field ones, and the aroma of wind and rain and the tang of autumn that comes into the kitchen with a basket of field mushrooms'. For a truly mind-boggling insight into the whole world of mushrooms, read *The Mushroom Feast* by Jane Grigson, the ultimate culinary mushroom bible.

Anyway, here I shall only cover the mushroom most commonly available, the cultivated.

It comes in roughly three stages of growth; as a *button*, which is picked just before the membranes between cap and stalk separate to reveal the gills; the *cup* or medium-sized mushroom which is a little larger, with the cap partially open; and the *flat* or *open* which is the largest and strongest tasting, with dark brown gills. Mushrooms in general are a health-giving food: they contain no sugars, not much carbohydrate (good for slimmers therefore), vitamins and minerals, and have a good proportion of protein (closer to meat than any other vegetable).

Buy the kind which suits the recipe you want to follow: the buttons for cooking whole, or in pale sauces; the cups for slicing and sautéing; the open for grilling or stuffing etc. Mushrooms which are not fresh will turn brownish, all over or in patches, and don't buy if they are at all greasy or sweaty. Prepare them as quickly and simply as possible: wipe over with a damp cloth rather than wash, and peel only the flat ones which look very ragged and perhaps a little bruised at the edges. Take a small slice off the stalk if necessary, and twist the stalks out if you want to use only the caps. Chop, slice or leave the mushrooms whole, as required. Use as soon as possible, and store in the salad drawer of the fridge for only a day or so.

Always *keep* and *use* the stalks. They contain a great deal of flavour, and make a good soup along with whole mushrooms, or can be added to chopped mushrooms in sauces, in duxelles, or my mushroom pâté. They can be stir-fried, finely chopped, with any other vegetable, or incorporated into croquette potatoes or cottage pie topping.

Mushrooms can be cooked in any variety of ways, and I consider them a *must* for any serious-minded cook. They make wonderful soups, sauces, starters and snacks; they go well with meat or fish, or indeed other vegetables; they can be steamed, sautéed, grilled, baked, deep-fried, and sliced raw in salads. They can be canned, pickled, made into ketchups, frozen or dried. They are incredibly versatile.

103

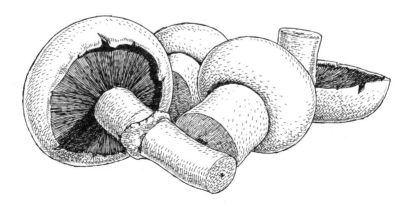

MUSHROOM SOUP

This is one of the best ways of using up mushroom stalks, but any mushroom can be used, the flavour and colour being dependent on maturity and variety.

Basic recipe (see page 11)
2lb (900g) mushrooms

Marsala instead of sherry is pleasant, and garnish finally with toasted almond flakes.

MUSHROOM PÂTÉ

Anyone who has bought and used my other books – or who has been to Miller Howe – will be familiar with my mushroom pâté. It can be eaten by itself, used as a constituent of many other dishes (a quick mushroom sauce can be made by adding a few ounces of the pâté to a plain white sauce), or it can be used as a stuffing or topping. As far as vegetables are concerned, it can stuff courgettes, marrow or tomatoes, line the leaves of cabbage, and top a baked potato. Its uses are endless!

4oz (100g) butter
8oz (225g) onions, finely minced
2lb (900g) mushrooms, finely minced
Sea salt and freshly ground black pepper
1 pint (550ml) red wine

Melt the butter in a saucepan over a gentle heat, then add the onions. Simmer slowly for about 10 minutes, then add the mushrooms, a good pinch of sea salt and pepper. Stir well then add the red wine. Leave to simmer over the lowest possible heat for about 2–3 hours, stirring occasionally. You want the liquid to evaporate to leave the mixture fairly dry.

When cold, store in a plastic container in the fridge. It will also freeze very well.

BAKED MUSHROOMS

So often I've had a grilled steak in a restaurant accompanied by those mushy watery mushrooms (or worse, canned), which immediately turn my stomach over. If you are entertaining and you wish your mushrooms to be firm, tasty, juicy and good, do bake the caps instead of frying or grilling. Serve two per person as a tasty garnish.

FOR 6 PEOPLE
8oz (225g) cup mushrooms (or 12 good even-sized mushrooms)
Butter
Salt and freshly ground black pepper

Remove the stalks from your fresh white mushrooms (these will weigh about 2oz or 50g, but *don't* throw them out!).

Butter and season a baking tray well, then lay the mushroom heads, gills down, on this. Carefully paint the top of each mushroom cap with more melted butter. (You could give added zest by skinning a clove or two of garlic and rubbing this over the tray prior to buttering.)

Preheat the oven to 350°F/180°C/Gas 4, and bake the mushrooms for:
10 minutes – crisp
12 minutes – firm
15 minutes – soft
You could also add a scattering of any finely chopped herbs from the garden before baking.

MARINATED MUSHROOMS

This is ideal for a starter on a hot summer's evening. Simply serve each mushroom with a blob of cheese and herb pâté in the concave middle (see page 16), and lots of fresh chopped herbs and grated radish to add colour.

FOR 6 PEOPLE
1lb (450g) cup mushroom caps or button mushrooms
½ pint (300ml) white wine
¼ pint (150ml) olive oil
3 tablespoons tarragon vinegar
1 tablespoon whole coriander seeds
1 tablespoon sugar
1 teaspoon English mustard powder

Place the mushrooms in a shallow bowl. In a saucepan, bring the remaining ingredients to the boil. Simmer for 4 minutes, then strain immediately, hot and bubbling, over the raw mushrooms.

When cool, transfer to the fridge, covered, and leave for at least 24 hours.

When I serve them, I prefer to transfer the mushroom caps to kitchen paper which absorbs any surplus marinade, so that the mushrooms are dished up fairly dry. Remember to see that the dishes you are going to use spend the afternoon in the fridge, to get them nice and chilled.

ALTERNATIVE MUSHROOM MARINADE

½ pint (300ml) white wine
¼ pint (150ml) wine vinegar
¼ pint (150ml) good oil
Juice and rind of 2 limes
2 cloves garlic, crushed with 1 teaspoon salt

Liquidise all the ingredients together and then put in a saucepan and bring to the boil.

As above, simply pour over the cleaned mushroom caps (this particular marinade is, in fact, sufficient to marinate 2lb or 900g of mushrooms), and leave to go cold. Put in the fridge, cover and leave for at least 24 hours, turning from time to time.

105

NETTLE

URTICA DIOICA

MOST PEOPLE CONSIDER nettles to be nothing more than a nuisance in the garden, but their leaves have quite a long history as food, particularly in the north of Europe. They were once raised under glass in Scotland as a vegetable, and they were eaten in Ireland and in eighteenth-century Scandinavia (where they also used the fibres of the stalks to make a cloth: nettle shirts are a feature of the fairy tale, *The Twelve White Swans*). As a child in the north of England, where nettles were considered purifying after the stodge of the winter, spring was heralded by good mutton broths liberally sprinkled with chopped fresh nettles to get rid of any lingering winter ailments.

And nettles *are* good for you. The folk belief that they are good for the blood is perfectly true: they contain numerous chemicals, including iron, histamine and formic acid (the stinging element) which do cleanse the blood, have a generally toning effect on the whole body, and can help relieve the symptoms of rheumatism and sciatica.

To use nettles in cooking, pick the young shoots – with gloves on – no later than May: thereafter they become tough and bitter. Wash them briefly and make into a purée rather like spinach, with only the water clinging to the leaves. (Cooking destroys the sting.) Add lots of butter, seasoning and nutmeg to offset the rather bland taste. They are also good as a soup, cooked as the basic recipe on page 11, and garnished with croûtons. Nettles are also made into beer, and dried, into a herbal tea.

One last thought: butterflies like to lay their eggs on nettles, so to kill two birds with one stone – to have a healthy vegetable on hand *and* to help our dwindling butterfly population – encourage some nettles to grow in a corner of your garden.

OKRA

HIBISCUS ESCULENTUS

KRA IS A PLANT NATIVE TO Africa, and African languages have been responsible for the two most common names – okra and gumbo. Okra – long, elegant and *green* – is also known as ladies' fingers! It is grown in hot climates, in the West Indies, the southern states of North America, in India, eastern Europe and the Middle East, and in each of these areas it has assumed its own culinary character, although each cuisine uses it for its mucilaginous qualities – the sticky juices which act as a thickener for soups and stews. It was probably brought from Africa by slaves – the first recorded usage of the word in the OED is 1707 – and it still features most strongly in West Indian and Creole recipes. The plant is a member of the mallow family, and is related to cotton, so is a fibre plant (and indeed the stalks are sometimes used to make paper).

Okra is available in Britain in cans, but can also be bought fresh from ethnic shops, and is

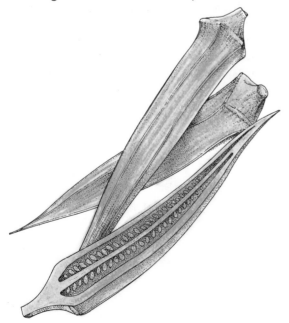

becoming more widely seen in supermarkets. Look for bright fresh green pods – it is the immature seed pods of the plant that are eaten – of about 3–4 inches (8–10cm) long, with as little brown as possible. To prepare, wash briefly and cut off the conical cap – but carefully if you don't want the juices to seep out, which happens if you cut off too much, exposing the seeds. If you are using whole, cook gently so that they retain their shape. If cutting, slice into rings so that the wonderful wheel shape is exposed, or into lengths as your recipe describes. If you wish to diminish the sticky nature of the vegetable, you can salt and drain them (like aubergine), or can soak them in water acidulated with a little vinegar. Dry thoroughly before proceeding to cook, and always beware of *overcooking*.

Okra or gumbo is an essential ingredient of the Creole gumbos, mixed with tomatoes – okra's most delicious partner – as well as seafood or chicken in tasty, hot, thick soupy stews. In India, where it is known as bindi, okra is a side vegetable, is eaten fresh like asparagus, and is pickled. The West Indians stew pork with okra, and there are many dishes from the Middle East, where it is known as bamia.

I once had a 'Southern-style' cup of coffee in the Bahamas, which I found revolting, but my host obviously enjoyed. Afterwards I discovered that it had been made from mature, roasted okra seeds. I can only advise you to avoid it like the plague. And my test cook and I attempted to cook an okra soup with potatoes and many other ingredients. The end results were more like wallpaper paste than soup, and they looked disgusting and tasted even worse. But a little okra can be added to tomato or marrow soup as a thickening agent. (They're obviously best in the ethnic dishes mentioned above, which are rather beyond the scope of this book.)

ONION

ALLIUM CEPA

THE ONION IS THOUGHT TO have originated in Central Asia, but is now grown, eaten and cooked all over the world, an absolutely essential flavouring in countless dishes in almost every cuisine, as well as a worthy vegetable in its own right. The Babylonians and Egyptians used them extensively (drawings of onions are to be seen in many Ancient Egyptian murals); Alexander the Great is said to have found onions in Egypt and taken them back to Greece as he believed they inspired his martial (or was it marital?) ardour. Onions (probably a little over-cooked) were found in the ruins of Pompeii. Considered generally to be the food of the poor, onions have been popular in England since at least the thirteenth century, and the common or maincrop onion was first planted in Massachusetts in the mid-seventeenth century (although many native varieties existed).

The bulb of a member of the *Liliaceae* family (along with asparagus, tulips etc), the genus *Allium* includes onions large and small – Spanish, maincrop, shallots, spring onions (or scallions in the USA), and chives – as well as leeks and garlic (which latter two are discussed separately). Cooked or raw, onions are used every single day by the modern cook, and I defy you to have a three-course meal in any restaurant in which the onion, obviously or not so obviously, does not play a part.

Maincrop onions, the type most commonly available, are round and strong-flavoured, while the Spanish, Italian red onion, or those bought from the Breton onion-seller, are even rounder and larger, as well as milder, often with pink-tinged flesh. Shallots have the essential onion flavour, and are stronger than the largest onion, while not having such an overpowering smell. They grow from one bulb which reproduces a tightly packed cluster of bulbs, thus their rather more elongated shape, and much smaller size. Welsh onions (actually from Siberia, the word *walsch* meant they were foreign) and tree onions are similar, being small: the former a cluster of bulbs like shallots, the latter with underground bulbs as well as bulbs at the end of stalks instead of flowers. Both can be pickled, but the common pickled onion – also known as button, silverskin or cocktail – is the maincrop onion picked when the plant has just formed its bulbs. Spring or salad onions are also a maincrop variety, but picked *before* the bulb has had time to form properly, or simply as

thinnings. Chives too have tiny bulbs, but it is the green onion-flavoured stalks which are eaten – as they have been for thousands of years – and cut continuously to encourage growth, not allowing it to develop into its pretty purple ball flower. (In fact, any onion's green shoots or leaves can be used as onion flavour, like chives.)

Everyone knows how to prepare onions and how to use them in general, so I'll limit myself (saving expensive paper into the bargain) to a few snippets of Tovey wisdom. I am constantly being asked how to peel and prepare onions without crying. I'm afraid I haven't found a way, and I've tried them all – under a running cold tap, beside an open window, with a slice of bread in my mouth, while sniffing smelling salts, even wearing those onion-peeling goggles sold in trendy kitchen shops. Perhaps to sit down and peel and cut in front of you, instead of leaning over, is the answer.

Onions are as health-giving as garlic, the juice being antiseptic (it was also believed once to cure baldness!). It contains a substance thought to delay blood-clotting and reduce the risk of heart attacks. They're best raw for health, so cut slices of those sweet, mild Spanish onions, and use in sandwiches, salads or with your ploughman's lunch (more often, originally, bread, onions and ale, *without* the cheese, in hard times).

Don't cut onions too long before you use them, they can become bitter. Remember to leave the skin on when adding a whole onion to the stock pot – it gives a brown colour – and the skin can also be wrapped around hard-boiled eggs for Easter to give a nice yellowy brown mottled effect.

I have been told that in certain parts of India, onions are only handled and prepared by men as they are believed to have aphrodisiac properties that could cause infidelity amongst wives!

CREAM OF ONION SOUP

For this recipe, the cooking method is slightly different, and *milk* is used instead of stock.

Proceed as in the basic recipe (see page 11), but then add the sherry, 2lb (900g) onions and 2 pints (a good litre) of milk (instead of the stock), *all at the same time*. Cook the whole mixture gently until mushy – about 45 minutes – and then liquidise.

Fresh sage is the ideal accompaniment to the soup, and could be added with the onions if you like. If you haven't got sage, any fresh herb from the garden will do, providing it won't dominate the soup.

Fried croûtons the size of an old half-crown piece are lovely with this. Top them with grated Cheddar cheese, press down, and heat under the grill.

ONIONS BAKED IN MILK WITH NUTMEG

Onions weighing about 5–6oz (150–175g) are best for this dish – about the size of a tennis ball. For a substantial vegetable for six, you will need 6 onions, but double the quantities for a supper dish.

FOR 6 PEOPLE
6 onions, about 5–6oz (150–175g) each
1 pint (550ml) milk
Salt and freshly ground black pepper
1 whole nutmeg, finely grated
4oz (100g) white breadcrumbs
6oz (175g) Cheddar cheese, grated

Top, tail and skin the onions, then place in an ovenproof dish that will hold them compactly in one layer. Cover with the milk mixed with salt, pepper and grated nutmeg.

Put in the preheated oven at 375°F/190°C/Gas 5, and bake for:
55 minutes – crisp
60 minutes – firm
65 minutes – soft
Remove onions from casserole and keep warm.

109

Put the breadcrumbs, grated cheese and milk in a pan and bring quickly to the boil. Serve as sauce over the onions. Add chopped parsley and a pinch of mustard to the sauce, if you like.

BABY ONIONS CASSEROLED IN MILK

FOR 6 PEOPLE
12 onions, about 1oz (25g) each
¼ pint (150ml) milk
1 bay leaf
Salt, freshly ground black pepper and nutmeg

Top, tail and skin the onions. Preheat the oven to 375°F/190°C/Gas 5. Place onions in a suitable ovenproof dish (I often use the *lid* of a round Pyrex dish), and add the milk, bay leaf, salt, pepper and nutmeg.

Place in oven, and bake for:
40 minutes – crisp
45 minutes – firm
50 minutes – soft

GLAZED BABY ONIONS

It's not my favourite job, the topping, tailing and peeling of these onions – about the size of a large olive – but worth the effort when they are available.

FOR 6 PEOPLE
24 onions, peeled, topped and tailed
½oz (15g) butter
Salt
1 teaspoon demerara sugar

All the onions should sit comfortably on the bottom of either your frying pan or saucepan without overlapping. Pour in sufficient cold water just barely to cover them, then add the butter, sugar and a little salt. Bring up to the boil as quickly as possible, and boil until the water evaporates, then reduce the heat. Keep on shaking the pan over the lower heat until the onions brown on all sides.

If done at the last minute to accompany your meat course they are superb, but they can be cooked earlier on in the day and then simply reheated in the oven. This takes about 5 minutes if the oven is over 375°F/190°C/Gas 5 with your roast or main course in.

BABY ONIONS FRIED IN DRIPPING

FOR 6 PEOPLE
12 onions, about 1oz (25g) each
2oz (50g) dripping of choice

Top, tail and skin the onions. Put your dripping in a frying pan and heat. Add the onions and fry, stirring occasionally with a wooden spoon, for:
25 minutes – crisp
30 minutes – firm
35 minutes – soft
Star anise or ground coriander may be added during the frying, as well as parsley stalks.

BAKED ONIONS STUFFED WITH CHEESE

This is a supper dish, rather than a vegetable accompaniment. To make it even more substantial, serve on a round baked croûton lined with mushroom pâté (see page 104).

FOR 6 PEOPLE
6 large onions, about 8oz (225g) each
1 batch savoury cheese breadcrumbs (see page 19)
6oz (175g) butter

Skin the onions, slice the tops off each (retain them) and then, with a sharp knife, scoop out hollows which should leave you with 'cases' weighing about 4oz (100g) each. (Use the insides up in cream of onion soup or savoury minced onions.)

Divide the savoury breadcrumb mixture between the six 'cases' and top each with 1oz (25g) butter and an onion 'lid'. Place onions on a greased baking tray or in a greased Pyrex dish, cover completely (with foil or the dish lid), and bake in a preheated oven at 400°F/200°C/Gas 6 for:

40 minutes – crisp
45 minutes – firm
50 minutes – soft

If you like, you can put some more grated cheese on top at the end and flash under the grill.

SAVOURY MINCED ONIONS

FOR 6 PEOPLE
1lb (450g) onions, peeled and minced
2oz (50g) breadcrumbs
8oz (225g) Cheddar cheese, grated
4oz (100g) peanuts, chopped
Salt and freshly ground black pepper
Melted butter

Mix all the ingredients together except for the butter, with which you should liberally paint the sides of six 3 inch (8cm) ramekins. Season them with salt and pepper.

Divide the onion mixture between the ramekins and bake in a bain marie (a roasting tray with boiling water to come half-way up the sides of the ramekins) at 350°F/180°C/Gas 4 for:

30 minutes – crisp, but onion dominates
40 minutes – delightful firm blend
45 minutes – soft

Extra grated cheese may be put on the top after the baking, and then the ramekins can be flashed under the grill.

ONION CUSTARD

FOR 6 PEOPLE
2oz (50g) butter
6 medium onions, finely chopped
2 eggs, beaten
8fl. oz (225ml) milk
Salt and freshly ground pepper
Pinch nutmeg or curry powder

Melt the butter over medium heat and cook the onions until golden. Beat together the remaining ingredients, then add the onions and pour into a buttered 2 pint (1 litre) casserole dish. Bake uncovered for 25–30 minutes at 375°F/190°C/Gas 5, or until the custard has set.

DEEP FRIED ONIONS

This is a simple version, but for even more taste, use the batter in the deep-fried courgette recipe (see page 69).

FOR 6 PEOPLE
3 medium onions
Milk
Seasoned flour
Oil for deep-frying

Top, tail and peel the onions, and then slice them crosswise into ¼ inch (5mm) slices. The resulting circles should be loosened and separated.

Toss circles liberally in cold milk, and then, a few at a time, dab them into a tray of seasoned flour. Shake off the surplus.

Heat the deep-fryer to 360°F/182°C and fry for:
6 minutes – *crisp*

And that is how they should be served – *crisp* and immediately!

ONION AND BLACKCURRANT SAUCE

This sauce is ideal for coating the cabbage platter on page 41, or to accompany roast chicken.

1lb (450g) medium onions, peeled and quartered
¾ pint (425ml) milk
1 tablespoon Crème de Cassis

Pop your peeled and quartered onions into an ovenproof casserole, cover with the milk, and put the lid on. Cook in a preheated oven at 350°F/180°C/Gas 4 for 45 minutes.

PARSNIP

PASTINACA SATIVA

Remove the onions and put into food processor with 2 tablespoons of the milk. Purée and then pass through a plastic sieve. Fold into this the Crème de Cassis, and put in the top of a double saucepan until needed.

You will have about ½ pint (300ml) milk left, which can be frozen when cold and eventually used with stock for soup.

112

FRIED SPRING ONIONS

There is a time in the summer when 'spring' onions become nice and round at the base (rather like the mini gobstoppers I used to love sucking as a kid). Individual spring onion bulbs weigh about ½oz (15g) each and, allowing three per person, you should buy about 1½lb (675g). This means a lot of waste, of the green leaves, but these can be added to the stock pot.

FOR 6 PEOPLE
About 1½lb (675g) spring onions
1 tablespoon olive oil
1oz (25g) butter
1 tablespoon cooking sherry

Prepare the spring onions by removing the stalk base and then cutting off the green top.

In a small frying pan of about 8 inches (20cm) in diameter, heat the oil and then add the butter. Put in the eighteen or so onions and, using a wooden spoon to turn them occasionally, cook for:

    5 minutes – crisp
    8 minutes – firm
   10 minutes – soft
    After 3 minutes, add the sherry.

THE PARSNIP, A ROOT vegetable and an umbellifer like carrot, has been eaten for some 2000 years, and is thought to be native to Europe. It was eaten by the Greeks and Romans – in fact it is said that the Emperor Tiberius had parsnips especially imported from the Rhineland to his clifftop villa on the isle of Capri; he was addicted to them, and considered the German variety superior to any other vegetable. The Middle Ages in England was when the parsnip came into its culinary own: because they contain a lot of nutritive starch, they were eaten on the many fast days when meat was renounced (parsnips and broad beans were the basic foods of Lent). They also had medicinal value, being considered good for a variety of ailments, including coughs. As they contain a lot of sugar, they were made into sweet puddings, mixed with spices and eggs. The newly introduced potato (the first eaten was probably the sweet potato) is said to have appealed so much because it was sweeter and finer than the home-grown parsnip. A valuable vegetable throughout the centuries because it could be stored over the winter, it also grows wild in Europe and North America – where it was cultivated by the Indians in the late seventeenth century.

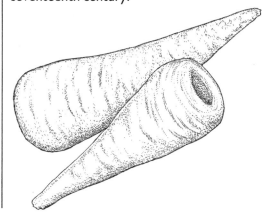

Thought of as a winter vegetable, the parsnip is basically available all year round, although best in the winter months. It is said to be sweeter and more tender after the first frost, but it should not really be left in the ground too long, as larger and older roots can develop a woody core. When buying, look for smaller roots, with few whiskers and knobbles (which make for waste); try to avoid any with brown patches on the creamy yellow skin as this could indicate rottenness inside. They usually come with the leaves cut off (these are inedible, but were fed to cattle in Britain as late as the nineteenth century, because they produced a richer milk), and try to avoid buying them washed in hygienic plastic packs, which can hide sins, and also make the vegetable sweat.

To prepare parsnips, cut off the thick leaf end and the end of the tail. Scrub young parsnips well, and peel only those which are old, if possible. In general, after topping, tailing and peeling, you should be left with about 12oz (350g) from a basic 1lb (450g). Leave them whole, or cut into slices, chunks, chips, depending on the recipe. Remove the woody core from older parsnips before or after cooking if you can.

Many people have a love-hate relationship with parsnips, but all seem to love the puréed version with the toasted pine kernels, or simply with lots of butter and nutmeg. I've often seen the astonished reaction: 'I hated parsnips until I had them done this way.' They can be boiled, steamed, baked, fried (see page 143 for a delicious mixture of fried turned vegetables), roasted alongside beef (traditional before potatoes), and stewed, when they act as a thickener. They always need some other enriching element – 'fine words butter no parsnips' – and go well with butter, cream and cheese. They also make a fine home-made wine.

PARSNIP SOUP

Basic recipe (see page 11)
2lb (900g) parsnips, topped, tailed and washed

Enhance the soup with fresh or preserved ginger, or a curry powder to taste.

PURÉE OF PARSNIPS WITH TOASTED PINE KERNELS (see also page 13)

FOR 6 PEOPLE
1 lb (450g) parsnips
1oz (25g) butter
¼ pint (150ml) single cream
2 tablespoons pine kernels, toasted

Peel the parsnips, cut them into even-sized pieces, and simmer in salted water until tender. Drain well, and put back over a low heat, and toss in the butter to dry.

Blend in the food processor with the single cream. (You will need a little more cream if you use a liquidiser rather than a food processor.) See you really liquidise them well, and then pass them through a very fine plastic sieve into a double saucepan that that has been brushed inside with butter.

When needed, reheat in the double saucepan, and top the dished-up purée with the toasted pine kernels.

ROASTED PARSNIPS

FOR 6 PEOPLE
1 lb (450g) parsnips
3oz (75g) dripping of choice
Sea salt and freshly ground black pepper

Top and tail the parsnips, peel and then cut into approximately ½ inch (1cm) cubes.

Put the dripping into a small roasting tray or Pyrex dish measuring about 12 × 4 inches (30 × 10cm), and then into a preheated oven at 400°F/200°C/Gas 6. Allow 5 minutes or so for the fat to melt and become hot.

Add the parsnip cubes and cook for 15 minutes until they are crisp and fatty like mini roast potatoes. Drain on kitchen paper prior to serving, and be liberal with sea salt and freshly ground pepper.

BAKED PARSNIP WITH CREAM AND CHEESE

FOR 6 PEOPLE
1 lb (450g) parsnips
Butter
Freshly ground black pepper (optional)
4 tablespoons onion, finely diced
½ pint (300ml) double cream
3oz (75g) Cheddar cheese, finely grated

Peel the parsnips, and then slice crosswise about ⅛ inch (3mm) thick, using only the fairly large top ends of the parsnips – usually about 1½ inch (4cm) wide. (Use the rest for soup or purée.)

Butter the base of a round 8 inch (20cm) Pyrex dish, and add pepper if you like. Then, starting from the middle, make circles of the parsnip slices, getting larger and larger, building up to about three layers ultimately.

Cover with the finely diced onion and the double cream mixed with the cheese. Bake in the preheated oven at 375°F/190°C/Gas 5 for 30 minutes, when they will be *crisp* and absolutely superb.

PARSNIP CROQUETTES

FOR 6 PEOPLE
1 lb (450g) parsnips
3oz (75g) butter
2 eggs
Seasoned flour
4oz (100g) breadcrumbs (or sesame seeds)
2 tablespoons oil
Salt and freshly ground black pepper

Prepare and cook the parsnips as in the purée recipe (see page 113), until they are soft. Drain and return to the pan to dry off over low heat.

Mash them with 1oz (25g) of the butter and the yolk of one of the eggs. The mixture does not really have to be smooth, but easy enough to make into six sausages, about 2 inches (5cm) long, and 1 inch (3cm) round.

Roll the 'sausages' in the seasoned flour and then in the lightly beaten egg plus remaining egg white. Turn into the breadcrumbs (or sesame seeds), which have been seasoned with a little salt and pepper.

Leave to chill until they are quite firm, about 3–4 hours at least. They could be frozen at this stage.

Place the oil and remaining butter in a frying pan and fry the croquettes for 8–10 minutes, as you would sausages! You could also deep-fry them, at 360°F/182°C, for 8 minutes.

114

PEAS

PISUM SATIVUM

THE CULTIVATED PEA IS usually called the garden or shelling pea, to differentiate it from its presumed wild ancestor, the field pea. The pea is thought to come from the Near East – odd, as it is a plant that flourishes in cooler climates – and has been eaten for centuries. They have been found in Stone Age lake dwellings in Switzerland, and in Bronze Age and Iron Age sites in France and England respectively. It was the field pea which was eaten until the Middle Ages: it was dried and used as a valuable winter staple, and it was also, like parsnips, a popular Lenten food. The Italians developed the garden pea in the sixteenth century, and from there, possibly with Catherine de Medici, it travelled to France where these *petits pois* eventually became so popular at the Court of Louis XIV, that ladies (according to a contemporary letter) would sup well with the king, then go home and eat *more* peas before going to bed (at the severe risk of indigestion, one presumes).

British gardeners started to grow garden peas in the seventeenth century, and only now if you grow your own, can you taste the pea as it truly should taste, for with freezer companies seizing the bulk of the new fresh crop, the remainder available to greengrocers is decidedly second-best (I *still* think frozen peas

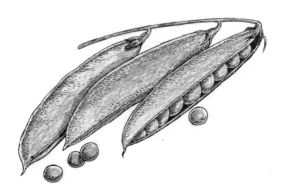

are the best). Peas were introduced to the United States by Columbus, and were grown by the Indians; Thomas Jefferson, that indefatigable vegetable gardener (and sometime American President), cultivated up to thirty varieties of his favourite vegetable.

When buying peas in their pods, look for bright, firm, plump and smallish pods, that rustle when picked up. Avoid any pods which look a bit wizened or dusty grey. Although not particularly easy to grow, home-grown peas have the best flavour and texture, and can be one of the major taste delights of the gardener's year. They are available from the end of May until the beginning of October.

To prepare peas, simply pod or shell them. Jane Grigson suggests boiling the peas while still in their pods, and then eating them from the pods, sucking like asparagus after dipping in melted butter. This could be sensible (as well as delicious) as a lot of the pea flavour contained in the pods can go into the cooking water, to be used as the base for a pea soup, or a vegetable stock for other uses. In fact, often the pods themselves, if young enough, can be used for soup – boiled and then pressed through a sieve to leave the parchmenty inner skin behind. (The classic pea pod is, of course, the mange-tout, which I discussed earlier.)

Fresh green small garden peas or petits pois are one of the most marvellous accompanying vegetables, simply steamed or boiled with a little mint, and sugar if necessary. They can be fried, made into soup – the classic pea soup is Potage St-Germain – and act as a wonderful garnish for any number of dishes, lending taste, texture and colour. They are also available dried, whole or split, when they are a valuable source of protein, like other pulses, and make delicious purées and pease pudding (marrowfat particularly).

PEA SOUP

Apart from making good soups in themselves, fresh uncooked whole peas also add a biting crunch to fennel and almond soup, sweetcorn soup, tomato soup and many others.

Basic recipe (see page 11)
2lb (900g) peas, podded

Tastes much nicer with a handful of fresh mint (including stalks) added at the beginning of cooking.

LEMON, PEA AND SWEETCORN SOUP

Basic recipe (see page 11)
1lb (450g) peas, podded
1lb (450g) sweetcorn kernels
1 lemon

Cut the lemon into quarters, and add the quarters and juice at the beginning of cooking.

STEAMED FRESH GARDEN PEAS

Unless you grow your own peas, or you have friendly neighbours who do, you will only have access to the commercial ones appearing in the vegetable shops which are often dreary. I am positive the harvesting machines of the frozen pea industry literally suck the land dry of those gorgeous peas I remember as a kid.

For 6 people
1½lb (675g) fresh pea pods
1 pint (550ml) water
1 teaspoon salt
2 tablespoons sugar
Juice of ½ lemon
Lots of fresh mint
Butter

Shell the peas, after which you will be left with about 10oz (275g).

Put the water, salt, sugar and lemon juice into a pan and bring to the boil. Put the peas, along with the mint, into a colander over the boiling water, cover with a lid (or foil) and steam:
5 minutes – crisp
7 minutes – firm
8 minutes – soft
As soon as they are cooked to your liking, serve immediately with a generous knob of salty butter.

Having spent endless hours attempting to reproduce the peas my Nan served me when I was young, this is the best method to use, *but* my test cook and I also realised to our cost that the above cooking times are for peas that have been freshly picked that day. Peas bought from a greengrocer have taken up to *double* that time to produce similar textures.

GARDEN PEAS WITH LETTUCE AND RED PEPPER

Follow the previous recipe for steamed peas, but mix into the colander with the peas, some shredded lettuce (which disappears so quickly you might have to use a whole head) and 4 tablespoons finely diced red peppers. The colour contrast is appealing, and the taste rather nice!

MUSHY MARROWFAT PEAS

FOR 6 PEOPLE
12oz (350g) marrowfat peas, soaked
EITHER
2 tablespoons dry English mustard powder
8oz (225g) onions, finely chopped
OR
Generous sprig of fresh mint
2 tablespoons clear runny honey

When buying peas from your health shop, always make sure they are sold with the special bicarbonate

PEPPER

CAPSICUM ANNUUM

tablets, and follow the packet instructions carefully.

Measure out 1 ½ pints (850ml) cold water. Add the soaked peas to the water along with the other ingredients of your chosen flavouring, and simmer for 45–60 minutes, until they become mushy.

BUTTERED FRESH YOUNG GARDEN PEAS

FOR 6 PEOPLE
1 ½lb (675g) fresh young pea pods
2oz (50g) butter
1 teaspoon sugar
1 teaspoon salt

Shell the peas and put them into a small saucepan with the butter, sugar and salt. Cook gently as follows:

    4 minutes – crisp
    5 minutes – firm
    8 minutes – soft

OLD GARDEN PEAS FRIED WITH MINT

Follow the previous recipe for buttered peas, but fry older peas in 2 tablespoons dripping instead of the butter (turkey is nice). Add lots of chopped fresh mint.

THE FAMILIAR PEPPER IS KNOWN variously as sweet pepper, bell pepper, capsicum, green, red, white or yellow pepper, as well as pimiento or pimento . . . all very confusing. There's also the chilli pepper (*Capsicum frutescens*), which is a close relation. They are all members of the *Solanaceae* family – which includes potatoes, tomatoes and nightshade (would you believe) – and are native to tropical America and the West Indies. They were not known in Europe until Columbus discovered the New World – wild varieties had been eaten in South America since about 5000 BC – and, although introduced to Spain in the sixteenth century, were slow to become established. They feature substantially in Mediterranean cuisines, but in a historical culinary sense, are relative newcomers. The paprika dishes so characteristic of Hungary, for instance, were not established until about the late seventeenth century, and peppers were, in fact, virtually unknown in Britain until well after the Second World War.

117

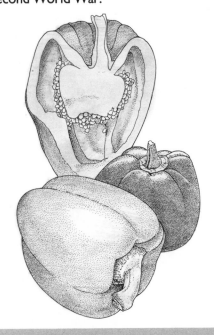

Commercially, peppers of all varieties are available throughout the year; home-grown varieties in late summer. The green pepper, if left on the plant, will turn red or yellow, according to variety, and there are also white or purple peppers (the Dutch have been experimenting cleverly). The flavour differs minimally, but I think the riper red is definitely sweeter, while the green can sometimes be indigestible (it is often said that peppers can cure stomach and kidney ailments, and counteract flatulence). They have little food value, but contain a lot of Vitamin C.

There are over thirty varieties of sweet peppers, and although it is fairly easy to be sure in Britain, it is a more hazardous business buying abroad: our round or almost square sweet peppers can be pointed like chillies on the Continent. Chillies, fortunately, are usually red or green and characteristically pointed in shape.

While I'm about it, I shall clear up the various queries which always seem to attach themselves to the pepper family. Sweet are just that, with a sweet-tasting flesh; occasionally the seeds can be bitter or a little hot. It is the flesh of a Hungarian pointed variety of sweet pepper that is dried and ground to make paprika. This comes in grades, basically sweet or hot, and it is the addition of the dried seeds that makes the seasoning hot rather than sweet. The Spanish word for pepper is *pimiento* (usually a smaller, more triangular variety), and dried, these make *pimentón*, the Spanish equivalent of paprika.

Chilli peppers, which I shall not discuss in detail here as they are usually used as a seasoning only, are closely related to the sweet pepper, but are distinctly hot and spicy in flavour. They are graded in heat from I to 120, apparently, and the hottest I've encountered, the jalapeño, is only rated at 15! Chillies need to be handled with extreme care, as their volatile oils can make the skin tingle, cause blisters, and can affect the eyes (many cooks advise preparing them with gloves on). Dried and ground chillies make red or Cayenne pepper. Chilli pepper is another name for Cayenne, and chilli powder or compound is a tastier mixture of Cayenne plus spices, most notably cumin.

That out of the way, when buying peppers, look for an appropriate size for the intended usage (big and stable for stuffing, say), and for shiny, glossy skins; avoid any which have bruises, softening or wrinkling. (Occasionally, though, if you grow your own and take the green off the plant to ripen to red, there may be a little wrinkling of the skin.) Store in the salad drawer of the fridge.

To prepare peppers, you must first get rid of the seeds and bitter white pith. If to be used sliced, cut in half, and scrape seeds and pith out. Wash and dry thoroughly, then slice as required. If to be stuffed, cut off the topmost ½ inch (1cm) or so, along with the stalk, and reach in with a teaspoon to scrape out seeds and pith. Many people like their peppers skinned, but I think this takes away quite a lot of the flavour as well as all of the skin's dietary value – as fibre!

Peppers are used a lot in salads where their colourful crispness contributes flavour and texture. They also feature cooked in many cuisines: in pipérade, rouille (the red pepper sauce of Provence, so wonderful with bouillabaisse), in ghoulash, ratatouille, caponata, and peperonata. They can be stuffed and baked and served hot, or I stuff them raw with cheese and herb pâté, before slicing into colourful tasty rings as a starter.

I think red peppers are the tastiest, but in any of the following recipes, excluding perhaps the soup, yellow, white or green peppers can be substituted.

RED PEPPER SOUP

Basic recipe (see page 11)
2lb (900g) red peppers

Simply wipe the peppers and then chop evenly (pith, seeds, tops and all). It's a delicious soup – and what a rich colour it turns out!

FRIED RED PEPPERS WITH ONION

This is a favourite dish of mine, as I adore sweet things, and red peppers are just that. A similar fried mixture, a wonderful supper dish for one, is on page 136.

PER PERSON
2oz (50g) red peppers, prepared as in method
Oil and butter
¹/₂oz (15g) onion, finely chopped

Wipe the pepper clean with a damp cloth and then slice through making round rings about ⅛ inch (3mm) thick. Remove any pith or seeds from the circles, then, taking about four at a time, lay them flat and cut into little pieces. A tedious task it may be, but *well worth* the effort.

Put a drop of oil in the frying pan, with some butter, and fry off the onions until golden. Add the chopped red peppers and stir-fry for about 3 minutes, and serve at once.

Maybe not for you, but if I'm serving cold breast of chicken or just pieces of cold chicken leg, I top them with this warm dish.

BAKED STUFFED RED PEPPER

A pepper weighing about 6oz (175g) will be a main supper dish for one, or give you four slices (one per person) as a starter.

Remove the stalk end and then scrape out all the seeds and pith (a good idea here is to wash the inside out under a running cold tap).

Fill a piping bag with one of the cooked stuffings – see page 19; you'll need about 8oz (225g) for each pepper – and pipe into the hole. Put the 'lid' back on, and wrap each pepper well in a piece of foil about 10 inches (25cm) square.

Place in a roasting tray with a little boiling water in the bottom, and cook in a preheated oven at 375°F/190°C/Gas 5 for:

25 minutes – crisp, but only warm
30 minutes – firm, and warmish
40 minutes – soft and hot

RATATOUILLE

The whole idea of making ratatouille is that you *eat* this lovely summery dish, but if any is left over it can be liquidised, sieved, and then with some added stock, will make a delicious soup.

FOR 6 PEOPLE
6 cloves garlic, crushed to a paste with 1 teaspoon salt
8oz (225g) onions, finely chopped
4oz (100g) fennel, finely chopped (optional)
4 tablespoons hazelnut or walnut oil
4 tablespoons olive oil (or oil of choice)
12oz (350g) red peppers
6oz (175g) green peppers
8oz (225g) aubergines
1¹/₂lb (675g) tomatoes
1 teaspoon sugar
8oz (225g) baby courgettes

Prepare the garlic paste, and finely chop the onions and fennel (if using). In a 10 inch (25cm) frying pan, heat 2 tablespoons of each oil (4 tablespoons!) and fry off the garlic, onions and fennel until golden.

Slice the red and green peppers into four lengthwise, remove pith and seeds, and then cut into thin strips. Wipe the aubergine and then cut into similar strips. Skin and seed the tomatoes and chop roughly, covering with the sugar. Wipe clean the baby courgettes and top and tail them. If you wish to take the trouble – and they do look much nicer when serving – score lengthwise about four or five times each, then slice thinly.

POTATO

SOLANUM TUBEROSUM

Add red and green peppers to the onions, along with the balance of oil, plus the aubergines. Cook for 10 minutes over a medium heat, stirring from time to time with a wooden spoon, in order to spread the ingredients evenly around.

Add the tomatoes and sliced courgettes and cook for a further 10 minutes.

Serve immediately garnished with lots of freshly chopped herbs of your choice, or leave to get cold, and serve as a cold starter. Sometimes I find the latter becomes a bit soggy, so I transfer the dish from the frying pan to a colander and leave the juices to strain. These I then quickly reduce in a small saucepan over a high heat before re-combining with the vegetables.

T HE HISTORY OF THE POTATO IS a convoluted one. No one actually seems to agree on anything, but we do know that the potato is native to the Andes, and was an important staple for the Incas. It was brought to Spain by the *conquistadores* and gradually spread throughout Europe. Both Sir Francis Drake and Sir Walter Ralegh are credited with the introduction, in the late sixteenth century, of the potato – but one of these introductions could have been of the *sweet* potato. Ralegh grew the tuber which was the most likely ancestor of our modern varieties on his estate in County Cork, so he can probably claim the larger responsibility.

Despite the fact that potatoes are now one of the four major world crops, they weren't at all liked at first. Many thought they caused leprosy, the dread disease of the time. Potatoes, related to the deadly nightshade, even today contain slightly poisonous alkaloids, called solanines; centuries ago, the solanine content would have been higher, and could cause a rash thought to be the onset of leprosy. Many criticised them because of their lack of taste – which is not easily denied. Most thought they should be animal fodder or a food for the very poor only – which on the whole they became. The Scots weren't keen because their preachers said they were an ungodly food, as they weren't mentioned in the Bible. In our weight-conscious

120

society, we were, until recently, warned constantly to eschew (rather than chew) the potato – so the poor potato has had a bad press all round.

However it did become established eventually, particularly in Scotland and Ireland – where the failure of the crop in 1845 through blight (and it was a one-crop country) caused famine. The North Americans probably first encountered the potato through Irish immigrants in the eighteenth century, and they were known as Murphys (thus, presumably, the name of that medieval-looking, potato-baking implement, the Spike-Murphy). The French disdained potatoes for years until they were championed by a M. Parmentier – after whom many potato dishes have been named. They eat a lot now – almost all the famous potato dishes have French titles, and think of French fries!

Potatoes are, in fact, quite good nutritionally: they contain over 70 per cent water, and have less carbohydrate than the equivalent amount of bread – so can be acceptable to the diet-conscious. (It's generally what you put *on* the potatoes that makes them fattening – all that butter or soured cream on your baked potatoes!) They contain a good amount of Vitamin C and potassium: both these, however, can be leached out into the cooking water, thus steaming, and certainly baking, are better cooking methods by which to retain the goodness. The nutrients are also near the skin, so it is always advisable to bake in their jackets, or to boil or steam in their skins (which can be slipped off afterwards). In fact, for the really diet- and health-conscious, a baked potato skin is the best part to eat: the discarded starch of the flesh can be used in soups or as a thickening for those less concerned with their shape. (But never use potato *when making stock*, as the stock will go cloudy.)

Apparently over fifty varieties of potato are

known in Britain, but even for those growing their own, the choice from seedsmen is considerably smaller. And for those of us simply buying potatoes from the market or greengrocer, there's hardly any choice at all.

Potatoes in the limited varieties on offer are white or red, waxy or floury. Waxy are good for boiling, frying, roasting and for salads; the floury are obviously better for baking or mashing. Although you don't want to pay for clumps of soil, it is really better to buy potatoes which are a bit dirty as this protects them from light and thus from turning green – those for sale, washed, in plastic bags, haven't got a lot going for them nutritionally. The best maincrop potatoes are those in the autumn, although they're available throughout the year. But the tastiest potato, to my mind, is the fresh new potato, available locally grown in Britain from about June.

Everyone knows how to prepare potatoes, or to boil them to their correct degree of done-ness (it so depends on their size and quality), so I'll just specify everything in the individual recipes – apart from the baby new potatoes. Meanwhile, just think of the many ways in which this most versatile of vegetables can be cooked and served: as a constituent of soup; boiled; mashed (as duchesse, croquette, dauphine as well as the simple buttery mash to accompany sausages – perhaps with a sprinkling of nutmeg on the top); sautéed (in slices, as shreds like the Swiss rösti, in cubes in Spanish tortilla); stewed (the classic Scottish dish of stovies); baked (whole, or in slices in the oven with cheese or milk); roasted; made into scones, cakes, gnocchi; served cold in salads . . . I could literally go on for ever! And the potato is made into a flour useful for those on gluten-free diets, as well as being over-processed into dry powders or granules which are *disgusting*!

BOILED NEW POTATOES

For six people having three other vegetables as well, you will need to purchase the amount specified, but whatever you do, try to get potatoes of the same small size – about that of walnuts.

FOR 6 PEOPLE
1¼lb (550g) small new potatoes
1 pint (550ml) water
2 teaspoons salt
2oz (50g) butter

Don't peel the potatoes, but simply scrub them lightly with a kitchen 'greenie'. If you have to prepare them a few hours before you wish to cook, soak them in cold water with a pinch of salt and a hint of fresh lemon juice.

When ready to cook, drain the potatoes and put in a pan with the water and salt and bring to the boil. Then let them simmer for:
    5 minutes – crisp
    9 minutes – firm
    15 minutes – soft
Strain them and return to saucepan. Add the butter and heat gently to dry them off and glaze with the melted foaming butter.

STEAMED NEW POTATOES

Using the same ingredients, and preparing the potatoes as above, bring the salted water to the boil. Place the potatoes in the colander over the boiling water and cover with a lid (or foil). Steam for:
    18 minutes – crisp
    22 minutes – firm
    30 minutes – soft
Glaze with the butter when ready to serve.

BAKED POTATOES

The best sized potatoes are about 6oz (175g) each in weight, and they should be cleaned really well with a nail-brush or a kitchen 'greenie'. Dry the potatoes and make a small cross with a sharp pointed knife on the top of each.

Cover the bottom of a small roasting tin completely with a layer of good sea salt – to a depth of about ¾ inch (2cm) – and bed the potatoes down in this.

In an oven preheated to 425°F/220°C/Gas 7, bake the potatoes for at least 2 hours. Remove the potatoes from the tin – you may have to use brute force to get off the salt encrusted round the bases – and push in and up towards the centre of each potato, opening up the cuts. Pipe some cheese and herb pâté, some port and Stilton cheese or a flavoured butter (see pages 15–16) into the opening.

GOLDEN POTATO WEDGES

FOR 6 PEOPLE
3 large baking potatoes
3oz (75g) butter
6oz (175g) fine dry breadcrumbs
Salt and freshly ground black pepper

Preheat oven to 350°F/180°C/Gas 4. Peel potatoes, wash and dry them, then cut each into four wedges lengthwise. Melt 2oz (50g) of the butter, dip the potato wedges in, then dredge with the seasoned breadcrumbs.

Place in a shallow greased baking dish, and dot with the remaining butter. Bake for 1 hour, then increase heat to 425°F/220°C/Gas 7, and bake for 20–30 minutes more until brown and crisp.

POTATOES BAKED WITH CREAM AND CHEESE

FOR 6 PEOPLE
About 1 ½lb (675g) potatoes, peeled
Sea salt
½ pint (300ml) double cream
2–3oz (50–75g) Cheddar cheese, grated
Chopped parsley

Try to mould and 'turn' the potatoes so that they are all about 2½ inches (6cm) in length and more or less evenly shaped. (If you have the time and patience, try to make them look like small rugby balls.) Use any trimmings in a soup or purée.

Cover with cold water and a pinch of sea salt, and bring to the boil. Simmer for 5 minutes only. Drain well, and place in a casserole dish. Pour the cream in so that it comes half-way up the sides of the potatoes, and then cover the whole dish with the grated cheese.

Bake at 375°F/190°C/Gas 5 for approximately 1 hour. Remove from the oven, and sprinkle liberally with chopped parsley.

SAVOURY POTATOES

FOR 6 PEOPLE
2 tablespoons bacon fat
6oz (175g) bacon, derinded and finely chopped
8oz (225g) onions, finely chopped
½ teaspoon dried thyme
About 1 ½lb (675g) potatoes, peeled and sliced
Salt and freshly ground black pepper
1 ½ pints (850ml) good chicken stock
Melted butter

Heat the bacon fat and fry the bacon for a few minutes before adding the onion. Cook until nice and golden, then add the thyme.

Butter the base and sides of a suitable ovenproof casserole dish, and start to build the potato slices up in layers. Spread a little of the onion/bacon mixture plus some seasoning between each layer.

Before adding the final layer of potatoes, pour in the chicken stock. Carefully overlap the final layer of slices for a better effect when served, and brush the top with melted butter. Bake at 400°F/200°C/Gas 6 for 1 hour.

ROAST POTATOES

I prefer to roast my potatoes without parboiling – which takes longer, of course, and they take up so much more fat. I like them to be extremely well done on the outside, really dark brown, in fact, and as crisp as a toffee apple, so that when you cut into them, lots of delicious fat spurts out.

First of all, though, I'll be more righteous. The parboiling of the following recipe helps to give the potatoes a slightly old-fashioned texture of inside fluffiness.

FOR 6 PEOPLE
1 lb (450g) potatoes
1 ½ pints (850ml) boiling water
Sea salt
2 tablespoons dripping (see below)

Try to buy potatoes that weigh in at about 4oz (100g) each. Peel and then cut each potato into three even-sized pieces.

Add the potatoes to the boiling water (with 2 teaspoons salt added), bring back to the boil with the lid on, and boil for 8 minutes. Strain and dry off on kitchen paper.

Put the dripping – turkey, chicken, lamb, pork or beef fat (never oil, butter or margarine) – into a roasting tray, and melt in a preheated oven set at 375°F/190°C/Gas 5. Sprinkle the potatoes with a little coarse sea salt, and put in the roasting tray. Baste and turn once or twice, and they will take only 30 minutes to be cooked crisp.

RICH ROAST POTATOES

FOR 6 PEOPLE
1lb (450g) potatoes
4 tablespoons dripping (see previous recipe)
Sea salt

124

Prepare potatoes exactly as before, but *do not parboil*. Melt the dripping in a roasting tray in a preheated oven at 375°F/190°C/Gas 5, then add the dry potatoes which have been sprinkled with sea salt. Roast for 40 minutes, and turn every 15 minutes with a wooden spoon. They will be even more heavenly after 60 minutes!

FANNED ROAST POTATOES

These potatoes are an unusual variant on the roasting theme – they fan out attractively during the cooking, and are deliciously crisp. I like to use duck fat or beef dripping for extra taste.

FOR 6 PEOPLE
At least 12 medium potatoes
Walnut oil
Salt and freshly ground black pepper
Fat for roasting (see above)

Peel the potatoes and cut to approximately the same size and shape. Take a small slice off the base of each so that the potatoes will stand firm and square in the roasting tin, then, using a small sharp knife, make cuts into the potato, going from the top to two-thirds down, all along the length of the potato, so that it resembles a cock's comb.

Paint each potato with walnut oil – inside the edges as well – sprinkle with salt and pepper, and then roast in your chosen fat for at least 1 hour at 375°F/190°C/Gas 5.

PARISIAN POTATOES

FOR 6 PEOPLE
About 1½lb (675g) potatoes, peeled
2oz (50g) butter
1 tablespoon oil

Using a 'baller' or Parisian scoop, cut into the peeled potatoes to make those lovely round shapes like grapes. (Use the leftover potato 'skeletons' for purées or in soups.)

Heat a mixture of the butter and oil (or even better, duck fat), and fry the potato balls over a low heat for about 40 minutes.

I prefer to cook them slowly, and tend just to leave them in the frying pan at the side of the stove until I want to serve them. They gradually become more brown, crisp and buttery. When they are ready, don't put them in a covered dish to keep hot, or cover the pan, or else they will become soggy. Just before serving, drain on kitchen paper, and sprinkle liberally with salt.

MASHED NUT POTATOES

FOR 6 PEOPLE
2lb (900g) potatoes, peeled and evenly cut
Pinch of sea salt
1 egg, lightly beaten
4 tablespoons double cream
2oz (50g) butter
7oz (200g) packet broken walnuts

Cover the potatoes with cold water, add sea salt, and bring to the boil. Reduce heat and simmer until the potatoes are soft, about 15 minutes.

Strain well and dry out briefly over heat, then mash well. When smooth, add the egg, double cream and butter, and beat until light.

Roughly crush the broken walnuts, and fold them into the smooth, creamy potatoes.

HERBED POTATO SCONES

Normally croquettes are made from mashed or leftover potatoes, as below, but this recipe is one my Nan used to serve on washday Mondays to go with the inevitable cold Sunday joint leftovers.

FOR 6 PEOPLE
4 medium potatoes, peeled and coarsely grated
1 medium onion, peeled and coarsely grated
1oz (25g) flour, sieved
2 eggs
2 tablespoons freshly chopped garden herbs
Pinch curry powder or powdered ginger
Salt and freshly ground black pepper to taste
Oil
Butter

Simply mix the potatoes, onion, flour, eggs, herbs and seasonings in a large bowl until well blended.

Heat oil and butter in your frying pan (see page 9 for suggested proportions), and drop large serving spoonfuls of the mixture in. Fry on each side until golden brown, and serve at once.

OATMEAL POTATO CROQUETTES

FOR 6 PEOPLE
1lb (450g) potatoes, peeled and evenly chopped
Salt
½oz (15g) butter
2oz (50g) onions, finely diced
1oz (25g) walnuts, finely chopped
1 tablespoon fresh parsley or chives, chopped
2 tablespoons double cream
2 eggs
8 tablespoons porridge oats
Oil for deep-frying

Cover the potatoes with generously salted water, bring to the boil, and simmer until tender. Meanwhile, heat the butter in a frying pan, and fry the onion, walnuts and herbs.

Strain the potatoes, then dry over a low heat before mashing them smooth. Beat in the double cream and one of the lightly beaten eggs. Fold in the cooked onion mixture. Divide the mixture into twelve even portions (two per guest), and roll each out into a sausage shape. Put on a tray, cover and chill in the fridge for at least a couple of hours (or overnight if you like).

Lightly beat the remaining egg with 1 tablespoon water, and place the porridge oats in a flat dish. Immerse each sausage in the egg momentarily before rolling in the oats. Once again, chill and leave until firm.

Preheat the deep-fryer or pan of oil to 360°F/182°C and fry for 10 minutes. Serve immediately after draining on kitchen paper.

POTATO, CHEESE AND GARLIC BREAD

This bread is absolutely delicious served straight from the oven, accompanied by a good strong cheese and some pickled onions. It's good with soup, too. It's quite light when hot, and very filling. As it cools, it becomes a trifle heavier, but is still tempting.

4oz (100g) Cheddar cheese
2 cloves garlic
2 teaspoons salt
12oz (350g) self-raising flour
2 teaspoons English mustard powder
12oz (350g) potatoes, peeled
1 egg
5 tablespoons milk

Grate the cheese and crush the garlic with the salt. Mix the flour, mustard, garlic/salt and cheese.

Coarsely grate the peeled potatoes and add to the dry ingredients. Then, using the dough hook on your Kenwood (or a strong arm and hand), fold in the beaten egg and milk until you have a smooth dough.

Shape into a ball on a sheet of greaseproof paper, and mark in wedges. Bake in the preheated oven at 375°F/190°C/Gas 5 for 45–50 minutes until golden.

PUMPKIN AND SQUASH

CUCURBITACEAE

THE ALL-EMBRACING SQUASH family includes gourds, cucumbers, squashes, courgettes, marrows, pumpkins and chayotes. The family is *Cucurbitaceae* from the Latin for gourd. The word *squash* itself comes from the American Indian, *askootasquash*, which clearly reflects the major growing and eating area of pumpkins and squashes. Both have been grown in South and North America for thousands of years, and to a certain extent in Europe and the Middle East. The first British to taste them were probably the Pilgrim Fathers, whose original Thanksgiving dinner consisted of wild turkey, cranberries and pumpkin – thus the traditional pumpkin pies of present-day American Thanksgiving dinners. Neither pumpkins nor squashes actually reached British shores until about the mid-nineteenth century, and we're still working out what to do with them!

The pumpkin is available in Britain in about October to November (thus its tendency to appear, hollowed out, with a jolly face as a Hallowe'en lantern). It comes in all sorts of colours and shapes, but all taste much the same. The rind is hard, most commonly an intense orange, and the whole pumpkin, if suspended uncut in a net, can keep for several months.

The Americans use pumpkin in two traditional dishes – the aforementioned pie, and a soup – but it can also be served as an accompanying vegetable: baked in chunks then puréed with cream and butter, or boiled and served with a good tasty sauce (it *needs* a sauce because the taste is rather bland). Pumpkin can be used in breads, to eke out apples, cooked with sweetcorn and cornmeal dishes, and made into jams.

Pumpkin seeds, beloved of parrots, hamsters and vegetarians, are also edible, being rich in the B vitamins, phosphorus, iron and zinc. They can be baked and salted for nibbles, or they can be sprouted. An edible oil is also made from pumpkin seeds.

Squashes are rarer in Britain than in the States and other sub-tropical climes like South Africa, but two varieties are occasionally found in autumn: the butternut squash and the custard squash or marrow. The former looks like an overgrown fig, with a pale yellow skin; the latter like a round yellow-white cushion with scalloped edges. They can be steamed, boiled, baked, stuffed, made into jams, preserves and pickles.

PUMPKIN SOUP

A *must* for the Hallowe'en party, but oh, do be careful when you make it, as it can bubble like a witches' brew if left too long or reheated too swiftly.

Basic recipe (see page 11)
2lb (900g) pumpkin flesh
Generous pinch ground cinnamon

To carve out the flesh, having cut off a lid, try painstakingly to scoop out the flesh without cutting through the sides so that the empty rind may be used as a soup tureen (or a lantern). Slice a thin piece off the base or else, as you take it to the table, it will wobble over!

PUMPKIN AND SAFFRON SOUP

Basic recipe (see page 11)
2lb (900g) pumpkin flesh
2 good pinches saffron infused in 2¹/₂fl. oz (75ml) hot
milk

ROAST PUMPKIN

Pumpkin flesh can be cut into 2 inch (5cm) squares, coated with ground cinnamon, then roasted in a moderate oven in duck fat for about 15 minutes. As the squares go soft so quickly, I then transfer them to a cooling wire tray over the roasting tray to finish off and dry out a little — only a few minutes more.

STEAMED SQUASH

PER PERSON
1 squash, about 3oz (75g)
Salt and freshly ground black pepper
1–2oz (25–50g) flavoured butter (see pages 15–16)

Wipe the outside of the squashes with a clean damp cloth and then, depending on the size, cut either into halves if very small, or quarters if larger. Lay on pieces of seasoned foil and top with a generous blob of your favourite flavoured butter. Wrap the squash up firmly in foil.

Place in a colander over a pan containing 1 pint (550ml) boiling salted water, and steam for:
  15 minutes – crisp
  18 minutes – firm
  20 minutes – soft

RADICCHIO, see ENDIVE
RED CABBAGE, see CABBAGE

RUNNER BEANS

PHASEOLUS MULTIFLORUS

RUNNER BEANS ARE ANOTHER green bean, like the French bean, which was unknown in the Old World before Columbus discovered America. Originally native to Central America, runners are also known as scarlet runners because of the profusion of red flowers on the commonest species (although in fact there are purple, violet and white variants too). Scarlet runners were introduced by John Tradescant, famous plant collector and gardener to Charles I, and the plants were probably used decoratively rather than nutritionally at first.

Green beans are, of course, all very similar, but runners have larger, coarser and stronger flavoured pods than French beans, and are flat in shape rather than rounded. As with many vegetables, the pod should be plucked and eaten as young and small as possible: if left on the plant to grow (sometimes larger than 10 inches or

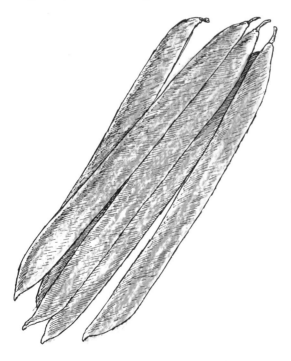

25cm in length), the pod has to be sliced, and much of the vitamin goodness and flavour will be lost in the cooking water.

Home-grown runners are available in Britain from July to October. When buying, try to snap the end of one to see if it *does* snap (the prime sign of freshness), and try to choose the smaller pods. If you can't use them straight away, put ends of stems in a little water in a cool place, or pop them in a plastic bag in the chilling compartment of the fridge.

To prepare for cooking, runners need a little more work than French beans. Wash, top and tail, but then you *must* remove the strings, by snapping off the ends and pulling the string off; or you may have to actually *shave* the sides with a potato peeler – the older they are, and the larger, the more string will have to be removed. (Incidentally, I *have* come across some tender, long, dark green runner beans – about 8–10 inches, or 20–25cm long, and ¾ inch (2cm) wide at the widest part – that seem to have lost their stringy sides, but only very occasionally I'm afraid!) Chop the pods into diagonal lengths of about 2 inches (5cm) – or you can push them through a bean cutter.

Like French beans, quick boiling or steaming – the very simplest methods – are best with runner beans (I think the steamed are best). But because runners are more robust, even a mite tough sometimes, they can stand up to more energetic treatment: they can be added to casseroles, to gratins of vegetables to be grilled or baked; they are good with crispy bacon and bacon fat, or in a cream sauce, and can also be served cold in vinaigrette.

I don't think they are any good for soup – sorry! – but if you have a glut and are desperate, cook them with rosemary sprigs, and do the best you can. I've always found them too stringy to pass through the sieve after liquidising.

SPINACH

SPINACIA OLERACEA

BOILED OR STEAMED RUNNER BEANS

If you can find the tender long beans without the string, you can cook them whole; if not, cut your runners into 2 inch (5cm) chunks, after washing and stringing.

If you want to perk them up a little, add a little coarse sea salt and chopped garlic immediately after steaming, or coat them with a little tomato provençale (see page 140).

FOR 6 PEOPLE
1 lb (450g) runner beans
1 pint (550ml) boiling water
1 teaspoon salt

WHOLE BEANS
Steamed, over boiling salted water:
    5 minutes – crisp
    6 minutes – firm
    8 minutes – soft
Boiled, in boiling salted water, and after being
    brought back to boil:
    4 minutes – crisp
    5 minutes – firm
    6 minutes – soft
CUT BEANS
Steamed, over boiling salted water:
    4 minutes – crisp
    5 minutes – firm
    6 minutes – soft
Boiled, in boiling salted water, and after being
    brought back to boil:
    3 minutes – crisp
    5 minutes – firm
    6 minutes – soft

RUTABAGA, see TURNIP AND SWEDE
SCALLION, SHALLOT, SPRING ONION, see ONION
SNOW PEAS, see MANGE-TOUT

THOUGHT BY MOST EXPERTS TO hail originally from Persia – the name comes from the Persian word *aspanakh* – the Arabs introduced it to Europe (one Arab commentator actually called spinach the 'prince of vegetables') in the thirteenth century. It was not cultivated in Britain until about the sixteenth century, and in America it only made an appearance at about the beginning of the nineteenth century, when Thomas Jefferson grew it in his garden. Its main areas of cultivation over the centuries were France and Italy, and the dishes which now bear the name Florentine (denoting their spinach content) must surely be the French raising their berets to the superior green thumbs of the gardeners of Florence.

A highly nutritious plant, it was first thought of as a laxative (a property it does possess mildly), and more recently as a source of iron

129

and calcium. This value is debatable, though, because of the amount of oxalic acid the leaves contain, which tends, apparently, to 'lock up' nutrients like iron and calcium, rendering them unavailable. But spinach also contains a lot of Vitamin A, the vitamin which is held in all dark green vegetable leaves. My years of suffering as a child, when I was made to drink the supposedly iron-rich spinach cooking water, weren't entirely wasted then perhaps. And was that why Popeye was invented, to laud the properties of spinach for its vitamin content? Or was it just to boost the market for American spinach?

Spinach is available all year round on the whole. It has a number of relatives and rivals: a wild spinach is known as Good King Henry; there is also a mountain spinach called orache. New Zealand spinach is not related to true spinach, but can be cooked in the same ways; and spinach beet or chard is a coarser version. None is as delicate in flavour as the true spinach.

When buying spinach, as Jane Grigson says, 'assess its liveliness. It should have a bouncing, bright appearance. As you stuff it into your basket or string bag, it should crunch and squeak.' What more need I say!

To prepare it for cooking, wash it very well because, as a ground hugging plant, it will have picked up a lot of grit from the soil and rain splashes. It *can* be bought needing practically no attention, just a quick wipe, but it's better washed. Take off the large stalks, and put the leaves into a sieve. Dip into a sink of cold water and swish around as quickly as possible. Shake the sieve vigorously, and keep on repeating until clean. You could also immerse the leaves in several changes of water in the sink, but don't *leave* them immersed.

Spinach should be cooked briefly and tenderly, in only the water adhering to its leaves. It collapses quickly, leaving a green puddle at the bottom of a pan which you had initial difficulty in covering with the lid. Spinach absorbs butter to an incredible degree (see the purée recipe on the following pages), and its slightly sour taste marries well with a variety of other flavours. Spinach goes well with fish and cheese, with eggs in omelettes, quiches and soufflés, holds its own in pastry, roulades and pancake fillings (the English before the eighteenth century used to make a sweet spinach tart), and as an accompanying vegetable, as a purée, a cream, in moulds, galettes, as wrapping etc. The Indians cook spinach wonderfully; the Italians use it to turn their pasta green, and to make the frailest and most delicious gnocchi; and the Turks wrap it in filo pastry for the tantalising börek.

Spinach is also wonderful *raw*, in salads, and is one of my favourite salad leaves, because of its bright colour and really crisp texture.

SPINACH SOUP

Basic recipe (see page 11)
2lb (900g) fresh spinach leaves

This soup is very tasty, if thinner than the other soups in the book. The merest hint of Pernod in the finished product adds a little 'oomph', otherwise be generous with grated nutmeg!

BOILED SPINACH WITH NUTMEG

FOR 6 PEOPLE
2lb (900g) fresh spinach
1 teaspoon sea salt
1oz (25g) butter
1/4 teaspoon grated nutmeg

This amount of fresh spinach will give you 1 1/4–1 1/2lb (550–675g) when the stalks are removed.

Wash well in cold water, drain, then place the wet spinach into a saucepan. Add the sea salt and bring to the boil. Cook for 5 minutes, turning the spinach over once.

Drain off any water, then put between two similar-sized dinner plates and gently squeeze all surplus liquid out. Put back over heat with the butter and nutmeg for a few moments. Serve immediately.

STEAMED SPINACH

I know that less vitamins and goodness are lost when spinach is cooked this way, but it is – believe it or not – rather soggy at the end, so have a triple thickness of kitchen paper to hand, to dry it out.

12oz (350g) prepared spinach
1 pint (550ml) boiling water
Salt, freshly ground black pepper and nutmeg
Butter

Put the stalkless spinach leaves into the colander over the saucepan of boiling water with 1 teaspoon salt added. Cover (with lid or foil) and steam for:
    4 minutes – crisp
    5 minutes – firm
    6 minutes – soft
    Immediately put the spinach leaves onto the kitchen paper. Pat dry, then remove to a warm dish, season with freshly ground black pepper and salt, and – if you like it – a touch of freshly ground nutmeg. Top with a knob of butter.

SPINACH PURÉE

This is a rather simpler – and less rich and fattening – version of a spinach purée given in *Table Talk with Tovey* in which 1lb (450g) spinach was blended with (dare I say it) 12oz (350g) butter! It can be prepared earlier in the day, then simply reheated in a double saucepan.

FOR 6 PEOPLE
3lb (1.5kg) fresh spinach – about 2–2 1/4lb (1kg) when prepared
4oz (100g) butter
Salt, freshly ground black pepper and nutmeg

Wipe or wash the leaves and remove and discard the stalks. Tear the leaves up into small pieces.

Melt half the butter in a saucepan, add the spinach, and cook for 8 minutes. Liquidise and pass through a plastic sieve. Melt half the remaining butter in a saucepan, add the purée, and again cook for 5 minutes.

When you wish to reheat, melt the remaining butter in the top of a double saucepan (or a Christmas pudding-type bowl over a saucepan), add the purée and season with salt, freshly ground black pepper and a touch of nutmeg. It will take 12–15 minutes to reheat over a pan of boiling water.

SPINACH FRIED IN BACON FAT WITH CHOPPED WALNUTS

FOR 6 PEOPLE
1lb (450g) fresh spinach
1 tablespoon bacon fat
2 tablespoons walnuts, finely chopped

132

Wipe the spinach leaves, cut out any tough stalks, and dry well. Roll the leaves up into cigar-shaped lengths and then, with a sharp knife, cut through into ¼ inch (5mm) pieces.

Melt the bacon fat in a frying pan, and stir-fry the cut spinach for:

3 minutes – quite crisp
5 minutes – still pleasantly firm

Add the finely chopped walnuts and serve immediately.

This recipe can be adapted by using, instead of the bacon fat, the soy sauce with raspberry vinegar mixture or the sesame oil with raspberry vinegar mixture (see page 10).

SPINACH SOUFFLÉS

These make wonderful starters, and they're quite delicious served with some Hollandaise (see page 17).

TO FILL 6 × 3 INCH (8CM) RAMEKINS
8oz (225g) fresh spinach, after removing stalks
Butter
Salt and freshly ground black pepper
1 level tablespoon plain flour
¼ pint (150ml) milk, warmed
4 eggs, separated
1oz (25g) strong Cheddar cheese, grated
Pinch of ground nutmeg

Lightly butter and season six ramekins, and preheat the oven well to 400°F/200°C/Gas 6.

Chop up the stalkless fresh spinach, wash it and then cook it without any extra water in a saucepan over medium heat for 3–5 minutes (depending on freshness of spinach, but you want it to be simply *tender*, not overcooked). Drain it well and squeeze out any excess moisture between two dinner plates over the sink. Finely chop the spinach (*do not* purée it), and cook off briefly in 1oz (25g) butter.

In a separate saucepan melt another 1oz (25g) butter. Add the flour and mix well to a roux, gradually adding the warmed milk, a little at a time. Beat constantly until you have a thick smooth sauce. Remove from the heat and beat in the egg yolks, one at a time, making sure the mixture is still lovely and smooth after each addition. Beat in the grated cheese then fold in the spinach. Taste and add salt, pepper and nutmeg to taste.

Beat the egg whites until very stiff and lightly fold these in. Spoon into ramekins and bake on a baking tray for 25 minutes. Serve at once.

SPROUTS, see BRUSSELS SPROUTS
SPRUE, see ASPARAGUS
SQUASH, see PUMPKIN AND SQUASH
STRING BEANS, see RUNNER BEANS
SUGAR PEAS, see MANGE-TOUT PEAS
SWEDE, see TURNIP AND SWEDE

SWEETCORN

ZEA MAYS

ALONG WITH GREEN BEANS AND the potato – and perhaps the tomato – maize or corn was the most important culinary result of the discovery of the Americas by Columbus in 1492. It has been grown there for over 5000 years, and had been the staple food, let alone cereal, of the Inca, Mayan, and Aztec civilisations. It was brought to Europe by the Spanish in the late fifteenth century, and was planted in Andalucia; but didn't reach Britain until at least the middle of the sixteenth century.

Southern Europe appreciated the cereal – evident in the maize meal polenta of Italy and the Rumanian mamaliga – but the rest of the continent fed it primarily to their animals. It became starvation rations – food for the poor, for the masses – during times of famine or poverty (during the potato blight in Ireland and elsewhere, for instance, and during the Industrial Revolution in the nineteenth century). It was not until, at the earliest, after the First World War, and at the latest, after the Second World War, that America was able to show Europeans how truly to appreciate its only native crop – and in fact, probably because of her closer relations with America, Britain is still the major European consumer of corn on the cob or sweetcorn.

More than half the world's crop of maize is grown in America (with the Soviet Union close behind), and that is mainly in the corn belt of the Mississippi basin. From these southern climes come the resonant names of southern culinary literature – cornpone, cornbread, ashcake, hoecake, hominy grits. Further west it is still a major ingredient in the Mexican culinary tradition – used ground as flour in tortillas and tamales. (In fact the green husks of corn are used as the outer cooking wrapper for the best

tamales.) Corn has spread, though, throughout the world, being grown in China (think of those miniature cobs which are so delicious in stir-fry dishes), in Africa (the 'mealie' or Kaffir corn), Europe and even, now, in temperate Britain. It is a hardy plant.

The variety of maize most popular for eating as a vegetable – sweetcorn or corn on the cob – was a later hybrid. The American Indians grew it at least by the beginning of the seventeenth century, and when they introduced it to settlers, it acquired its other name, Indian corn. Sweetcorn must be eaten when immature – 'botanically green but gastronomically ripe' as Waverley Root puts it in *Food* – and indeed should be eaten as soon as plucked from the plant. The kernels are high in sugar, and as soon as picked, this sugar starts to convert to starch. Mark Twain recommended lighting a fire in the middle of the cornfield, and putting a kettle of water on to boil; when it was boiling, then and only then should the corn be picked and chucked directly into the water!

For most of us that, sadly, is an impossibility, but a rough guide to freshness is a sneaky fingernail yet again. Stick your nail through the husk (or cellophane if you must) into a kernel; if it exudes a milky liquid it's still got some life in it; if there's no liquid it's well over the hill. Colour, too, is a pointer: the kernels should be the pale yellow of youth, not the dark gold of age (although, elsewhere, in the Americas, corn can be red, purple or brown!).

To prepare corn on the cob, hold the cob at the base, and gently tear away the outer leaves from the top down to the base, and rub and pull away the long silks too. Chop off the ends. To cook, boil or steam the cobs in plenty of water *without* added salt at first, as this – as with pulses – tends to harden the kernel skin. You could add a little salt half-way through the cooking time, and perhaps a little sugar to replace some of that originally in the vegetable. If you want to use the kernels only, you could take them off the cob before cooking or after. I find it a terrible fag, but it's made easier by using a shoehorn: the curve rips the corn off quite successfully!

Although here I talk mainly about cooking the cob, maize or corn is amazingly versatile. It can be ground into meal or flour to make all the ethnic specialities already mentioned; it makes a syrup and an oil, and bourbon whiskey is a product of fermented corn. Corn kernels make a delicious creamed vegetable, can be made into fritters (the traditional accompaniment to Maryland or Southern-style chicken), and a good soufflé with cheese. Popcorn too is a favourite, salted or sweet – and apparently not such a recent one, either, as it was known to the Incas!

SWEETCORN SOUP

I must confess to using frozen sweetcorn kernels for this soup as the actual bother of boiling the raw corn on the cob, and then painstakingly removing the kernels, is a task that doesn't turn me on.

Basic recipe (see page 11)
2lb (900g) frozen sweetcorn kernels
1 lemon

Add the juice to the initial mixture, plus the lemon itself, cut into quarters.

This soup is thick, and very, very quickly forms a skin between kitchen and table.

BOILED CORN ON THE COB

Corn on the cob with its golden kernels is bursting with stored sunshine and its sweet flavour is always tempting. But I love this particular vegetable as it can be made even nicer with an over-generous helping of salted butter when serving as a starter.

Whole cobs vary considerably in length and weight, but the average one, with silks and leaves, weighs about 6oz (175g).

FOR 6 PEOPLE
6 even-sized corn on the cob
2 pints (a good litre) boiling water
2 teaspoons salt

Trim the cobs well, then bring the water to the boil in a large saucepan (I occasionally add a tablespoon of olive oil or honey). Submerge the corn and when the water comes back to the boil, cook for:

   25 minutes – crisp
   27 minutes – firm
   30 minutes – soft

Add the salt about half-way through the cooking time. Please note that these cooking times are for fresh cobs. Frozen defrosted cobs take considerably less – but in my opinion simply cannot be compared to the fresh.

Stick sturdy cocktail sticks or those special cob-holders in each end to make for easier handling when turning the corn round in the lips and teeth – just as if you were a lathe turning a stick of wood! Be very generous with the butter, and flavoured butters (see pages 15–16) can ring the changes.

STEAMED CORN ON THE COB

FOR 6 PEOPLE
6 fresh corn on the cob
1 pint (550ml) boiling water
2 teaspoons salt

Make sure that your colander will take the amount of corn you intend to cook lying *flat*. Put the colander over the boiling salted water and cover. Steam for:

   40 minutes – crisp
   45 minutes – firm
 over 50 minutes – soft

Serve as boiled, with lots of butter or flavoured butter. Freshly ground black pepper is a good addition too.

SWEETCORN FRITTERS

This mixture makes twelve 2 inch (5cm) fritters which go well with a cold meat supper or as a starter dish served with a little warmed runny honey or yoghurt.

FOR 6 PEOPLE
4oz (100g) self-raising flour, sieved
1 egg
1 teaspoon olive oil
¼ pint (150ml) milk
1 teaspoon salt
Freshly ground black pepper and a pinch of nutmeg
11oz (300g) cooked sweetcorn kernels

Make a batter with the flour, egg, oil, milk and seasonings, and leave covered for 2–3 hours to rest. Then fold in the sweetcorn kernels.

Simply line the base of your frying pan with the merest smear of your favourite cooking oil and heat to smoking. Drop dessertspoonfuls of the thick batter mixture into the pan and, using a palette knife, gently press down on to the top of each fritter. After 2–3 minutes, flip over and cook for the same time on the other side. Remove to kitchen paper and serve as soon as possible. If you cannot serve immediately, keep very hot as they tend to go stodgy as they cool.

SWEETCORN, RED PEPPER AND LEEKS WITH PARSLEY

This is a super – and easy – supper dish for one, using leftovers. Use as much or as little as you have available, or mix up a similar mixture to your fancy.

Basically you'll need about ½oz (15g) butter and 1 tablespoon olive oil, and you should fry the sweetcorn kernels off first. Then add the sliced leeks and stir-fry for a few moments. Add the finely diced red peppers for the last minute or so. All in all, no longer than about 5 minutes.

You could then add a beaten egg to the mixture to make a funny kind of omelette. Serve garnished with fresh or deep-fried parsley sprigs. And what could be simpler or more delicious!

SWEET PEPPER, see PEPPER

SWEET POTATO
IPOMOEA BATATAS

SWEET POTATOES ARE NOW increasingly available in Britain, in ethnic shops and in markets, and they look like large, elongated, knobbly, red-skinned potatoes. They are a tuber of a plant of the convolvulus family, native to tropical America, and have become one of the fifteen most important food crops in the world; along with cassava, taro and yams (with which they are sometimes, wrongly, confused), they are the staple starch or carbohydrate in the diet of the poor in many tropical countries.

They were brought back to Spain by Columbus after the discovery of America, and were probably the potato first known in Britain – as opposed to the later 'white' or common potato. The potatoes mentioned by Shakespeare were probably the sweet variety; they were then used in sweet pies and were thought of as aphrodisiac. Sweet potatoes became popular in France briefly after their introduction by the Martinique-born Empress Josephine; and the Americans still roast them to accompany their Thanksgiving turkey.

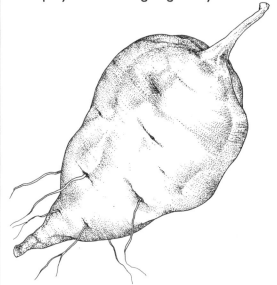

TOMATO

LYCOPERSICON ESCULENTUM

There are two basic varieties – a red-skinned one and a white-skinned one. Both have yellow flesh which contains Vitamin A; the latter are drier, less rich and have a fluffier texture when cooked.

Both can be cooked in most respects like common potatoes, but they do not keep so well. Wash them carefully before cooking, as their skins are more delicate than white potatoes, and boil with their skins on. Peel and roast alongside roast meat or poultry, sprinkled with a little seasoning such as brown sugar or cinnamon, or bake them, like ordinary baked potatoes – my favourite method of cooking them.

Choose even-sized small sweet potatoes, wash them and imbed in sea salt in a roasting tray (see page 122). Bake in a preheated oven at 375°F/190°C/Gas 5 for about 45 minutes – but test with a sharp-pointed knife. They are perfect when the skins begin to puff up a little. Serve with some cheese and herb pâté (see page 16) placed in a 2 inch (5cm) slit in the top.

BOTANICALLY SPEAKING, THE tomato is a fruit, but as it is used continually as a vegetable, it is included here (in fact it has been re-classified as a vegetable in the USA). Although such a familiar part of our culinary lives, it has been known in Europe for less than four centuries, arriving with the Spanish from Peru at the close of the sixteenth. It was only the Italians who took to it with any enthusiasm – and where would *they* be without their classic tomato sauces! For about two hundred years in Britain and elsewhere, the plant was used as a decoration rather than eaten, because it was known that it was a member of the *Solanaceae* family, along with deadly nightshade – and the potato, incidentally. (Although tomatoes aren't of course in themselves toxic, their leaves and stems can be, and tomato and potato seeds should never be sprouted like other seeds.)

In Britain we used the tomato first in ketchup, along with spices and vinegar, to render its 'toxicity' as safe as possible, presumably, and American cookbooks of the late nineteenth century recommend cooking tomatoes for no less than three hours! Even well into the twentieth century, tomatoes were thought to cause cancer. And my father, idiot that he could be at times, would never eat them in any form as he was convinced the seeds built up inside and caused appendicitis! It is really only in the last fifty years, perhaps even less, that tomatoes have become a major crop and cooking ingredient in both Britain and the States.

They were first known in Britain and France as the love apple (*pomme d'amour*), presumably deriving from the Italian name, *pomodoro* – golden apple – because the first tomatoes seen in Europe were small, round and yellow. (The present name tomato comes from the Mexican

137

tomatl.) Nowadays, tomatoes of all shapes and sizes are available: cherry (the very smallest); salad (the ubiquitous Moneymaker usually: it may make money but it doesn't do anything for the palate); plum (the fleshy elongated one which is peeled and canned); and the wonderful beefsteak varieties, huge and – usually – tasty. For sadly, after centuries of ignoring the tomato, we now seem, in the interests of large crops and lasting ability, to be ignoring it again, having bred out all taste. Perhaps this is why the tomato is the most common vegetable grown at home.

They are usually red, but can be yellow (called white by seedsmen), and there are, apparently, orange and pink varieties. The green tomato is unripe, and is wonderfully firm and tart in chutneys.

When buying tomatoes for salads, look for firmness and a bright unflawed skin. If soft, they can be used in sauces etc. If you want to stuff them, look for size; if you want them as a garnish, small ones are effective. To store them, place stalk side down, and don't put them in the fridge. Eat them up straight away and buy often.

I needn't say much about preparation, as everyone knows how to prepare a tomato. To skin them, though, is another matter. Many tomatoes today have bred into them a thicker, more indigestible skin, and this needs to be removed for a number of recipes. Make a small nick in the skin with a sharp knife, and place in a bowl. Pour over boiling water and leave for about 10–15 seconds. Drain, and slip off the top of the skinned tomato, scoop out all the seeds with a teaspoon and drain, upside down, to remove all the liquid. Chop finely to make a delicious and healthy raw tomato sauce or garnish – this is the tomato concasse mentioned in a few recipes.

Tomatoes, a reasonable source of Vitamin C, are used both raw and cooked. Raw, they are wonderful sliced in salads with their favourite ally, fresh chopped basil. They're also quite fond

of onions and garlic – and a sprinkling of walnut oil is a great taste treat. In sandwiches they're delicious with lots of creamy butter and freshly ground black pepper, and they can be stuffed raw with a variety of fillings – cheese and herb pâté (see page 16), prawns in mayonnaise, or an avocado mix. They make a delicious aspic mould, can even be made into an ice cream, and where would many restaurants be without their mixed salads with tomatoes, or their tomato garnishes, whole, halved or vandyked? Cooked, they are even more versatile: they can be stuffed and baked, grilled for breakfast, made into the children's favourite soup, made into classic sauces like the Italian napolitana, concentrates, purées, ketchups, a jam, and the juice for my Sunday morning Bloody Mary. They can be baked in tarts, and are an essential ingredient of ratatouille (see page 119).

TOMATO SOUP

Basic recipe (see page 11)
2lb (900g) tomatoes

Do not remove the stalks of the tomatoes. Just pile everything, flesh, skin, stalks and all, onto the golden cooked onions, and what a joyous sight it is!

Basil is the natural herb to go with this, or fresh garden mint. Chop finely with a little sugar and sprinkle over the soup as a garnish.

TOMATO, APPLE AND CELERY SOUP

Basic recipe (see page 11)
10oz (300g) tomatoes
10oz (300g) apples
10oz (300g) celery stalks

Leave the stalks on the tomatoes, and simply wipe the apples before cutting into eight sections.

BAKED TOMATOES

In my earlier days at Miller Howe, not an evening went by when a stuffed or baked tomato in some guise or other didn't flaunt itself on the main-course dinner plate. I thought the colour visually appealing, and the actual tomato could be a handy casing for using up leftovers. Simply baked whole and garnished with a sprig of parsley, it was an easy and attractive addition . . . until one year *The Good Food Guide* said extremely rude things and rarely since has a baked or stuffed tomato been served at the hotel. However, at home, I still adore them.

To bake tomatoes whole, place them on a buttered baking sheet, with the stalk side down, so that they balance. Put in the preheated oven at 350°F/180°C/Gas 4. Tomatoes weighing 2½–3oz (60–75g) will take 10 minutes until firm, but cooked. Tomatoes of 3½–4oz (90–100g) will take 12 minutes.

And tomatoes can be stuffed and baked – with mushroom pâté, cooked sausagemeat or any filling, leftover bacon and bits from breakfast (black pudding is a favourite of mine) – as well as stuffed, raw and cold, with something like cheese and herb pâté.

Simply hold the tomato firmly on your cutting board, stalk side down, and gently slice through two-thirds of the top (as if you were breaking into a breakfast boiled egg). Raise this up carefully to act as a hinged lid, and then using a Parisian scoop or teaspoon, take out the seeded centre. If your tomatoes are not particularly sweet, add the merest touch of castor sugar at this stage to bring out the dormant flavour.

Stuff the tomatoes with whatever you fancy (see above for some ideas), and bake exactly as the whole baked tomatoes. Insert a sprig of parsley in the open mouth just before serving.

TOMATO PROVENÇALE

This fresh tomato sauce has many uses. You can freeze it, and it will keep in the fridge for up to a week.

2oz (50g) butter
4 fat cloves garlic, peeled
2 teaspoons salt
4oz (100g) onions, finely chopped
1½lb (675g) tomatoes, peeled, seeded and roughly chopped

Melt the butter in a saucepan, and crush the garlic with the salt. Fry the garlic paste and onions in the butter until golden, and then add the chopped tomatoes. Simmer slowly for about an hour until thick, stirring occasionally.

MRS P.'S GREEN TOMATO CHUTNEY

FILLS ABOUT 4 × 1LB (450G) JARS
3½lb (1.6kg) green tomatoes
1lb (450g) onions
2 tablespoons salt
½lb (225g) apples, peeled and cored
VINEGAR MIXTURE
1¼ pints (700ml) malt vinegar
1lb (450g) demerara sugar
2 tablespoons English mustard powder
1 dessertspoon curry powder
½lb (225g) sultanas
1 teaspoon Cayenne pepper
1 teaspoon ground allspice

Roughly slice the tomatoes. Peel the onions and cut them up roughly. Cover with the salt, and leave overnight, covered. In the morning, strain away the salty juices.

Place the vinegar mixture ingredients into a saucepan and bring them to the boil.

Meanwhile, mince the tomatoes and onions, along with the peeled and cored apples (in a meat mincer rather than a processor – you don't want them *too* small).

When the vinegar is boiling and well mixed, add the minced ingredients, and boil until soft – normally about 35–45 minutes.

While this is boiling, pour boiling water into the jam jars to sterilise them. Dry them and fill when the mixture has cooled a little, then seal well. Store as you would any other preserve, and do not use for at least 6 weeks.

TURNIP AND SWEDE

BRASSICA RAPA and *BRASSICA CAMPESTRIS RUTABAGA*

TURNIPS AND SWEDES ARE members of the same family as cabbage, Brussels sprouts etc, and I have put them together because the cooking methods and recipes are so similar. I have also put them together because there is a great deal of confusion about these vegetables. When is a turnip a swede, and when is a swede a turnip?! As a northerner, *my* turnip is the big purple vegetable with a yellow flesh, and *my* swede is the tennis-ball, white-skinned vegetable. This is precisely the opposite of what everyone else considers to be turnips and swedes! The bashed neeps beloved of the Scots on Burns' Night to accompany the haggis, obviously derive from the suffix of tur*nips*, but neeps must be yellow, so they're swedes. And to confuse matters even further, when the Americans aren't calling swedes turnips they're calling them rutabagas! The following descriptions of the vegetables are the botanical ones, the common ones found in most reference books (obviously written by southerners), although *I* still think the swede is white and the turnip yellow! (Colour and size should govern in the recipes therefore.)

Historically, though, turnips and swedes differ considerably. Turnips were eaten by the Romans – their name comes from the Latin, *napus* – and were the staple food of the poor in Europe before the arrival of potatoes. Despite the fact that they now do magical things with them, the French so looked down upon turnips that they would call an unsuccessful picture, book or play a *navet* or turnip (what the British would call a flop, and the Americans a turkey – whatever did happen to the language in that Atlantic crossing?). Swedes in comparison are johnny-come-lately vegetables on the culinary and botanical scene, for in spite of their name (a contraction of Swedish turnip), they are thought to have originated in Bohemia in the seventeenth century.

Turnips (*Brassica rapa*) come in all shapes and sizes, but should really be eaten when they are young, about the size of an orange. They are at

141

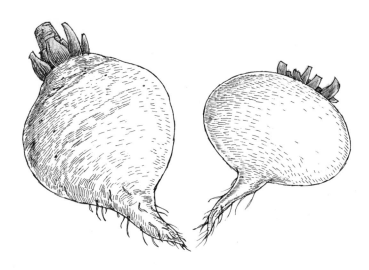

this stage in spring and summer, but can be left to grow larger and stronger in flavour (when they can also be a bit stringy). Young baby turnips are smooth-skinned white, pale green or violet, and can be boiled, steamed, baked whole, made into soup, glazed, buttered and used in pickles. Maincrop turnips can be used in stew – where, like swedes, they have a remarkable ability to absorb flavour, and are best used with fattier meats like mutton, duck, goose and smoked sausages – and are often mashed with butter, cream and other flavourings. The Japanese and Koreans julienne turnip into soups, mixed vegetable dishes and pickles, and raw grated turnip is good in salad. Turnip tops or leaves can be used as spring greens.

Swedes (*Brassica campestris rutabaga*) are larger than turnips, with a rougher skin – almost corrugated at the top – of a purplish-brown, white or yellow colour. Their flesh is bright yellow-orange, not white, and they taste sweeter than turnips. They are more for winter eating, although immature swedes pulled in late summer are good. They, too, can be boiled, steamed, baked and made into soups and purées (try mixing puréed swede with mashed potato as well). Swedes make a good tasty soufflé, and are also good in fatty stews and casseroles. In the American Mid-West, rutabagas are candied; in Finland, swedes are casseroled with cream and spices, and apparently swede root shoots or sprouts, which appear after the vegetable has been lifted and stored, are good boiled and served with butter like asparagus.

Buy bright looking vegetables, and avoid those that look too knobbly or faded. To prepare young turnips, scrub only or peel thinly; older turnips and swedes will need peeling quite thickly. Then slice, dice or quarter as the recipe demands, dropping pieces into acidulated water to prevent discoloration.

YELLOW TURNIP/SWEDE SOUP

Basic recipe (see page 11)
2lb (900g) turnip/swede, peeled
2 tablespoons dried dill

WHITE TURNIP/SWEDE SOUP

Basic recipe (see page 11)
2lb (900g) turnip/swede, peeled
1 teaspoon mustard or horseradish cream
Cranberries

Garnish with just defrosted but not softened whole cranberries. These can be fairly bitter, so the reheated soup may need a little sweetening.

BOILED OR STEAMED SWEDES OR TURNIPS

FOR 6 PEOPLE
1lb (450g) swedes or turnips
2 pints (a good litre) boiling water
2 teaspoons salt

Top, tail and peel and you will be left with about 12oz (350g). Cut into ¼ inch (5mm) cubes.

The cooking times are identical whether you are boiling them in the salted water or steaming them over it:
    4 minutes – crisp
    5 minutes – firm
    6 minutes – soft
You can boil them with 1 tablespoon dill seeds in the water, but it's sometimes embarrassing to denture wearers, so beware. I also adore caraway seeds, and they too go well with these vegetables, but they introduce the same dental problem.

DICED TURNIPS OR SWEDES WITH HONEY

FOR 6 PEOPLE
1lb (450g) turnips or swedes
2 tablespoons (at least) clear runny honey

Prepare the vegetables as in the previous recipe and then cook, by boiling or steaming, to the *crisp* stage only.

Drain well, and put back into the saucepan over a low heat for a few minutes to dry out. Then add runny clear honey to personal taste. Heat for a few moments, tossing, then serve immediately.

PIQUANT SWEDE OR TURNIPS

FOR 6 PEOPLE
1lb (450g) swede or turnip
Granulated sugar
2oz (50g) butter
2oz (50g) onion, finely chopped
2 tablespoons wine vinegar
Salt and freshly ground black pepper
2 teaspoons grated horseradish
½ teaspoon grated orange rind

Prepare and boil vegetable as in the previous recipe, with 1 teaspoon sugar added to the water, until crisp preferably. Melt the butter in a pan and fry the chopped onion gently. Stir in about 2 tablespoons sugar plus the remaining ingredients. Season to taste. Heat, stirring constantly, then combine gently with the crisp vegetable dice. Keep warm in a double boiler.

FRIED TURNED VEGETABLES

FOR 6 PEOPLE
8oz (225g) each of carrot, parsnip and turnip or swede, topped, tailed and peeled
Olive oil
Butter
Sea salt and freshly ground black pepper

Cut the vegetables into chip-sized pieces about 2 inches (5cm) long, and as thick as your thumb. With a small sharp stainless steel knife, shape each 'chip' from the middle to each end until it looks like a mini cucumber. Leave to soak in water while you finish the rest. Keep them separate.

In a saucepan large enough to hold a metal sieve, bring lots of salted water to the boil. Place the carrots in the sieve, and submerge in the water. Bring back to the boil, and cook for 2 minutes. Do the same, separately, with the parsnips and turnips or swedes, then drain them all thoroughly and dry.

When you wish finally to cook and serve, coat a small frying pan with a smear of olive oil and, when smoking, add a similar amount of butter (see page 9 for a hint on proportions). Place the parcooked, drained, dried vegetables in the pan, and stir-fry for 4 minutes. Season liberally with sea salt and freshly ground black pepper and serve at once.

These vegetables taste even better if you fry a tablespoon of finely chopped onions and mix them in with a generous sprinkling of chopped parsley.

CARROT, TURNIP AND HAZELNUT LETTUCE MOULD

FILLS 6 × 3 INCH (8CM) RAMEKINS
6oz (175g) carrots, peeled
6oz (175g) turnips or swedes, peeled
1oz (25g) butter
3 tablespoons double cream
2 tablespoons hazelnuts, skinned and chopped
3 egg yolks
2 egg whites
Good pinch each of onion salt and ground ginger
6 lettuce leaves, blanched

Cut the peeled vegetables in even, small pieces, and put in a saucepan of salted water. Bring to the boil and cook with the lid on for 15–20 minutes. Remove from the heat, and drain. Put back into the saucepan, add the butter, and simmer for a moment to dry out.

Put this mixture into your food processor or blender and add the cream and hazelnuts. Whizz around until the mixture is fairly smooth, adding the egg yolks one at a time. Beat the egg whites in a separate bowl until stiff, and add the onion salt and ginger. Fold the vegetable mixture gently into the stiff egg white. (The dishes can be prepared to this stage the day before.)

Grease and season the ramekins, and put a blanched lettuce leaf in the base and up the sides of each. Divide the mixture between the ramekins and then put them into a roasting tray. Pour in boiling water to come half-way up the sides of the ramekins, and cook in a preheated oven at 375°F/190°C/Gas 5 for 15–20 minutes. If the main course is not quite ready, turn off the oven and leave moulds for 5–10 minutes. They will come to no harm.

When serving, run a sharp knife round the edge of each ramekin, and turn out onto the individual serving plates. They look most attractive.

VEGETABLE MARROW, see MARROW
ZUCCHINI, see COURGETTES

INDEX

A

Acton, Eliza, 36
Alexander the Great, 108
alfalfa, beansprouts, 27
almond:
   cabbage with orange, 40
   fennel and almond soup, 75
   steamed whole cauliflower with
     toasted almonds, 52
anise, 45
Apicius, 33
apple:
   beetroot and apple soup, 29
   cabbage with cider, 40
   carrot and apple soup, 47
   celery baked with yoghurt,
     apple and red pepper, 60
   diced celeriac with grated
     apples and garden peas, 56
   Mrs P.'s green tomato chutney,
     140
   spiced red cabbage with apples
     and orange, 43
   tomato, apple and celery soup,
     139
apple cucumber, 70
artichoke, globe, *see* globe
   artichoke
artichoke, Jerusalem, *see* Jerusalem
   artichoke
artichoke hearts, 82
asparagus, 22–4, 34
   asparagus soup, 23
   baked asparagus, 24
   boiled asparagus, 23
   nutrients, 23
   preparation, 22–3
   quiche, 15
aubergine, 24–6
   aubergine soup, 26
   deep-fried aubergine chips, 26
   deep-fried aubergines, 26, 69
   degorging, 25
   preparation, 25
   ratatouille, 119–20
   savoury aubergine casserole,
     26
   slicing, 6–7
avocado oil, 9

B

baby onions fried in dripping, 110
bacon:
   bacon cabbage boats, 41
   baked broccoli with bacon, 36
   Jerusalem artichokes fried with
     bacon, onion and garlic, 85
   leeks cooked with bacon and
     cheese, 94
   savoury Jerusalem artichokes, 86
   savoury potatoes, 123
bacon fat, 9
   bacon walnut cabbage, 42
   broccoli fried in, 35
   leeks and mushrooms in bacon
     fat with croûtons, 93
   spinach fried in bacon fat with
     chopped walnuts, 132
baked vegetables:
   asparagus, 24
   broccoli with bacon, 36
   cabbage with garlic and juniper,
     42
   celery baked with yoghurt,
     apple and red pepper, 60
   celery with onions and pepper,
     60
   chicory with cheese and herb
     pâté, 63
   chicory with garlic, 63
   chicory with orange, 63
   chicory with star anise, 63
   courgette cups, 68
   courgettes baked in honey and
     raspberry vinegar, 67
   courgettes baked in honey and
     soya sauce, 67
   fennel quarters, 76
   kohlrabi with cream and cheese,
     88–9
   leeks baked in cheese pastry, 92
   lettuce, 97
   marrow rounds, 101
   mushrooms, 104
   onions stuffed with cheese,
     110–11
   parsnip with cream and cheese,
     114
   potatoes, 122

savoury cabbage, 42
savoury celery, 59
stuffed marrow, 101
stuffed red pepper, 119
tomatoes, 139
bamboo steamers, 8
bamia, *see* okra
banana, with stir-fried vegetables,
   8
basic double cream sauce, 18
basic vegetable soup, 11–12
basic white sauce, 17
basil: tomato soup, 139
batavia, *see* endive
Batavian endive, 73
batter:
   for deep-fried courgettes, 69
   sweetcorn fritters, 135–6
beans, broad, *see* broad beans
beans, French, *see* French beans
beans, runner, *see* runner beans
beansprouts, 27
   nutrients, 27
   to sprout, 27
beefsteak tomatoes, 138
Beeton, Mrs, 70, 87, 90
beetroot, 28–30
   beetroot and apple soup, 29
   beetroot, onion and cheese
     savoury, 29
   beetroot soup, 29
   grated beetroot fried with
     orange and walnut oil, 29
   preparation, 28
   steamed beetroot balls, 30
Belgian endive, *see* chicory
bell peppers, *see* peppers
bindi, *see* okra
blackcurrant and onion sauce,
   111–12
boiled vegetables, 8
   asparagus, 23
   broccoli, 35
   Brussels sprouts, 37
   corn on the cob, 135
   diced celeriac, 55
   fennel, 75
   French beans, 78
   garlic cloves, 80
   Jerusalem artichokes, 85

boiled vegetables – *cont.*
 kohlrabi, 88
 lettuce quarters, 97
 maincrop carrots, 48
 new baby carrots, 47
 new potatoes, 122
 runner beans, 129
 spinach with nutmeg, 131
 swedes, 142
 turnips, 142
borecole, *see* kale
bread:
 leeks and mushrooms in bacon
  fat with croûtons, 93
 potato, cheese and garlic bread,
  125
breadcrumbs:
 baked onions stuffed with
  cheese, 110–11
 celeriac croquettes, 56
 golden potato wedges, 122
 onions baked in milk with
  nutmeg, 109–10
 parsnip croquettes, 114
 savoury cheese breadcrumbs, 19
 savoury fillings, 19
 savoury ham filling, 19
 savoury minced onions, 111
broad beans, 30–3
 broad bean hazelnut soup, 31
 broad bean lemon soup, 31
 broad bean soup, 31
 broad beans with cheese sauce,
  32
 broad beans with French
  dressing, 32
 broad beans with wine sauce, 32
 dried, 31
 old broad beans cooked in
  sweet white wine, 33
 preparation, 31
 purée of broad beans, 32
 quiche, 15
 steamed broad beans, 32
broccoli, 33–6, 39, 51, 86
 baked broccoli with bacon, 36
 boiled broccoli, 35
 broccoli fried in bacon fat, 35
 broccoli fried with sesame and
  raspberry, 35

broccoli with Hollandaise, 35
broccoli with tarragon cream,
 35
broccoli polonaise, 35
broccoli soup, 34
preparation, 34
quiche, 15
steamed broccoli heads, 34
Brussels sprouts, 33, 36–8, 39, 86,
 141
 boiled or steamed Brussels
  sprouts, 37
 Brussels sprouts soup, 38
 fried Brussels sprouts with
  chestnuts, 38
 preparation, 37
 purée of Brussels sprouts, 38
buckwheat, beansprouts, 27
butter:
 flavoured butters, 15–16
 garlic, 16
 herb, 16
 horseradish, 16
 lemon, 16
 lime, 16
 orange, 16
 relish, 16
 for stir-frying, 9
 tomato, 16
 tomato and mustard, 16
 walnut, 16
buttered fresh young garden peas,
 117
butterhead lettuce, 95
butternut squash, 126
 see also squash
button onions, 108
buying vegetables, 5

C

cabbage, 39–44, 86, 141
 bacon cabbage boats, 41
 bacon walnut cabbage, 42
 baked cabbage with garlic and
  juniper, 42
 baked savoury cabbage, 42
 cabbage with cider, 40
 cabbage with orange, 40
 cabbage boats, 40–1

cabbage platter, 41
preparation, 40
stuffed cabbage, 43
stuffed cabbage boats, 41
see also Chinese leaf; red
 cabbage
cabbage lettuce, 95
cabbage-turnip, *see* kohlrabi
calabrese, 33
 see also broccoli
capsicum, *see* peppers
caraway seeds: glazed carrots with
 caraway and lemon, 48
carbohydrates, 5
cardoon, 81
carrot, 45–50
 boiled maincrop carrots, 48
 boiled new baby carrots, 47
 carrot and apple soup, 47
 carrot and coriander soup, 47
 carrot and ginger soup, 47
 carrot and orange soup, 47
 carrot and spinach soup, 47
 carrot soup, 47
 carrot, turnip and hazelnut
  lettuce mould, 144
 carrots glazed with coriander,
  49
 carrots glazed with fresh lime,
  49
 carrots glazed with marjoram,
  48
 carrots glazed with Pernod, 49
 carrots glazed with thyme, 48
 carrots mashed with black
  pepper and horseradish, 49
 carrots mashed with black
  pepper and orange, 49
 cold poached leeks with savoury
  yoghurt, 92
 deep-fried carrots, 50
 food values, 5
 fried grated carrots with
  radishes, 50
 fried turned vegetables, 143
 glazed carrots with caraway and
  lemon, 48
 grated carrots with orange and
  walnut oil, 50
 preparation, 46

purée of carrots, 49
slicing, 6–7
steamed maincrop carrots, 48
steamed new baby carrots, 48
cassava, 136
casserole, savoury aubergine, 26
Cassis: onion and blackcurrant
   sauce, 111–12
Cato, 39
cauliflower, 33, 39, 51–3
   cauliflower with cheese sauce,
      53
   cauliflower with chopped
      walnuts, 53
   cauliflower with fresh thyme,
      53
   cauliflower with grated cheese,
      53
   cauliflower with Hollandaise, 53
   cauliflower with mushroom
      sauce, 53
   cauliflower with nutmeg and
      diced ginger, 53
   cauliflower cheese soup, 52
   cauliflower purée, 53
   cauliflower soup, 52
   cauliflower stir-fried in sesame
      and raspberry, 54
   preparation, 52
   quiche, 15
   steamed whole cauliflower with
      toasted almonds, 52
   stir-fried cauliflower with
      coriander, 53–4
cayenne pepper, 118
celeriac, 54–7
   boiled diced celeriac, 55
   celeriac and courgette cake,
      56–7
   celeriac chips, 57
   celeriac croquettes, 56
   celeriac purée, 56
   celeriac soup, 55
   diced celeriac with cheese and
      chives, 56
   diced celeriac with grated
      apples and garden peas, 56
   diced celeriac with honey, 56
   diced celeriac with lemon and
      thyme, 55

grated celeriac with
   horseradish, 57
pan-fried celeriac balls, 57
preparation, 55
savoury stuffed courgettes, 68
celery, 58–61
   baked celery with onions and
      pepper, 60
   baked savoury celery, 59
   celery and dill soup, 59
   celery and fennel soup, 59
   celery baked with yoghurt,
      apple and red pepper, 60
   cream of celery soup, 59
   lightly curried, deep-fried celery
      strips, 61
   preparation, 59
   stir-fried celery with
      sesame-raspberry sauce, 60–1
   tomato, apple and celery soup,
      139
celery seeds, 58
cellulose, 5
celtuce, 96
chard, 28, 130
   see also spinach
Charles I, King of England, 45, 128
chayote, 126
cheese:
   baked fennel quarters, 76
   baked kohlrabi with cream and
      cheese, 88–9
   baked onions stuffed with
      cheese, 110–11
   baked parsnip with cream and
      cheese, 114
   baked savoury cabbage, 42
   baked savoury celery, 59
   beetroot, onion and cheese
      savoury, 29
   broad beans with cheese sauce,
      32
   cauliflower with cheese sauce,
      53
   cauliflower with grated cheese,
      53
   cauliflower cheese soup, 52
   cheese and mustard sauce, 17
   courgettes in cheese custard,
      69

diced celeriac with cheese and
   chives, 56
Jerusalem artichokes with cream
   and cheese, 85
leeks baked in cheese pastry, 92
leeks cooked with bacon and
   cheese, 94
onions baked in milk with
   nutmeg, 109–10
port and Stilton cheese, 16
potato, cheese and garlic bread,
   125
potatoes baked with cream and
   cheese, 123
sauce, 17
savoury cheese breadcrumbs, 19
savoury ham filling, 19
savoury minced onions, 111
savoury pastry, 14
savoury stuffed courgettes, 68
spinach soufflés, 132
   see also cream cheese
cherry tomatoes, 138
chervil, 45
chestnuts:
   fried Brussels sprouts with
      chestnuts, 38
   see also water chestnuts
chick peas, 31
   beansprouts, 27
chicken:
   savoury filling, 19
   stock, 11
chicory, 61–3, 72, 73
   baked chicory with cheese and
      herb pâté, 63
   baked chicory with garlic, 63
   baked chicory with orange, 63
   baked chicory with star anise, 63
   chicory braised in orange juice,
      62
   preparation, 62
   steamed chicory, 62
chilli peppers, 117, 118
chilli powder, 118
Chinese artichoke, 84
Chinese cabbage, 39
   see also Chinese leaf
Chinese leaf, 64
   preparation, 64

Chinese peas, see mange-tout peas
chives, 108
  diced celeriac with cheese and
    chives, 56
  steamed French bean parcels, 78
chopping, 6–7
chutney, Mrs P.'s green tomato,
    140
cider:
  cabbage with cider, 40
  old broad beans cooked in,
    32–3
cinnamon: roast pumpkin, 127
citrus rind, with stir-fried
    vegetables, 8
citrus twirls, 20
cocktail onions, 108
coconut:
  celeriac croquettes, 56
  with stir-fried vegetables, 8
coffee, dandelion, 72
cold poached leeks with savoury
    yoghurt, 92
collards, 39, 87
  see also kale
Columbus, Christopher, 70, 77,
    95, 100, 115, 117, 128, 133,
    136
cooking techniques, 8–10
coriander seeds, 10
  carrot and coriander soup, 47
  carrots glazed with coriander,
    49
  marinated mushrooms, 105
  stir-fried cauliflower with
    coriander, 53–4
corn, see sweetcorn
corn oil, 9
corn on the cob, 133
  boiled corn on the cob, 135
  preparation, 134
  steamed corn on the cob, 135
  see also sweetcorn
corn salad, 96
Cos lettuce, 95, 96
courgette, 65–9, 70, 100, 126
  baked courgette cups, 68
  celeriac and courgette cake,
    56–7
  courgette and fennel soup, 66

courgette and rosemary soup,
    66
courgette soup, 66
courgettes baked in honey and
    raspberry vinegar, 67
courgettes baked in honey and
    soya sauce, 67
courgettes braised with orange,
    67
courgettes in cheese custard, 69
courgettes with Marsala, 66
deep-fried courgettes, 69
degorging, 65–6
fennel and courgette soup, 75
grated courgettes with fresh
    lime, 67
grated courgettes with lemon,
    67
grated courgettes with orange,
    67
preparation, 65–6
quiche, 15
ratatouille, 119–20
savoury stuffed courgettes, 68
slicing, 6–7
courgette flowers, 66
cranberry: white turnip/swede
    soup, 142
cream:
  baked kohlrabi with cream and
    cheese, 88–9
  baked parsnip with cream and
    cheese, 114
  basic double cream sauce, 18
  Jerusalem artichokes with cream
    and cheese, 85
  potatoes baked with cream and
    cheese, 123
  savoury Jerusalem artichokes,
    86
cream, soured, Norwegian red
    cabbage, 44
cream cheese:
  bacon cabbage boats, 41
  baked chicory with cheese and
    herb pâté, 63
  cheese and herb pâté, 16
  see also cheese
cream of celery soup, 59
cream of onion soup, 109

Crème de Cassis: onion and
    blackcurrant sauce, 111–12
croquettes:
  celeriac, 56
  herbed potato scones, 125
  oatmeal potato, 125
  parsnip, 114
croûtons: leeks and mushrooms in
    bacon fat with, 93
cucumber, 65, 70–2, 126
  cucumber balls, 71
  Persian cucumber soup, 71
  preparation, 71
  ridge cucumber cups, 72
Culpeper, Nicholas, 79
cumin, 118
curly kale, 86
  see also kale
curry:
  deep-fried curried leek rounds,
    94
  lightly curried, deep-fried celery
    strips, 61
  parsnip soup, 113
custard:
  courgettes in cheese custard, 69
  onion, 111
custard squash, 126
cutting, 6

D

dandelion, 72–3
dandelion coffee, 72
dandelion flower honey, 73
dandelion flowers, 73
David, St, 90
David, Elizabeth, 65
deep-fried vegetables:
  aubergine, 26
  aubergine chips, 26
  aubergines, 69
  carrots, 50
  courgettes, 69
  curried leek rounds, 94
  garlic cloves, 80
  kohlrabi matchsticks, 89
  marrow balls, 101
  onions, 111
  parsley, 20

diced celeriac with cheese and
    chives, 56
diced celeriac with grated apples
    and garden peas, 56
diced celeriac with honey, 56
diced celeriac with lemon and
    thyme, 55
diced turnips or swedes with
    honey, 143
dietary fibre, 5
dill seeds:
    celery and dill soup, 59
    yellow turnip/swede soup, 142
Drake, Sir Francis, 120
dressings, see salad dressings
dripping, baby onions fried in, 110
duck fat, 9
Dutch white cabbage, 39
dwarf beans, see French beans

E

eggplant, see aubergine
eggs:
    onion custard, 111
    spinach soufflés, 132
Elizabeth I, Queen of England, 77
Emerson, Lucy, 79
endive, 61, 73–4
    preparation, 74
equipment:
    electric equipment, 7–8
    food processors, 12, 15
    frying pans, 9
    knives, 6
    liquidizers, 12
    steamers, 8
escarole, 73
Evelyn, John, 72

F

fanned roast potatoes, 124
fats and oils, 5, 9–10
    bacon fat, 9
    duck fat, 9
    garlic oil, 9–10
    sesame oil with raspberry
        vinegar, 10
fava beans, see broad beans

fennel (bulb), 45, 74–6
    baked fennel quarters, 76
    boiled fennel, 75
    celery and fennel soup, 59
    courgette and fennel soup, 66
    fennel and almond soup, 75
    fennel and courgette soup, 75
    fennel soup, 75
    preparation, 75
    quiche, 15
    ratatouille, 119–20
    steamed fennel, 76
    steamed whole fennel, 76
fennel leaves, 45, 74, 75
fennel seeds, 74
fenugreek, beansprouts, 27
fibre, dietary, 5
field mushrooms, 102
field peas, 115
fillings:
    savoury, 19
    savoury ham filling, 19
finocchio, see fennel (bulb)
flavoured butters, 15–16
Florence fennel, see fennel (bulb)
flowers:
    courgette, 66
    dandelion, 73
    marrow, 66
food processors, 12, 15
freezing:
    flavoured butters, 15
    soups, 12
    stock, 12
French beans, 5, 77–8, 128
    boiled or steamed French beans,
        78
    French bean salad, 78
    matchstick French beans, 78
    preparation, 77
    quiche, 15
    steamed French bean parcels, 78
French dressing, 18
    broad beans with, 32
fried vegetables:
    Brussels sprouts with chestnuts,
        38
    grated carrots with radishes, 50
    lettuce with nuts and pineapple,
        97

red peppers with onion, 119
spring onions, 112
turned vegetables, 143
see also deep-fried vegetables;
    pan-fried vegetables; stir-fried
    vegetables
fritters, sweetcorn, 135–6
frying pans, for stir-frying, 9
fuls, 30

G

garden peas, 115
garden peas with lettuce and red
    pepper, 116
garlic, 79–80, 90, 108
    baked cabbage with garlic and
        juniper, 42
    baked chicory with garlic, 63
    boiled garlic cloves, 80
    deep-fried garlic cloves, 80
    garlic butter, 16
    garlic oil, 10
    Jerusalem artichokes fried with
        bacon, onion and garlic, 85
    marinated mushrooms, 105
    potato, cheese and garlic bread,
        125
    preparation, 80
    ratatouille, 119–20
    shallow-fried garlic cloves, 80
    tomato Provençale, 140
garlic presses, 79
garnishes, citrus twirls, 20
Gerard, John, 71, 98
gherkin, 65, 70, 71
ginger, 84
    carrot and ginger soup, 47
    cauliflower with nutmeg and
        diced ginger, 53
    grated kohlrabi fried with
        ginger, 89
    marrow soup, 101
    parsnip soup, 113
    for stir-fried vegetables, 8
glazed baby onions, 110
glazed carrots with caraway and
    lemon, 48
glazed carrots with coriander, 49
glazed carrots with fresh lime, 49

glazed carrots with marjoram, 48
glazed carrots with Pernod, 49
glazed carrots with thyme, 48
globe artichoke, 81–2
    preparation, 81–2
golden beetroot, 28
golden potato wedges, 122
Good King Henry, 130
    see also spinach
goose fat, 9
gourds, 70, 100, 126
grated beetroot fried with orange
    and walnut oil, 29
grated carrots with orange and
    walnut oil, 50
grated celeriac with horseradish,
    57
grated courgettes with fresh lime,
    67
grated courgettes with lemon, 67
grated courgettes with orange, 67
grated kohlrabi fried with ginger,
    89
grating, 7–8
green beans, 133
    see also French beans; runner
    beans
green peppers, see peppers
Grigson, Jane, 28, 36, 51, 65, 82,
    90, 103, 115, 130
gumbo (okra), 107

H

ham, savoury ham filling, 19
haricot beans, 30, 77
haricots verts, see French beans
Hartley, Dorothy, 31, 59, 102
hazelnut oil, 9
hazelnuts:
    broad bean hazelnut soup, 31
    Brussels sprouts soup, 38
    carrot, turnip and hazelnut
    lettuce mould, 144
hemlock, 45
Henry II, King of France, 33
Henry VIII, King of England, 95
herbs:
    cheese and herb pâté, 16
    chopping, 7

herb butter, 16
herbed potato scones, 125
    see also individual types of herb
Hollandaise, 17
    broccoli with Hollandaise, 35
    cauliflower with Hollandaise, 53
honey:
    courgettes baked in honey and
    raspberry vinegar, 67
    courgettes baked in honey and
    soya sauce, 67
    diced celeriac with honey, 56
    diced turnips or swedes with
    honey, 143
    mushy marrowfat peas, 116–17
hop shoots, 82
horseradish, 83
    carrots mashed with black
    pepper and horseradish, 49
    grated celeriac with
    horseradish, 57
    horseradish butter, 16
    piquant swede or turnips, 143
    preparation, 83

I

Iceberg lettuce, 95, 96
Italian red onions, 108

J

jalapeño peppers, 118
Jefferson, Thomas, 25, 36, 74, 115,
    129
Jerusalem artichoke, 84–6
    boiled or steamed Jerusalem
    artichokes, 85
    Jerusalem artichoke soup, 85
    Jerusalem artichokes with cream
    and cheese, 85
    Jerusalem artichokes fried with
    bacon, onion and garlic, 85
    preparation, 84
    quiche, 15
    savoury Jerusalem artichokes, 86
Johnson, Dr, 70
Josephine, Empress, 136
juniper berries, baked cabbage
    with garlic and, 42

K

kale, 33, 39, 86–7
    preparation, 87
kidney beans, see French beans
knife racks, 6
knife sharpeners, 6
knives, 6
kohlrabi, 39, 87–9
    baked kohlrabi with cream and
    cheese, 88–9
    boiled kohlrabi, 88
    deep-fried kohlrabi matchsticks,
    89
    grated kohlrabi fried with
    ginger, 89
    preparation, 88
    steamed kohlrabi, 88

L

ladies' fingers (okra), 107
lamb, savoury filling, 19
leaf vegetables:
    nutrients, 5
    shredding, 7
    see also individual types of leaf
    vegetable
leek, 79, 90–4, 108
    cold poached leeks with savoury
    yoghurt, 92
    deep-fried curried leek rounds,
    94
    leek and potato soup, 91
    leek soup, 91
    leeks and mushrooms in bacon
    fat with croûtons, 93
    leeks baked in cheese pastry,
    92
    leeks cooked with bacon and
    cheese, 94
    leeks, spring onions and peas
    with tomato concasse, 94
    poached leeks, 91
    preparation, 91
    quiche, 15
    sliced leeks cooked in Noilly
    Prat, 93
    sliced leeks cooked in orange
    juice, 93

sliced leeks cooked in white
  wine, 93
sliced leeks cooked in yoghurt,
  92
steamed French bean parcels, 78
sweetcorn, red pepper and
  leeks with parsley, 136
lemon:
  broad bean lemon soup, 31
  citrus twirls, 20
  diced celeriac with lemon and
    thyme, 55
  glazed carrots with caraway and
    lemon, 48
  grated courgettes with lemon,
    67
  lemon butter, 16
  lemon, pea and sweetcorn soup,
    116
  sweetcorn soup, 135
lettuce, 95–7
  baked lettuce, 97
  boiled lettuce quarters, 97
  carrot, turnip and hazelnut
    lettuce mould, 144
  cold poached leeks with savoury
    yoghurt, 92
  fried lettuce with nuts and
    pineapple, 97
  garden peas with lettuce and
    red pepper, 116
  preparation, 96
lightly curried, deep-fried celery
  strips, 61
lime:
  carrots glazed with fresh lime,
    49
  citrus twirls, 20
  grated courgettes with fresh
    lime, 67
  lime butter, 16
  marinated mushrooms, 105
liquidizers, 12

M

Mabey, Richard, 83
maize, *see* sweetcorn
mange-tout peas, 5, 98–9, 115
  older mange-touts, 99
  preparation, 98
  steamed mange-touts, 99
  stir-fried mange-touts, 99
  see also peas
mangel-wurzels, 28
marinated mushrooms, 105
marjoram, carrots glazed with, 48
marrow, 65, 100–2, 126
  baked marrow rounds, 101
  baked stuffed marrow, 101
  deep-fried marrow balls, 101
  marrow soup, 101
  pan-fried marrow balls, 102
  preparation, 100
marrow flowers, 66
marrowfat peas, 116–17
Marsala, courgettes with, 66
mashed nut potatoes, 124
matchstick French beans, 78
meat:
  savoury fillings, 19
  serving vegetables with, 4
Medici, Catherine de, 33, 81, 115
Melba toast, 19–20
melon, 65, 70
milk:
  baby onions casseroled in milk,
    110
  boiled garlic cloves, 80
  cream of onion soup, 109
  onion and blackcurrant sauce,
    111–12
  onion custard, 111
  onions baked in milk with
    nutmeg, 109–10
  shallow-fried garlic cloves, 80
minerals, 5, 8
mint:
  mushy marrowfat peas, 116–17
  old garden peas fried with mint,
    116
  pea soup, 116
  tomato soup, 139
Mrs P.'s green tomato chutney,
  140
Mosimann, Anton, 66
moulds: carrot, turnip and hazelnut
  lettuce mould, 144
mung beans, beansprouts, 27
mushroom, 103–5

baked mushrooms, 104
cauliflower with mushroom
  sauce, 53
leeks and mushrooms in bacon
  fat with croûtons, 93
marinated mushrooms, 105
mushroom pâté, 104
mushroom sauce, 17
mushroom soup, 104
nutrients, 103
preparation, 103
quiche, 15
stuffed cabbage boats, 41
mushy marrowfat peas, 16–17
mustard:
  cheese and mustard sauce, 17
  mushy marrowfat peas, 116–17
  tomato and mustard butter, 16
  tomato and mustard cream, 18
mustard and cress, 27

N

Napoleon, Emperor, 28
Nero, Emperor, 90
nettle, 106
  preparation, 106
New Zealand spinach, 130
Noilly Prat, sliced leeks cooked in,
  93
Norwegian red cabbage, 44
nutmeg:
  boiled spinach with nutmeg, 131
  cauliflower with nutmeg and
    diced ginger, 53
  onions baked in milk with
    nutmeg, 109–10
nuts: fried lettuce with nuts and
  pineapple, 97

O

oak leaf lettuce, 95
oatmeal potato croquettes, 125
oils and fats, 9–10
  bacon fat, 9
  duck fat, 9
  garlic oil, 10
  sesame oil with raspberry
    vinegar, 10
  for stir-frying, 9

okra, 107
  preparation, 107
old broad beans cooked in sweet
  white wine, 32–3
old garden peas fried with mint, 116
olive oil, 9
onion, 79, 108–12
  baby onions casseroled in milk,
    110
  baby onions fried in dripping,
    110
  baked celery with onions and
    pepper, 60
  baked onions stuffed with
    cheese, 110–11
  beetroot, onion and cheese
    savoury, 29
  cream of onion soup, 109
  deep-fried onions, 111
  fried red peppers with onion,
    119
  glazed baby onions, 110
  Jerusalem artichokes fried with
    bacon, onion and garlic, 85
  mushroom pâté, 104
  mushy marrowfat peas, 116–17
  onion and blackcurrant sauce,
    111–12
  onion custard, 111
  onions baked in milk with
    nutmeg, 109–10
  preparation, 109
  quiche, 15
  ratatouille, 119–20
  savoury minced onions, 111
  savoury potatoes, 123
  spiced red cabbage with apples
    and orange, 43
  tomato Provençale, 140
onions, spring, *see* spring onions
orache, 130
orange:
  baked chicory with orange, 63
  cabbage with orange, 40
  carrot and orange soup, 47
  carrots mashed with black
    pepper and orange, 49
  celeriac soup, 55
  chicory braised in orange juice,
    62

citrus twirls, 20
courgettes braised with orange,
  67
grated beetroot fried with
  orange and walnut oil, 29
grated carrots with orange and
  walnut oil, 50
grated courgettes with orange,
  67
orange butter, 16
sliced leeks cooked in orange
  juice, 93
spiced red cabbage with apples
  and orange, 43
stuffed cabbage, 43
orange rind, with stir-fried
  vegetables, 8

P

pan-fried vegetables:
  celeriac balls, 57
  marrow balls, 102
  see also shallow-fried vegetables
paprika, 117, 118
Parisian potatoes, 124
Parmentier, M., 121
Parr, Catherine, 95
parsley, 45
  chopping, 7
  deep-fried, 20
  sweetcorn, red pepper and
    leeks with parsley, 136
parsnip, 45, 113–14, 115
  baked parsnip with cream and
    cheese, 114
  fried turned vegetables, 143
  parsnip croquettes, 114
  parsnip soup, 113
  preparation, 113
  purée of parsnips with toasted
    pine kernels, 113
  roasted parsnips, 114
pastry:
  leeks baked in cheese pastry, 92
  savoury cheese pastry, 14
  savoury pastry, 13
pâtés:
  bacon cabbage boats, 41
  baked chicory with cheese and

herb pâté, 63
  cheese and herb pâté, 16
  mushroom pâté, 104
  stuffed cabbage boats, 41
pe-tsai, *see* Chinese leaf
peanuts: savoury minced onions,
  111
peas, 115–17
  buttered fresh young garden
    peas, 117
  diced celeriac with grated
    apples and garden peas, 56
  garden peas with lettuce and
    red pepper, 116
  leeks, spring onions and peas
    with tomato concasse, 94
  lemon, pea and sweetcorn soup,
    116
  mushy marrowfat peas, 116–17
  old garden peas fried with mint,
    116
  pea soup, 116
  steamed fresh garden peas, 116
  see also mange-tout peas
pepper, black:
  carrots mashed with black
    pepper and horseradish, 49
  carrots mashed with black
    pepper and orange, 49
  seasoning with, 10
peppers, 117–20
  baked celery with onions and
    pepper, 60
  baked savoury cabbage, 42
  baked savoury celery, 59
  baked stuffed red pepper, 119
  celery baked with yoghurt,
    apple and red pepper, 60
  fried red peppers with onion,
    119
  garden peas with lettuce and
    red pepper, 116
  preparation, 118
  quiche, 15
  ratatouille, 119–20
  red pepper soup, 119
  savoury stuffed courgettes, 68
  sweetcorn, red pepper and
    leeks with parsley, 136
Pernod, carrots glazed with, 49

Persian cucumber soup, 71
petits pois, 115
pickled onions, 108
pies, vegetable savoury pie, 14
Pilgrim Fathers, 126
pimiento, *see* peppers
pine kernels:
    purée of parsnips with toasted
        pine kernels, 113
    savoury Jerusalem artichokes, 86
pineapple: fried lettuce with nuts
        and pineapple, 97
piquant swede or turnips, 143
plain-leaved kale, 86
Pliny, 82, 83
plum tomatoes, 138
poached leeks, 91
pork, savoury filling, 19
port and Stilton cheese, 16
potato, 112, 117, 120–5, 133, 137
    baked with port and Stilton
        cheese, 16
    baked potatoes, 122
    boiled new potatoes, 122
    celeriac and courgette cake,
        56–7
    cream of celery soup, 59
    fanned roast potatoes, 124
    golden potato wedges, 122
    herbed potato scones, 125
    leek and potato soup, 91
    mashed nut potatoes, 124
    nutrients, 121
    oatmeal potato croquettes, 125
    Parisian potatoes, 124
    potato, cheese and garlic bread,
        125
    potatoes baked with cream and
        cheese, 123
    preparation, 121
    rich roast potatoes, 124
    roast potatoes, 123–4
    savoury potatoes, 123
    slicing, 7
    steamed new potatoes, 122
potato, sweet, *see* sweet potato
preparation and cooking
        techniques, 6–10
protein, 5
pumpkin, 65, 70, 100, 126–7

pumpkin and saffron soup, 127
pumpkin soup, 127
roast pumpkin, 127
pumpkin seeds, 126
purées, 13
    broad bean, 32
    Brussels sprouts, 38
    carrot, 49
    cauliflower, 53
    celeriac, 56
    parsnips with toasted pine
        kernels, 113
    spinach, 131
Pythagoras, 39

Q

quiche, vegetable, 14–15

R

radicchio, 73, 74, 96
radish, fried grated carrots with,
    50
Ralegh, Sir Walter, 120
rape kale, 86
raspberry vinegar:
    broccoli fried with sesame and
        raspberry, 35
    cauliflower stir-fried in sesame
        and raspberry, 54
    courgettes baked in honey and
        raspberry vinegar, 67
    sesame oil with, 10
    soya sauce with, 10
    stir-fried celery with
        sesame-raspberry sauce, 60–1
ratatouille, 119–20
red cabbage, 39
    Norwegian red cabbage, 44
    spiced red cabbage with apples
        and orange, 43
    stuffed cabbage, 43
red lettuce, 73
red onions, 108
red pepper soup, 119
red peppers, *see* peppers
relish (flavoured butter), 16
rich roast potatoes, 124
ridge cucumber, 70

ridge cucumber cups, 71–2
roast potatoes, 123–4
roast pumpkin, 127
roasted parsnips, 114
Root, Waverley, 46, 134
root vegetables:
    simple soup, 13
    *see also individual types of root
        vegetable*
rosemary: courgette and rosemary
    soup, 66
runner beans, 77, 128–9
    boiled or steamed runner beans,
        129
    preparation, 128
    quiche, 15
rutabagas, 141, 142

S

saffron: pumpkin and saffron soup,
    127
sage: cream of onion soup, 109
salad burnet, 96
salad dressings:
    French dressing, 18
    see also sauces
salad, French bean, 78
salad onions, *see* spring onions
salad tomatoes, 138
salt, 10
sauces:
    basic double cream sauce, 18
    basic white sauce, 17
    cheese, 17
    cheese and mustard, 17
    Hollandaise, 17
    mushroom, 17
    onion and blackcurrant, 111–12
    savoury yoghurt, 92
    tarragon cream, 18
    tomato and mustard cream, 18
    tomato Provençale, 140
    see also salad dressings
savoury aubergine casserole, 26
savoury cheese breadcrumbs, 19
savoury cheese pastry, 14
savoury fillings, 19
savoury ham filling, 19
savoury Jerusalem artichokes, 86

153

savoury minced onions, 111
savoury pastry, 13
savoury potatoes, 123
savoury stuffed courgettes, 68
Savoy cabbage, 39, 40
scallions, see spring onions
scarlet runners, 128
scones: herbed potato scones, 125
Scottish kale, 86
sea salt, 10
seasonings:
  soup, 12
  vegetables, 10
sesame oil:
  broccoli fried with sesame and
    raspberry, 35
  cauliflower stir-fried in sesame
    and raspberry, 54
  sesame oil with raspberry
    vinegar, 19
  stir-fried celery with
    sesame-raspberry sauce,
    60–1
sesame seeds: parsnip croquettes,
  114
Shakespeare, William, 136
shallots, 108
shallow-fried garlic cloves, 80
sherry:
  baked celery with onions and
    pepper, 60
  basic vegetable soup, 12
shredding, 7
sieving soups, 12
silverskin onions, 108
simple root vegetable soup, 13
skinning tomatoes, 138
sliced leeks cooked in Noilly Prat,
  93
sliced leeks cooked in orange juice,
  93
sliced leeks cooked in white wine,
  93
sliced leeks cooked in yoghurt, 92
slicing, 6–7
snap beans, see French beans
snow peas, see mange-tout peas
Socrates, 45
sorrel, 96
soufflés, spinach, 132

soups:
  asparagus, 23
  aubergine, 26
  basic vegetable soup, 11–12
  beetroot, 29
  beetroot and apple, 29
  broad bean, 31
  broad bean hazelnut soup, 31
  broad bean lemon soup, 31
  broccoli, 34
  Brussels sprouts, 38
  carrot, 47
  carrot and apple, 47
  carrot and coriander, 47
  carrot and ginger, 47
  carrot and orange, 47
  carrot and spinach, 47
  cauliflower, 52
  cauliflower cheese, 52
  celeriac, 55
  celery and dill, 59
  celery and fennel, 59
  courgette, 66
  courgette and fennel, 66
  courgette and rosemary, 66
  cream of celery, 59
  cream of onion, 109
  fennel, 75
  fennel and almond, 75
  fennel and courgette, 75
  Jerusalem artichoke, 85
  leek, 91
  leek and potato, 91
  lemon, pea and sweetcorn, 116
  marrow, 101
  parsnip, 113
  pea, 116
  Persian cucumber, 71
  pumpkin, 127
  pumpkin and saffron, 127
  red pepper, 119
  sieving, 12
  simple root vegetable soup, 13
  spinach, 131
  sweetcorn, 135
  tomato, 139
  tomato, apple and celery, 139
  white turnip/swede soup, 142
  yellow turnip/swede soup, 142
soya beans, beansprouts, 27

soya sauce:
  courgettes baked in honey and
    soya sauce, 67
  soya sauce with raspberry
    vinegar, 10
Spanish onions, 108, 109
spiced red cabbage with apples and
  orange, 43
spices, for stir-fried vegetables, 8
  see also individual spices
spinach, 129–32
  boiled spinach with nutmeg, 131
  carrot and spinach soup, 47
  nutrients, 129–30
  preparation, 130
  quiche, 15
  shredding, 7
  spinach fried in bacon fat with
    chopped walnuts, 132
  spinach purée, 131
  spinach soufflés, 132
  spinach soup, 131
  steamed spinach, 131
spinach beet, 28, 130
spring cabbage, 39
spring greens, 39
spring onions, 108
  fried spring onions, 112
  leeks, spring onions and peas
    with tomato concasse, 94
sprouts, see Brussels sprouts
sprue (asparagus), 22
squash, 65, 70, 100, 126–7
  steamed squash, 127
star anise, baked chicory with, 63
steamed vegetables, 8
  beetroot balls, 30
  broad beans, 32
  broccoli heads, 34
  Brussels sprouts, 37
  chicory, 62
  corn on the cob, 135
  fennel, 76
  French bean parcels, 78
  French beans, 78
  fresh garden peas, 116
  Jerusalem artichokes, 85
  kohlrabi, 88
  maincrop carrots, 48
  mange-touts, 99

new baby carrots, 48
new potatoes, 122
runner beans, 129
spinach, 131
squash, 127
swedes, 142
turnips,142
whole cauliflower with toasted
    almonds, 52
whole fennel, 76
steamers, 8
Stilton: port and Stilton cheese, 16
stir-fried vegetables, 8, 9
    cauliflower with coriander,
        53–4
    celery with sesame-raspberry
        sauce, 60–1
    mange-touts, 99
stock, 11–12
string beans, see French beans;
    runner beans
stuffed cabbage, 43
stuffed cabbage boats, 41
sugar beet, 28, 46
sugar peas, see mange-tout peas
sugars, 5
sultanas:
    Mrs P.'s green tomato chutney,
        140
    with stir-fried vegetables, 8
swede, 141–3
    boiled or steamed, 142
    carrot, turnip and hazelnut
        lettuce mould, 144
    diced swede with honey, 143
    fried turned vegetables, 143
    piquant swede, 143
    preparation, 142
    white turnip/swede soup, 142
    yellow turnip/swede soup, 142
sweet peppers, see peppers
sweet potato, 112, 136–7
    preparation, 137
sweetcorn, 133–6
    boiled corn on the cob, 135
    lemon, pea and sweetcorn soup,
        116
    preparation, 134
    quiche, 15
    steamed corn on the cob, 135

sweetcorn fritters, 135–6
sweetcorn, red pepper and
    leeks with parsley, 136
sweetcorn soup, 135

T

taro, 136
tarragon cream, broccoli with, 35
tarragon vinegar:
    marinated mushrooms, 105
    tarragon cream, 18
thyme:
    carrots glazed with thyme, 48
    cauliflower with fresh thyme, 53
    diced celeriac with lemon and
        thyme, 55
Tiberius, Emperor, 70, 112
toast, Melba, 19–20
tomato, 117, 133, 137–40
    baked tomatoes, 139
    leeks, spring onions and peas
        with tomato concasse, 94
    Mrs P.'s green tomato chutney,
        140
    quiche, 15
    ratatouille, 119–20
    savoury aubergine casserole, 26
    savoury ham filling, 19
    savoury Jerusalem artichokes, 86
    to skin, 138
    tomato and mustard butter, 16
    tomato and mustard cream, 18
    tomato, apple and celery soup,
        139
    tomato butter, 16
    tomato Provençale, 140
    tomato soup, 139
Tradescant, John, 128
tree onions, 108
triticale, beansprouts, 27
turkey:
    savoury filling, 19
    stock, 11–12
turnip, 87, 141–4
    boiled or steamed, 142
    carrot, turnip and hazelnut
        lettuce mould, 144
    diced turnips with honey, 143
    fried turned vegetables, 143

piquant turnip, 143
preparation, 142
white turnip/swede soup, 142
yellow turnip/swede soup, 142
turnip-rooted celery, see celeriac
Twain, Mark, 51, 134

V

vegetable marrow, see marrow
vegetables:
    boiling, 8
    buying, 5
    chopping, 7
    cutting, 6–7
    fried turned vegetables, 143
    grating, 7–8
    nutrients, 5
    purées, 13
    seasoning, 10
    shredding, 7
    slicing, 6–7
    steaming, 8
    stir-frying, 9
    stock, 11–12
    storage, 5
    vegetable quiche, 14–15
    vegetable savoury pie, 14
    see also individual vegetables
vinegar: Mrs P.'s green tomato
    chutney, 140
vinegar, raspberry, see raspberry
    vinegar
vitamins, 5, 8
vitamin A, 5
vitamin C, 5

W

walnut oil, 9
    grated beetroot fried with
        orange and walnut oil, 29
    grated carrots with orange and
        walnut oil, 50
walnuts:
    bacon walnut cabbage, 42
    cauliflower with chopped
        walnuts, 53
    mashed nut potatoes, 124

walnuts – *cont.*
   spinach fried in bacon fat with
     chopped walnuts, 132
   walnut butter, 16
water chestnuts:
   fried Brussels sprouts with
     chestnuts, 38
   see also chestnuts
Webb's Wonderful lettuce, 95
Welsh onions, 108
Wesley, John, 45
wheat, beansprouts, 27
white, cabbage, 39
   see also cabbage
white sauce, 17
white turnip/swede soup, 142
wild mushrooms, 102
wine:
   broad beans with wine sauce, 33
   marinated mushrooms, 105
   mushroom pâté, 104
   old broad beans cooked in
     sweet white wine, 33
   poached leeks, 91
   sliced leeks cooked in white
     wine, 93
   spiced red cabbage with apples
     and orange, 43
   white sauce, 17
Woolton, Lord, 14
Worcestershire sauce, relish, 16

Y

yams, 136
yellow turnip/swede soup, 142
yoghurt:
   baked savoury cabbage, 42
   baked savoury celery, 59
   celery baked with yoghurt,
     apple and red pepper, 60
   cold poached leeks with savoury
     yoghurt, 92
   Persian cucumber soup, 71
   sliced leeks cooked in yoghurt,
     92

Z

zucchini, *see* courgette